SLOW
COOKER
CENTRAL
2

SLOW
COOKER
CENTRAL
2

SLOW COOKER
CENTRAL

2

Paulene Christie

ABC
Books

The ABC 'Wave' device is a trademark of the Australian Broadcasting Corporation and is used under licence by HarperCollinsPublishers Australia.

First published in Australia in 2016
by HarperCollins*Publishers* Australia Pty Limited
ABN 36 009 913 517
harpercollins.com.au

HarperCollins*Publishers*
Level 13, 201 Elizabeth Street, Sydney NSW 2000, Australia
Unit D1, 63 Apollo Drive, Rosedale Auckland 0632, New Zealand
A 53, Sector 57, Noida, UP, India
1 London Bridge Street, London, SE1 9GF, United Kingdom
2 Bloor Street East, 20th floor, Toronto, Ontario M4W 1A8, Canada
195 Broadway, New York NY 10007, USA

National Library of Australia Cataloguing-in-Publication entry:

Christie, Paulene, author.
  Christie, Paulene, author.
  Slow cooker central 2 / Paulene Christie.
  ISBN 978 0 7333 3511 2 (paperback)
  ISBN 978 1 4607 0654 1 (ebook)
  Electric cooking, Slow.
  Cookbooks
641.5884

Cover design by Hazel Lam, HarperCollins Design Studio
Internal design by HarperCollins Design Studio
Cover images by shutterstock.com
Author photograph by Tina Baills
Typeset in Adobe Jenson by Kirby Jones
Printed and bound in Australia by McPhersons Printing Group
The papers used by HarperCollins in the manufacture of this book are a natural, recyclable product made from wood grown in sustainable plantation forests. The fibre source and manufacturing processes meet recognized international environmental standards, and carry certification.

Dedicated to Simon and Caleb, Talyn and Ella
You are my life, my purpose, my everything
xx

Contents

INTRODUCTION

Welcome to book 2 in the Slow Cooker Central series!

To be honest I'm still a little shocked to be here myself :)

I'm a busy married mum of three young children, a nurse who juggles shift work with family life and like many of you – I'm always looking for ways to save time. Enter slow cooking …

When I began this journey I was just looking for new and exciting slow cooker recipes to try. I'd found myself using a slow cooker for the first time and loved the convenience of preparing my family meals earlier in the day and having them all ready to serve during those hectic evening hours.

I first created the Facebook page 'Slow Cooker Recipes 4 Families' just over three years ago hoping some friends may join and share some recipes along with mine. I never for a moment expected over 400,000 people from all over the world to join!

In August 2014 we launched our website www.slowcookercentral.com. To this day we continue to add recipes, blogs and all manner of slow cooking content to our website and Facebook group and are thrilled to be a part of igniting a passion for slow cooking in so many people all over the world.

What makes us unique is our user-submitted content. It's not just me publishing recipes … although I of course submit a large number of them. We help everyday people share their favourite recipes with the world too – on our Facebook group, on our website, and now in our books. That's what gives us our family feel. Members are always online helping each other and being helped.

Most of us aren't chefs; we don't use obscure exotic ingredients or have highly stylised images of our finished dishes like so many other recipe sources do.

We are real people, cooking in real kitchens, with regular ingredients.

Sure, some recipes are from scratch, some recipes are not. And that's totally ok – because everyone wants different things from their cooking and everyone has different dietary needs and preferences. We provide a wide range of options and let you choose what you like best.

But at the end of the day, everyone can achieve a great result with our recipes and deliver a delicious meal on the table! Now that's what I call success.

I am constantly humbled by the number of people who write to me telling me how slow cooking has changed their lives. In some cases people are finding confidence in cooking for the first time ever. They feel pride in what they achieve. They feel excitement at the prospect of trying the next new dish. They appreciate the time, money and stress they are now saving as a result of slow cooking. Just like me, they tried slow cooking and it changed their lives! How blessed I am to be even a small part of that.

Together we have created an amazing thriving community of slow cooking enthusiasts and together we all expand our skills, tastes and knowledge in all things slow cooking.

When ABC Books approached us to release the first Slow Cooker Central book I was shocked to say the least! What an incredible opportunity to be given to share our passion with an even wider audience.

The release of the first *Slow Cooker Central* book saw us rocket up the bestseller lists in Australia and we achieved the #1 bestseller position for nonfiction! To this day the book is selling well, and is in kitchens and on bookshelves all around the world.

If someone had told me a few years back that I would be involved in the publication of a bestselling book I would have surely laughed. Yet here we are, at the launch of *Slow Cooker Central 2*.

Congratulations to those whose recipes feature in these pages – I know from personal experience just how good it feels to see your name in print for the first time. Well done! Your recipes are now going to be cooked and enjoyed by people all over the world! How cool is that? Thank you for sharing :)

To all of you holding this book in your hands, to all our members and visitors to our website, to my amazing admin team who help run our Facebook group ... thank you so much for being a part of this journey with me.

I feel like the luckiest lady in the world some days. Here I am, after all, just doing something I enjoy, sharing an interest I'm passionate about. And yet every day people are thanking me for creating these groups and pages they enjoy.

It's not necessary to thank me – I am the one who is thankful! I get to share my passion for slow cooking with others and ignite it in them too! Seeing joy and confidence blossom in others is an amazing thing. To be even a small part of that means I am truly blessed.

So thank YOU!

Now settle in ... sit back ... and start finding your new favourite recipes!

Paulene Christie

SLOW COOKER
HINTS & TIPS

Here's a great little collection of tips and tricks and frequently asked questions that we have gathered from the experience in our slow cooking community.

If you are cooking a cake or dessert in the slow cooker, be sure to read the section on cake tins first. The section on the tea-towel trick helps explain what that little strategy is all about – you will see it mentioned a lot in our recipes. It helps us make many of the unique and unusual dishes we create in our slow cookers! We've also covered some really important safety do's and don'ts to help you to get the very best out of your slow cooking experiments while minimising the risks that other cooks may unknowingly take.

So have a read through this section FIRST – and then your hardest decision will be deciding which great recipe from the book to cook!

Can I use frozen meat in the slow cooker?

This is a hotly debated topic. The shorter answer is yes, you can. In fact many people will tell you they have done so for years and it's never hurt them.

Health concerns

It is up to you to make an educated and informed risk assessment for yourself. Although many people cook frozen meat in their slow cookers, the health and food technology experts say that for food safety reasons you should bring your food to temperatures of 60°C (140°F) as quickly as possible. It varies between machines, but in a slow cooker the LOW setting often cooks at around 94°C (200°F) and HIGH at 150°C (300°F) (check the manual that came with your machine and test it using a thermometer), which is why some people prefer to start the cooking process on HIGH (or AUTO – see more on the auto function below) to ensure the food reaches this safe temperature as quickly as possible.

The bottom line is that cooking with frozen food significantly increases the amount of time it takes for that food to reach the safe temperature, and thus significantly increases the chances of you and your family getting food poisoning. And because of that, I for one WILL NOT take that risk with my loved ones. But as I said previously, you are free to weigh up this risk for you and your family.

Cooker care

Cooking meat from frozen also increases the risk of a ceramic slow cooker bowl cracking as a result of the wide difference in temperature between the frozen food and the heating bowl. If the bowl cracks, your slow cooker is unusable.

On a similar note, you should always remove the food from your slow cooker dish before refrigerating it. The nature of the thick ceramic bowl means it retains heat and thus takes a lot longer to cool down to safe refrigeration temperatures, once again leaving your food too long in the danger zone.

How can I thicken slow-cooker recipes with a high liquid content?

There are several methods you can use to thicken a sauce before serving a dish.

Cornflour (cornstarch)

Combine 2 tablespoons cornflour (cornstarch) with 2 tablespoons cool tap water and mix until it becomes a thin smooth paste. Put this paste straight into the slow cooker dish 20–30 minutes before serving it, and stir briefly around whatever meat or vegetables are in the pot. Allow the dish to continue cooking, preferably on HIGH, or on LOW if the recipe requires.

This added cornflour will thicken the liquids in the recipe. If this amount of cornflour doesn't thicken the liquids sufficiently, you can repeat the process. But take care not to add too much cornflour to your recipe – one or two additions are usually all that's needed. Some people ladle the liquid out of the slow cooker into a saucepan on the stove and add the cornflour there. How you do it is totally up to you.

Gravy granules/powder

Substitute gravy granules for cornflour and follow the method as described above. The suitability of this option will depend on the recipe and if the addition of gravy will suit it.

Grated potato

Grate 1–2 raw potatoes and add them to the slow cooker about 30–45 minutes before serving. Stir them as much as you can around the solid ingredients. This will very quickly thicken the dish and continue to thicken it during the remaining cooking time.

Grated potato will only suit some recipes – those with vegetable or potato already in them, or that would work well with the addition of potato.

Instant potato flakes can also be used.

Lift the lid

Another option is to remove the lid of the slow cooker, or at least place it ajar, for the last 30 minutes of cooking, to enable the sauce to thicken through evaporation. This goes against the very nature of the slow cooker – having a sealed environment in which the cooking temperature is maintained constantly – but it is an available option if you choose to.

Use less liquid to begin with

Another natural consequence of slow cooking is the increased moisture content thanks to the drip condensation from the lid down into the food during cooking. Many people think meat has to be covered in liquid to slow cook it, but in fact it needs very little liquid. If you find a dish is regularly ending up with far too much liquid, reduce the amount you add initially next time you cook it.

The tea towel (dish towel) trick

Quite a few of the recipes in this book, and many in the Sweets chapter, will ask you to 'Cover the slow cooker, putting a tea towel (dish towel) under the lid, and cook on HIGH.' The tea towel, which lies between the top of the slow cooker bowl and the lid of the slow cooker, acts to absorb condensation and stop it from dripping down into the food cooking inside. It's often used when you wouldn't want the cake or bread being cooked ending up soggy.

This trick has been devised by home slow cooker enthusiasts and is not recommended officially or declared a safe practice by slow cooker manufacturers.

When using the tea towel trick, regular users suggest you fold up any excess fabric onto the lid of the slow cooker lid, securing it to the lid handle, so it doesn't hang down over the hotter outer casing of the slow cooker. The tea towel absorbs liquid during the cooking process, so it stays damp and is unlikely to burn.

If you have concerns about the fire hazards related to this practice, you can research the safety issues involved and inform yourself about the pros and cons. It is totally up to you to appraise the risks and decide whether it is safe to use the tea towel trick with your slow cooker.

It is not recommended to use the tea towel in general slow cooking, but just as an optional measure to reduce liquid in a dish. You should use the technique, if you do decide to use it, only for cakes and breads where water dripping onto them is a major issue.

Please make your own decision regarding the safety of this practice. If in any doubt, do not do this. I personally recommend you don't leave your home when you are using a tea towel in this way, so that you are able to keep an eye on your slow cooker and the towel.

How can I remove oil and fat from a slow cooker dish?

There are several methods you can use to remove oil from your dish. First and foremost, you can reduce the amount of fat going into the dish from the beginning.

Be choosy
Choose lean cuts of meat, trim visible fat from meat and add little to no oil to your slow cooker recipes.

Prep it
Pre-browning or sealing meat in a frying pan is one way to remove some of the fat before cooking it in the slow cooker (read more about pre-browning and sealing meat on page 9).

Skim and discard
Perhaps the most obvious solution is to spoon that fat right out of there! Towards the end of the cooking process, the fat will often gather at the top of your dish so you can use a ladle or spoon to gently remove and discard it.

The ice-cube trick
Placing ice-cubes briefly on top of the dish will cause the fat to 'stick to' the ice-cubes (because the lower temperature causes the fat to solidify). You can then discard the ice-cubes and the oil right along with them.

The bread trick

Very briefly lay a piece of bread along the top of the dish. This will soak up the fat, which will be discarded with the bread or fed to a four-legged friend. But be very careful and always remove the bread with tongs, as it will be hot!

Some people use paper towel instead of bread to soak up the fats and oils, but if something is going to break down in my food, I would rather it were bread than paper.

Cool and skim

If you have the time or you are cooking a recipe in advance, you can cool the entire dish in the fridge overnight. The fat will solidify on top and you can remove it before reheating and serving the dish.

What does the AUTO function on my slow cooker do?

Many slow cookers have LOW, HIGH, KEEP WARM and AUTO settings. The AUTO function often means the dish will begin cooking at HIGH for approximately 2 hours, then the slow cooker will switch itself down to the LOW temperature setting. (The dial itself doesn't move and will remain pointing to AUTO.)

This feature varies with different slow cooker models and brands, so always consult your user manual.

Is it safe to leave my slow cooker unattended all day while I am out of the house?

In short, yes ... with precautions.

Slow cookers are designed to run all day unattended without posing a fire hazard. There are, however, further precautions you can take if you're concerned.

- I always place my slow cookers on top of my ceramic cooktop. This surface is designed to withstand high temperatures, after all. Just be sure never to accidentally have a hotplate turned on (I lost my first ever slow cooker to this happening when I melted its legs off!). If you don't have this option, placing the cooker on a glass-top trivet or cutting board works in a similar way.

- Ensure flammable objects are not left touching or anywhere near the slow cooker.
- Move the slow cooker away from the wall and any curtains, etc.
- Always have a working smoke alarm and electrical safety switch in your home so that if you are home and the worst somehow happens, you and your family will be alerted to the danger and the electricity supply will shut off.

Is it okay to open the lid of my slow cooker to stir my dish or check on it?

Many of us have heard the tale that each time you open the lid of your slow cooker, it adds 30 minutes to the cooking time.

In practice, I have never personally found this to be true. If I am at home I am a habitual lid-lifter, often pausing to look at, stir, taste or even smell my dish throughout the day. And if anything, my dishes often cook much faster than I might expect.

However, slow cookers rely on the slow build-up of heat to cook food to perfection. Lifting the lid during cooking lets built-up heat escape and will lower the temperature in the slow cooker considerably. Stirring the contents allows even more heat to escape from the lower layers of the food. Once the lid is replaced, it will take a significant amount of time for the food to heat back up to its previous temperature.

So the choice is up to you. Resist if you can, or don't. You will soon come to know your own slow cooker (or if you are like me and have several, you will get to know each of their little quirks and cooking times and temps).

Do I need to pre-brown, pre-cook or seal my meat before placing it in the slow cooker?

In short, no, you do not.

Some people like to do this step to add more depth of flavour (in their opinion) to the dish or to seal in juices.

Pre-browing can also help to liquefy fat from the meat, which can then be discarded before you add the meat to the slow cooker.

However, it does add another step in the preparation of your dish, and more washing up to go with it.

So it's totally your choice, but for what it's worth, I rarely pre-brown, pre-seal, or pre-cook anything.

Can I prepare a meal in advance and store it in the slow cooker bowl in my fridge overnight, then put it on the next morning?

Yes, you can if you wish. But it comes with risks!

Heating a cold bowl can lead to it cracking.

Also, the bowl and its contents will retain that cold for a long time and thus take even longer to reach safe food cooking temperatures once you begin cooking, placing you at increased risk of food poisoning.

A great way around this is to prepare the dish in advance but store it in the fridge in another large bowl, for example a mixing bowl. The food can then be poured into the slow cooker bowl in the morning and turned on. You still have all the convenience but without any of the risk.

What is the best way to clean my slow cooker bowl?

It happens to all of us sometimes! We finish cooking our recipe only to find a baked-on ring of cooked or burnt residue inside our slow cooker or on the base. Or maybe the inner casing of your slow cooker has stains in it? Don't despair – we've got the solution!

Basics

- The sooner you get it off the better!
- Avoid harsh abrasive chemicals or cleaning scourers.
- Always unplug the unit from the power source before cleaning.

Cleaning inside the cooking bowl

Most slow cooker bowls can simply be washed by hand in the sink. Some are OK for washing in the dishwasher after use. Be sure to check your manual for what is suitable for your model as not all models are dishwasher safe.

However, if you find yourself with a baked-on ring around the bowl that's hard to remove, the easiest way to get rid of it is remove the food, add water to a level above the baked-on ring and leave the slow cooker turned to LOW for a couple of hours. The ring should clean away much more easily then.

Some suggest placing a dishwasher tablet or even a denture cleaning tablet in the slow cooker while the water is heating in it for up to 2 hours but it is advisable to check with your user manual if this is safe for your model.

Like any ceramic, the stoneware and lid will not withstand sudden temperature changes. Do not fill the bowl with cold water when it is hot.

Some ceramic bowls have a porous base and should not be left standing in water for extended periods because they might absorb water. It's fine to fill the bowl with water and leave it for any amount of time, but avoid leaving it standing IN water.

Cleaning inside the main casing of the slow cooker

The metal housing of the slow cooker and electrical lead should NOT be placed in water! Be sure to completely unplug your unit from the power source and allow it to cool before any cleaning.

Over time you will find some of your food will splash down into the main casing of your slow cooker – under the cooking bowl.

It is important to ALWAYS CHECK YOUR INSTRUCTION MANUAL FIRST as to how your manufacturer recommends you clean your slow cooker.

Normally, electrical cables inside the base unit are fully sealed, but you should still exercise extreme caution in washing this main base unit – and again, never place the unit itself in water. If you can see heating elements inside the base do not clean or add water in this area and instead contact the manufacturer for advice.

For those who wish to proceed with cleaning inside the main casing, here are some suggestions I have gathered from members of the Slow Cooker Central community.

- Simply wipe the spill off with a soft, damp cloth and a small amount of dish detergent, especially if the spill is fresh or new.
- Clean using a mix of baking soda and vinegar on a cloth or sponge.
- Use a chalk-based cleaning paste like Gumption, which you can find in your supermarket cleaning aisle.
- Use baking soda and lemon juice. Combine and allow to foam-up then apply with a soft pad, sponge or scourer.

- While a soft green scrubbing type pad scourer should be OK please think carefully before using a stronger steel wool type scourer as you could scratch your inner casing or bowl. A gentle sponge or rubber based scrubbing tool is ideal .
- Some report using a thin coat of oven cleaner (a fume-free version if you can), left for an hour or so then wiped off. If doing this I would recommend wiping over a few times with a damp cloth to minimise any smells next time you use the unit. Note: oven cleaners can be caustic and may even dissolve paint on the outside of your cooker, so use sparingly and cautiously.

Prevention is best

Rather than deal with the clean-up, try to prevent spills where you can!

- Spray your slow cooker bowl with some non-stick cooking spray before beginning.
- Line your slow cooker with baking paper for baked items or ones you think may stick.
- Use a slow-cooker liner bag or even an oven bag to slow-cook your dish.
- Follow cooking time recommended in the recipe and avoid overcooking and burning.
- Do not overfill your slow cooker, which would increase the likelihood of spilling and staining in the casing area.

Are there any 'diet' recipes for slow cookers?

Almost every recipe can be adapted for weight loss or to make it healthier (with some obvious dessert-type exceptions).

Ways to adapt recipes to make them more waist-friendly include:

- using leaner cuts of meat
- adding extra vegetables to bulk out your meal
- choosing low-sodium versions of soups, stocks and sauces that go into your dish
- choosing low-fat versions of cream and milk that go into your dish

- serving healthy side dishes like brown rice, salads and vegetables
- using wise portion control when serving
- storing leftovers in portion-controlled healthy serves to serve instead of bad impulse meals and snacks when you are time poor.

Does it cost less to run a slow cooker for 8 hours than an oven for 1 hour?

It certainly is cheaper!

Of course there are many variables to consider, including the size and model of your slow cooker, and the size and efficiency of your conventional oven, but overall the stats are well in favour of your slow cooker being the cheaper way to cook – even if it takes over 8 hours instead of 1 hour!

Energy provider Ergon Energy advises that a slow cooker costs 4 cents per hour to run, while an oven costs 60 cents per hour!

So running your slow cooker for 8 hours will cost 32 cents compared to 60 cents for just one hour of the oven (and that doesn't even account for oven pre-heating time).

Bargain!

Is it toxic to slow cook raw red kidney beans?

Yes, it is! One example that I think explains it best is found at www.choosingvoluntarysimplicity.com:

'Raw kidney beans contain especially large amounts of [phytohaemagglutinin], and amazingly, eating just four or five raw or improperly cooked kidney beans can make a person extremely ill. Ingesting larger amounts can actually cause death. Other beans, including white kidney beans, broad beans and lima beans, contain the same toxin in smaller but still dangerous amounts.'

If you'd like to read further on this issue, these websites would be good starting points:

- www.choosingvoluntarysimplicity.com/crockpots-slow-cooking-dried-beans-phytohaemagglutinin/
- www.medic8.com/healthguide/food-poisoning/red-kidney-bean-toxins.html

Slow cooking on a budget

There are several ways your slow cooker can help you save money if you are on a budget.

Save money on cooking costs

It is cheaper to slow cook than it is to run other appliances like ovens.

Of course there are many variables to consider including the size and model of your slow cooker and size and efficiency of your wall oven but overall the stats are well in favour of your slow cooker being the cheaper way to cook (see prices on page 13).

Save money on shopping costs at your butcher

Slow cooking saves you money at the butcher. The very nature of long slow cooking means your meat will be lovely and tender. So you can buy a much cheaper cut of meat. That's more money in your pocket!

Cook in bulk and save

A lot of slow cooker fans are cooking bigger meals and storing leftovers.

For instance, many people are using a large slow cooker with a six litre bowl to cook a soup. They fill it and store leftovers for another day.

Using 'dump bags' for slow cooking is another easy way to buy ingredients in bulk to save money! It involves doing the prep work for several recipes all at once and bagging up the contents to freeze for later cooking. Then all you need to do is defrost your bag, pour it into the slow cooker on the day and turn it on. So easy.

You can find menu plans and shopping lists for these on our website at www.slowcookercentral.com.

Save money on take-away and impulse buys

Who hasn't got to the end of a long day and out of sheer exhaustion just decided to grab take-away for dinner instead of cooking a meal from scratch. We've all been there! Throw in some tired, hungry kids into the mix and it's a recipe for disaster.

So save yourself and slow cook! Come dinner time, you'll have dinner already cooked, smelling amazing and just ready to serve. It's actually faster and easier than going out for take-away ... and so much cheaper on the hip pocket!

Save money with smart choices

Some recipes are going to be more budget-friendly than others based on their core ingredients.

For example, skip the seafood and steak category and head to these kind of recipes first:

- sausage recipes
- chicken recipes
- mince recipes
- soups
- vegetable dishes

Use leftovers in a new meal

For example, use a moist meat or meat and veg meal from the night before to make a pie for the next night.

Use shredded meat in a new form on wraps, pizzas or tacos the next night.

Get creative and start saving today!

Slow cooking cakes

Cooking cakes in slow cookers is out of the norm for a lot of traditionalist slow cooker users, so we wanted to include some advice on what can and can't be used in cake making in your slow cooker, and also to provide some general tips for getting the most out of your slow cooker cake making .

First and foremost, as detailed on page 6, the 'tea towel trick' is very important to prevent condensation dripping on your cakes when cooking them in the slow cooker.

Slow cookers can be used to cook packet (box) cake mixes as well as your own favourite from-scratch recipe.

But what do you cook the actual cake in?

There are three options:

1. Line your slow cooker inner bowl and cook your cake directly in it.
When doing this I find lining the bowl with non-stick baking paper not only prevents sticking but also gives you something to hold onto so you can lift the cake out at the end of the cooking time.

2. Cook your cake in a metal cake tin.

If you are concerned about using a metal cake tin dry in your slow cooker (ceramic bowls in particular) simply fill the bottom of the slow cooker bowl with 2–3 cm (1 in) of water first, then sit your cake tin gently in this water.

You can also elevate the cake tin off the bottom of the slow cooker to allow heat to circulate evenly around your cake. This can be achieved by resting the cake tin on a metal trivet, on metal egg rings or even on scrunched up balls of aluminium foil.

3. Cook your cake in a silicone cake tin.

Silicone cake tins (full size and cupcake size) are also safe to use in your slow cooker and will not melt. After all, they are intended for the high heat of conventional ovens.

When using non-ceramic slow cooker bowls I personally sit my silicone cake tins/cups directly onto the bottom of the slow cooker, without water, with no concerns. But if you prefer, you can elevate your tin using the methods described above.

As with all non-traditional slow cooking, be sure to check your manual first and only do what you are comfortable doing.

Slow cooker fudge faqs

Our members LOVE cooking fudge! We have over 120 different varieties on the website, so you can browse for fudge online or use one of the recipes in this book. I've compiled some commonly asked questions about fudge to help you along the way.

What type of chocolate can I use?

Any type. Change the flavour of the chocolate to change the taste of the fudge. Milk chocolate, white chocolate, hazelnut chocolate, cookies and cream chocolate ... the options are unlimited. Some members use cooking chocolate, but others say the taste is not the same, so use your judgement. (Cooking chocolate does tend to melt at higher temperatures, so regular chocolate is ideal for the lower temp of the slow cooker.) If you are using chocolate that has a liquid-type filling, eg Caramello, you will need to increase the chocolate amount to account for this.

Can I add chocolate and lollies to my fudge

Yes. You can mix or top your fudge with anything you like. Make the base fudge, stir through whatever you like to add, then pour it into the lined tin to set. For example, you could add chopped nuts, biscuits, Mars bars, lollies (candies) … whatever you like. Or pour your fudge into your tray to set then decorate the surface with these types of toppings. Again the options are endless.

How do I actually cook it? Do I need to stir it?

Break up the chocolate and place it in your slow cooker. Pour over condensed milk and add the butter and vanilla. LEAVE THE LID OFF your slow cooker and turn it on low and walk away. Every 10–15 minutes just pass by and give it a stir. It's that easy. As you near the end of the cooking time you may need to keep a closer eye on it but really it's just the odd stir along the way and there is nothing else to do.

Can I use any spoon to stir?

It's ideal to use a metal spoon when stirring your fudge. A wooden spoon can absorb some of the liquid from your fudge so it's best to avoid these. (Not to mention the fact that a metal spoon is a little nicer to lick clean!)

My fudge has seized – how can I fix it?

If things don't go to plan, your fudge might seize, which means it turns hard and weird instead of glossy. This problem can result from water getting into the fudge – remember, lids off for fudge to avoid condensation drips. Using a wooden spoon can do the same – remember, use a metal, plastic or silicone spoon for stirring fudge. There are a few approaches our members use to rescue seized fudge. Try stirring the living daylights out of it to bring it back to glossy. Others add a little splash of milk or condensed milk or even a bit more chocolate then stir like the clappers to bring it all back together. All is not lost. This is fixable – stir stir stir!

How do I know when it's done?

Everyone's slow cooker takes a different amount of time to cook. Simply melting the chocolate is not enough. After some time, you'll notice a very slight 'crust' on the surface as you stir, and the mixture will come away from the edges of the bowl slightly. This is the best sign that it's done. Some larger (hotter) machines may achieve this in half an hour. My 1.5 litre cooker that I use for fudge takes more like 90 minutes to achieve this. You will get to know yours.

What do I do with it once it's cooked?

Stir through any extras you want to add, then pour your fudge into a slice tray (bar tray) lined with baking paper. You can use silicone moulds instead if you choose. Smooth the surface down to flat and decorate with any additions you are adding. If nothing is being added then simply place your tray in the fridge until set. Then use the baking paper to lift out your fudge from the tray. Remove the paper and cut the fudge quickly. Dipping your knife into hot water first can help cut cleanly.

How should I store my fudge?

Store your fudge in a sealed container in the fridge (make it a non-transparent container if you want to keep it from being rapidly gobbled up by the fudge fanatics in your home *wink*). The fudge will keep up to 3–4 weeks in a fridge. It can also be frozen for up to 3 months.

My fudge didn't set. What did I do wrong?

Please review the above tips. One of them will most likely reveal the reason your fudge did not set. You could also try returning your fudge to the slow cooker to reheat, add more chocolate, then cook for longer.

Pantry staples

One of the best ways to ease into trying new recipes is to have a supply of staple items in your pantry – on hand and at the ready for your next kitchen session. These may include:

+ Baking powder
+ Balsamic vinegar
+ Canned or dried fruits
+ Canned or dried vegetables
+ Canned soups: condensed cream soups in various flavours (especially cream of mushroom and cream of chicken)
+ Coconut cream and milk
+ Cornflour
+ Couscous
+ Curry powder
+ Dry packet soups such as French onion and chicken noodle
+ Flour: plain (all-purpose) and self-raising
+ Garlic: fresh or minced in jar
+ Ginger: fresh or minced in jar

- Gravy powder/granules
- Herbs and spices: fresh in your garden, frozen in tubes or dried in jars and packets – as many as you can gather!
- Honey
- Lentils
- Mustard powder
- Parmesan: fresh or dried
- Pasta
- Pepper
- Powdered milk or UHT milk
- Rice
- Salt
- Sauces: sweet chilli, BBQ, tomato, worcestershire, soy, mint, oyster, hoisin
- Stock: powder, cubes or long life liquid (especially beef, chicken and vegetable)
- Sugar: brown and white
- Sweetened condensed milk
- Tinned tomatoes
- Tinned tuna
- Tomato paste
- Vinegar
- Wine: red and white
- Yeast

This is by no means an exhaustive list but it's a great start!

Goodbye, oven. Hello slow cooker! Converting oven and stovetop recipes for your slow cooker

Now you're hooked on slow cooking, I bet you'll find there are heaps of your family's favourite recipes that you have always cooked in the oven or on the stove top that you want to convert for a slow cooker. And, for almost all of them, there is no reason you can't!

Here are some simple pointers:

- Reduce the amount of liquid. The condensation that forms in your slow cooker when in use, means that recipes cooked in slow cookers need much less liquid then their traditional stovetop or oven counterparts. As a general rule try reducing the total recipe liquid by approximately one quarter.
- Use cheaper cuts of meat. Remember that almost any cut of meat – even the cheapest and toughest – is sure to be tender after slow cooking. So feel free to replace more expensive cuts of meat with a cheaper option.

- Adjust the amount of herbs and spices. Many people recommend reducing them by one half when converting a regular recipe for a slow cooker.
- Adjust the time. See the chart below to convert your stove and oven times to slow cooker times.
- Arrange the ingredients. When filling your slow cooker, put the root vegetables around the bottom and sides of your slow cooker, then place your meat on top.
- Take notes and experiment. It may take some trial and error to tweak your old favourites but it'll be worth it. Adjust liquids as you go (adding or removing) and keep an eye on cooking times. Take notes as you try new things so you'll always know just what worked the best for you. Soon you'll have a recipe you can use anywhere!

Stovetop & Oven Cooking Times	Slow Cooking on LOW Cooking Times	Slow Cooking on HIGH Cooking Times
15–30 mins	4–6 hours	1½–2½ hours
45 mins–1 hour	6½–8 hours	3–4 hours
1½–2½ hours	9–12 hours	4½–6 hours
3–5 hours	12½–18 hours	5–7 hours

SNACKS & LIGHT MEALS

Overnight Steel Cut Oats
with Apple & Chia Seeds

I first made this recipe because I love a nice healthy bowl of oats in the morning for breakfast, but being a working mum I don't have time to stand at a stove cooking steel cut oats on a weekday morning. This way, I prepare my oats before I go to bed and everyone in my house wakes up to a deliciously warming and nutritious breakfast! And the clean up afterwards is super easy which is a bonus.

Serves 4–5 • Preparation 10 mins • Cook 7 hours • Cooker capacity 4.2 litres

4 cups milk of choice
1 cup steel cut oats
120 g (4½ oz) apple purée
1 apple, peeled, cored and cubed
½ cup sultanas (golden raisins)
3 tablespoons chia seeds
1 tablespoon butter
½ teaspoon cinnamon
Toppings of your choice, to serve

1. Mix all of the ingredients with 2 cups water in a heatproof bowl that will fit in the bowl of a slow cooker.

2. Put the bowl into the slow cooker and pour water into the gap between the heatproof bowl and the slow cooker bowl until it comes up to about halfway.

3. Cover and cook on LOW for 7 hours.

4. When ready to serve, stir then spoon the desired amount into bowls and add your toppings of choice. I like to top mine with a drizzle of honey, pecans and fresh berries.

Emily O'Brien

⇒— Asian Brekkie Eggs —●

My dad used to make this for me as a kid. Now at 37 I make it for my kids. It's a bit different from a normal brekkie. You can serve it with rice, cooked mushrooms or steamed Asian greens. And sometimes I make it for dinner.

Serves 6 • Preparation 10 mins • Cook 1 hour 20 mins • Cooker capacity 6 litres

100 g (3½ oz) vermicelli noodles
6 eggs
3 teaspoons sesame oil
3 lap cheong Chinese sausages, chopped
¼ cup chopped spring onions (scallions)
Tempura noodle sauce or kecap manis (sweet soy sauce), to serve
Fried shallots, to serve
Finely chopped fresh red chilli, to serve

1. Soak the noodles in hot water for 5 minutes. Drain and set aside.

2. In a large bowl, whisk the eggs. Add the drained noodles and sesame oil, season with pepper and mix well.

3. Transfer the noodles to a rectangular baking dish that will fit inside a slow cooker. Top with the chopped sausage and spring onions.

4. Pour enough water into the slow cooker to create a water bath. Transfer the baking dish to the slow cooker.

5. Cook on HIGH for 1 hour 20 minutes, or until the noodles are firm.

6. Cut up and serve with the noodle sauce, fried shallots and fresh chilli.

Michelle Lee

Vegetable-Loaded Breakfast Eggs

Mornings are a busy time for most people. This is my most commonly cooked breakfast dish: I can put it on, get busy with my morning chores, then come back and enjoy. No two days have to be the same, depending on what different veg you add. I like mine served with a side of baked beans for a filling, healthy start to my day. Keep any leftovers for an easy lunch, served with a side salad.

Serves 2–4 • Preparation 5 mins • Cook 30–45 mins • Cooker capacity 3 litres

4 eggs
100 g (3½ oz) bacon, diced
2 tablespoons finely diced red onion
4 small mushrooms, finely chopped
¼ red capsicum (pepper), finely diced
2 shallots, finely sliced

1. Line slow cooker with non-stick baking paper.

2. In a large bowl, whisk the eggs. Add the bacon and chopped vegetables and stir to combine. Pour the egg mixture into the slow cooker.

3. Cover, putting a tea towel (dish towel) under the lid, and cook on HIGH for 30–45 minutes, or until the egg is firmly set.

4. Using the edges of the baking paper to assist you, lift the egg out of the slow cooker.

5. Slice into quarters and serve.

Paulene Christie

Banana Pikelets

My kids love banana pikelets, but I don't like the time standing by the stove to cook them the traditional way. I cooked these pikelets in silicone cupcake cases to prevent them spreading, because the slow cooker wasn't as hot as a regular frying pan, and it worked great – the kids love these in their lunchboxes at school!

Makes 30 • Preparation 10 mins • Cook 45 mins • Cooker capacity 7 litres

2 cups self-raising flour, sifted
1½ cups milk
⅓ cup sugar
2 eggs, whisked
1½ tablespoons butter, melted
Pinch of salt
2 ripe bananas
Sliced banana, maple syrup or honey, to serve (optional)

1. In a large bowl, combine all of the ingredients except the bananas and mix well. Mash the bananas then stir through the batter.

2. Put 2 tablespoons batter into each silicone cupcake case – this will fill them about halfway. Transfer to a slow cooker.

3. Cover, putting a tea towel (dish towel) under the lid, and cook on HIGH for 45 minutes, or until a skewer inserted into the middle of a pikelet comes out clean.

4. Serve with slices of banana and a drizzle of maple syrup or honey for breakfast, or just as they are in lunchboxes for a healthy snack option.

Paulene Christie

Choccy Fruit Oat Bites

These are perfect for home snacks or as an addition to a fruit side for school lunches. Made from scratch, you can be sure of what goes in, and be proud of your results.

Makes 12 • Preparation 15 mins • Cook 30–40 mins • Cooker capacity 7 litres

1 cup rolled (porridge) oats
½ cup plain (all-purpose) flour
½ cup mixed dried fruit
¼ cup caster (superfine) sugar
¼ cup milk
2 tablespoons light brown sugar
1 egg
100 g (3½ oz) butter, melted
½ teaspoon cinnamon
3 teaspoons cocoa

1. In a large bowl, combine all of the ingredients and mix well. Transfer to 12 individual silicone cupcake moulds. Put the moulds in a slow cooker.

2. Cover, putting a tea towel (dish towel) under the lid, and cook on HIGH for 30–40 minutes, or until cooked through.

Simon Christie

Bees Neez Bars

These bars are a healthier and cheaper option than store-bought bars. I love that I control what goes in them: all of my favourite fruits and nuts and seeds. These bars can be frozen.

Makes 10–12 bars • Preparation 10–15 mins • Cook 1 hour • Cooker capacity 7 litres

2 cups rolled (porridge) oats
1 cup Rice Bubbles (Rice Krispies)
1–2 cups unsalted mixed nuts and unsweetened dried fruit, roughly blended
¼ cup desiccated coconut
2 tablespoons wholemeal (wholewheat) self-raising flour
2 tablespoons your favourite seeds (I used sunflower seeds and pepitas)
1 tablespoon chia seeds (optional)
50 g (1¾ oz) butter
¾ cup honey
1–2 tablespoons golden syrup (optional)
Melted dark chocolate, to drizzle

1. Grease and line the base of a slow cooker with baking paper and preheat to HIGH.

2. In a large bowl, combine all of the dry ingredients.

3. Melt the butter in a small saucepan and stir in the honey and golden syrup (if using). Pour this mixture into the dry ingredients and combine.

4. Pour the mixture into the prepared slow cooker and press down firmly.

5. Cover, putting a tea towel (dish towel) under the lid, and cook on HIGH for around 1 hour, or until cooked through. Allow to cool, then drizzle over the melted chocolate.

6. Remove the slice from the slow cooker, using the baking paper to lift it out, and set aside in the fridge for at least 2 hours to set.

7. Cut into slices and store in an airtight container in the fridge, or wrap each slice in plastic wrap and set aside for lunchboxes.

Robyn Clark

Pumpkin soup scones

I hate to waste any food so I came up with this quick and easy recipe to use up my left-over slow-cooked soup.

Makes 10 • Preparation 15 mins • Cook 2 hours • Cooker capacity 5.5 litres

3 cups self-raising flour
2 cups slow-cooked pumpkin (squash) soup (or tinned soup)
Butter and/or jam and cream, to serve

1. Line a slow cooker with baking paper.

2. In a large bowl, combine the flour and pumpkin soup to form a dough.

3. On a floured surface, roll out the dough to about 2 cm (¾ in) thick. Using a cutter or egg ring, cut out 10 rounds (you may need to recombine the dough and roll out again). Place in the lined slow cooker, leaving some space between.

4. Cover, putting a tea towel (dish towel) under the lid, and cook on HIGH for 2 hours.

5. Serve warm with butter or cooled with jam and cream.

Melissa Lee

Wholemeal Pumpkin Bread

This was originally a banana bread recipe; I played around with it because I wanted pumpkin (squash) bread. I cut the slices about 2 cm (¾ in) thick, and eat them for afternoon tea and even toasted for a quick breakfast on the run. This bread also freezes well.

Serves 8–10 • Preparation 10 mins • Cook 1½ hours • Cooker capacity 5.5 litres

2 eggs
⅓ cup milk
50 g (1¾ oz) melted butter, plus extra, to serve
1 cup mashed pumpkin (squash) (I used butternut)
½ cup lightly packed light brown sugar or raw sugar
2 teaspoons mixed spice
1½ teaspoon bicarbonate of soda (baking soda)
2 cups wholemeal (wholewheat) self-raising flour

1. Pour 2.5 cm (1 in) water into a slow cooker and place a metal trivet that sits just above the water line in the bottom. Preheat the slow cooker to HIGH. Line a loaf tin that fits inside the slow cooker with baking paper.

2. Using an electric mixer, beat together the eggs, milk and butter. Add the pumpkin and mix to combine. Add the brown sugar, mixed spice, and bicarbonate of soda and mix. Lastly add the flour and mix until combined.

3. Pour the mixture into the prepared loaf tin and transfer to the slow cooker, sitting the tin on the trivet.

4. Cover, putting a tea towel (dish towel) under the lid, and cook on HIGH for 1½ hours or until a skewer inserted into the middle of the bread comes out clean.

5. Serve warm with butter.

Karen Stuckings

Caz's Knotted Garlic Bread

This is just so yummy, it's hard to stop at one piece. I always make this for get-togethers and it's always devoured. You can put as much garlic in as you want. This is a fabulous accompaniment to lasagne and spaghetti bolognese, and it makes such delicious pizza bread as well – tying it in knots makes it easier to pull apart. Definitely need to try, guys!

Serves 16–20 • Preparation 1 hour + rising time • Cook 2 hours • Cooker capacity 5 litres

1¾ cups warm water
2 teaspoons yeast
1 teaspoon sugar
4 cups bread flour
2 tablespoons olive oil
½ teaspoon salt
Grated cheese and oregano, for topping

DIPPING OIL
3 tablespoons melted butter
2 tablespoons crushed garlic
2 teaspoons olive oil

1. In a small bowl, combine the warm water, yeast and sugar. Allow to sit for about 15 minutes or until frothy.

2. Mix the flour, oil and salt in a large bowl then pour in the yeast mixture. Turn the dough out onto a floured bench top and knead for about 10 minutes. Place in a large oiled bowl, cover with plastic wrap and set aside somewhere warm to rise for about 1 hour.

3. Meanwhile, combine the dipping oil ingredients in a small bowl. Grease the bowl of a slow cooker.

4. Turn the dough out onto a floured bench top and knead for about 2 minutes. Break into golf ball-sized pieces and roll into sausages. Loosely tie into knots.

5. Dip each knot into the dipping oil and place into the slow cooker, leaving a little space between the knots. Sprinkle the tops with cheese and oregano. You may need to do two layers of knots – try to place the second layer over the gaps. Drizzle any remaining dipping oil over the top.

6. Cover, putting a tea towel (dish towel) under the lid, and cook on HIGH for about 2 hours.

NOTE: You can flavour these with whatever you want – try making pizza knots by adding onions, capsicum, bacon, cabanossi, etc.

Carol Wilkinson

Slow-Cooker Garlic Bread

Garlic bread is a great side dish to so many meals. It's perfect to pop into your slow cooker and serve warm straight from the cooker onto the table. So simple, so easy! Why buy garlic bread when you can make your own?

Serves 6 • Preparation 10 mins • Cook 1 hour • Cooker capacity 6 litres

1 rustic baguette (about 30 cm/12 in)
100 g (3½ oz) butter, in once piece
About 3–4 teaspoons crushed garlic

1. Slice into the bread every 3 cm (1¼ in) or so along the length, but do not cut all the way through.
2. Slice the butter into thin slices then cut into squares. Insert a square of butter and approximately ¼ teaspoon of garlic into each slice in the bread.
3. Wrap tightly in foil and cook in a slow cooker on HIGH for 1 hour. Take care when opening the foil parcel as steam will be released.

Paulene Christie

⚱— Cheesy Garlic Bread Loaf —•

More lush than regular garlic bread, this is an open-style loaf piled with melted cheese. It's a great side dish for your next barbecue or party.

Serves 6 • Preparation 10 mins • Cook About 1 hour • Cooker capacity 7 litres

1 rustic baguette (about 30 cm/12 in)
About 3–4 tablespoons butter, softened
About 3–4 teaspoons crushed garlic
1 cup grated tasty cheese
Finely chopped fresh parsley

1. Slice the baguette lengthways into halves. Spread each half generously with the softened butter. Smear the crushed garlic over the butter (add as much as you like), top with grated cheese and scatter over the parsley.

2. Lay the bread halves, butter side up, on a sheet of foil in a slow cooker.

3. Cover, putting a tea towel (dish towel) under the lid, and cook on HIGH for up to 1 hour – the bread is ready when the cheese is melted and the loaf is crisp on the bottom.

Paulene Christie

Loaded Cheese & Bacon Cob Loaf Pull-Apart

Who doesn't love a cob loaf or pull-apart bread at a party? There are so many options to fill it with. I chose cheese and bacon for this one because ... well, cheese and bacon are meant to be! Turn up to a party with this bad boy and you'll be the talk of the night! You could also prepare this ahead of time for your own party, then just pop it in the slow cooker in time for your guests to arrive!

Serves 10 • Preparation 20 mins • Cook 2 hours • Cooker capacity 7 litres

1 x 450 g (1 lb) crusty cob loaf
200 g (7 oz) diced bacon
1 onion, diced
2–4 garlic cloves (according to taste)
125 g (4½ oz) butter
½ cup finely sliced spring onions (scallions)
230 g (8 oz) grated tasty cheese

1. Make five deep cuts across the top of the cob loaf, but don't slice all the way through. Rotate the loaf 90 degrees and make three more cuts in the opposite direction. You should have a checkerboard pattern of cuts.

2. In a small frying pan, cook the bacon, onion and garlic in 25 g (1 oz) of the butter over medium heat for 5–10 minutes, or until the onion is translucent and the bacon is lightly cooked. Transfer to a bowl and stir through the spring onions and 130 g (4½ oz) of the grated cheese.

3. Take two long sheets of aluminum foil (about 60 cm/2 ft each) and lay them crossways over each other to form an X shape. Place the cob loaf in the middle.

4. Carefully spoon the bacon mixture into the cuts of the cob loaf.

5. Melt the remaining butter and pour over and in the cracks of the cob loaf.

6. Top with the remaining grated cheese.

7. Wrap the loaf securely in the foil and put it into a slow cooker.

8. Cover and cook on HIGH for 2 hours.

9. Unwrap the loaf carefully, as it will be hot.

NOTE: If you like, you can brown the bread in a preheated oven for a few minutes before serving.

Paulene Christie

Mexican Scrolls

This recipe is a new take on the many versions of scrolls available. I had some leftover taco mince on hand so I thought, why not make something a little different with it. I deliberately used ready-made puff pastry, as this is intended to be a quick, easy recipe, but you could of course make your own, if you prefer. This may take longer than your regular scroll to cook and crisp because the filling is quite wet, so use your own cooker as your guide.

Makes 24 • Preparation 15 mins • Cook 1½ hours • Cooker capacity 7 litres

2 sheets ready-made puff pastry, slightly defrosted
1½ cups taco mince (see page 105)
1 cup grated tasty cheese
1 egg, beaten

1. Line a slow cooker with greased baking paper.

2. Lay out each sheet of puff pastry on a clean bench top. Top each sheet with ¾ cup taco mince and spread out over the pastry. Scatter the cheese over the top of both sheets.

3. Roll each sheet from one side to the other into a tight log. Cut each log into slices approximately 2 cm (¾ in) thick and place, cut side up and close together, in the slow cooker. Brush the scrolls with the beaten egg (you won't need all of the egg).

4. Cover, putting a tea towel (dish towel) under the lid, and cook on HIGH for 1½ hours.

Paulene Christie

Loaded Mac 'n' Cheese

An easy and filling dish that all the family will love. LOW cost but HIGH in taste!

Serves 4 • Preparation 10 mins • Cook 2 hours 40 mins • Cooker capacity 3 litres

2 tablespoon butter
4 rashers bacon, diced
1 onion, diced
1 tablespoon crushed garlic
2 cups milk
30 g (1 oz) packet cheese sauce mix
200 g (7 oz) mushrooms, sliced
80 g (2¾ oz) parmesan cheese, grated
½ punnet cherry tomatoes, halved
2 tablespoon chopped parsley
1½ cups grated cheese, plus extra, to top
Pinch of smoked paprika
250 g (9 oz) spiral pasta, cooked

1. Melt the butter in a frying pan over medium–high heat and sauté the bacon, onion and garlic until browned. Transfer to a slow cooker.

2. In a bowl, combine the milk and the cheese sauce mix. Pour into the slow cooker along with the remaining ingredients except the pasta.

3. Cover and cook on HIGH for 2½ hours.

4. Meanwhile, preheat the oven to 200°C (400°F).

5. Add the pasta and mix through. Transfer to an oven dish and top with the extra cheese. Bake for 5–10 minutes, or until the cheese topping is melted.

Jaime Caillot de Chadbannes

Potato Gem Quiche

I love this recipe as it only takes 15 minutes to prepare. I have cooked this for a lunch and a dinner and served it with salad and vegies. It's loved by all.

Serves 4 • Preparation 15 mins • Cook 2½ hours • Cooker capacity 6 litres

750 g (1 lb 11 oz) potato gems
4–6 rashers bacon, diced
1 onion, diced
Grated cheese (as much as you like)
8–12 eggs
½ cup milk

1. Line a slow cooker with baking paper and put the potato gems on top.

2. Add the bacon, then sprinkle the onion and cheese over the top.

3. In a large bowl, whisk the eggs and milk and pour into the slow cooker.

4. Cover, putting a tea towel (dish towel) under the lid, and cook on for HIGH 2½ hours.

NOTE: This recipe can be easily adapted to use prosciutto instead of bacon and spring onions (scallions) instead of onion.

Jo McKinnon

Individual Creamy Potato Bake Cups

I love creamy potato bake. It is such a great side dish to so many meals. Serving it in individual ramekins like this really adds a nice touch to your plated presentation. They are the perfect serving size!

Serves 4 as a side dish • **Preparation** 15 mins • **Cook** 4 hours • **Cooker capacity** 6 litres

2 large potatoes, peeled and thinly sliced
¼ onion, finely diced
50 g (1¾ oz) bacon, diced
1 teaspoon crushed garlic
2½ cups grated tasty cheese
250 ml (8½ fl oz/1 cup) cooking cream
Paprika, to garnish

1. Lightly grease four ramekins.

2. Layer half of the potato slices in the ramekins. Scatter the onion, bacon and garlic over the potato, and sprinkle ½ cup grated cheese, divided over the four cups. Top with the remaining potato slices and pour over the cream.

3. Pour water into a slow cooker to create a water bath approximately 2 cm (½ inch) deep. Lay a metal trivet in the water and place the ramekins on top, to elevate them out of the water.

4. Cover, putting a tea towel (dish towel) under the lid, and cook on HIGH for 3½ hours.

5. Top each ramekin with ½ cup of the remaining grated cheese. Lightly sprinkle some paprika over the top to give a browned appearance.

6. Continue cooking for 30 minutes.

NOTE: You can also finish the dish in a hot oven, to brown.

Paulene Christie

Cheesy Potato Smash

This is a new option for a potato side dish at your next barbecue. It's so easy to serve directly from the slow cooker too! This recipe will easily serve six but could be halved or even doubled, if you wished. It's great served with a sizzling steak and side salad.

Serves 6 • Preparation 10 mins • Cook 3 hours 30 mins • Cooker capacity 7 litres

4 large washed, unpeeled potatoes, cut into 2 cm (¾ in) cubes
2 tablespoons diced bacon
1 small onion, diced
2 tablespoons butter
Cracked black pepper
1 cup grated tasty cheese

1. Put the potatoes in a single layer in the base of a slow cooker. Scatter the bacon and onion over the top and dot the butter over the potato. Season with cracked black pepper.

2. Cover and cook on HIGH for 3 hours 30 minutes, or until the potato is tender but not too soft. When 15–20 minutes from cooked, scatter the cheese over the potato smash to melt.

3. Serve straight from your slow cooker – delicious!

Paulene Christie

Pizza Potatoes

This is a great side dish for any meal.

Serves 2 • Preparation 10 mins • Cook 3–6 hours • Cooker capacity Any

2 large potatoes

FILLING AND TOPPING
Ham
Slices of salami
Slices of cheese
Olives
Cubes of feta
Diced red capsicum (pepper)

1. Push a skewer longways through the bottom of each potato, but don't push all the way through. The skewer will stop the knife going all the way through the potato.

2. With a sharp knife, make lots of fine slits, about 2 cm (¾ in) apart, across the top of the potatoes (this makes the potato more flexible and easier to fill – you don't have to fill all of the slits).

3. Remove the skewer then fill the slits with the ham, salami and cheese slices. Top the potatoes with a few olives, cubes of feta and some capsicum and place in a slow cooker.

4. Cover and cook on HIGH for 3 hours or on LOW for 5–6 hours.

Samantha Steele

Beef 'Biscuits'

For something a little different as finger food, or as a protein with a fresh salad, these 'biscuits' are sure to surprise.

Makes 12 biscuits • Preparation 15 mins • Cook 2 hours • Cooker capacity 7 litres

4 flatbreads (tortilla-wrap style)
500 g (1 lb 2 oz) minced (ground) beef
½ cup grated tasty cheese
⅓ cup breadcrumbs
1 egg
1 tablespoon barbecue sauce
1 teaspoon sesame seeds
½ teaspoon thyme
½ teaspoon crushed garlic

1. Using a round biscuit cutter approximately 8 cm (3 in) in diameter, cut out 24 circles of flatbread.

2. In a mixing bowl, combine the remaining ingredients.

3. Transfer the beef mixture to a clean bench top and flatten to approximately 1 cm (½ in) thick. Cut out circles of mixture with the same biscuit cutter. Re-flatten any leftover mixture and repeat until completely used. You should have 12 circles.

4. Put half of the flatbread circles in a slow cooker. Lay a mince circle on top of each flatbread circle and top with the remaining flatbread. Lightly press each 'biscuit' by hand to help them stick. (You might find it easier to do this outside the slow cooker.)

5. Cover, putting a tea towel (dish towel) under the lid, and cook on HIGH for 1 hour.

6. Using tongs, gently turn the biscuits over and continue cooking for 1 hour.

Simon Christie

Cheat's Chicken & Cheese Dip

I first made this as a dip to take to barbecues and family gatherings, but it was such a hit with the kids and adults alike that I decided to adapt it into a main meal. The reason I call it 'cheat's chicken and cheese dip' is that you can buy already-cooked chicken breast or use leftovers from the previous night's dinner.

Serves 6–8 • Preparation 15 mins • Cook 2½ hours • Cooker capacity 5.5 litres

450 g (1 lb) gouda cheese, roughly grated
225 g (8 oz) cooked chicken breast, diced
225 ml (7½ fl oz) chunky tomato salsa
225 ml (7½ fl oz) sour cream
350 g (12½ oz) packet corn chips
3 spring onions (scallions), thinly sliced, to garnish

1. Put the chicken, cheese and salsa into a slow cooker and stir well to combine.

2. Cover and cook on LOW for 2 hours.

3. Stir in the sour cream and cook on HIGH for 20 minutes on or until heated all the way through.

4. Serve hot, garnished with spring onion and with corn chips on the side.

Melissa Lee

Peg's Pasta Salad Sauce

I make this sauce the night before we have a barbecue and pour it over cooked pasta shells. This sauce can be kept in the fridge for up to a week and used hot or cold. It never lasts long in my house when I make it.

Serves 6+ • Preparation 10 mins • Cook 1 hour • Cooker capacity 1.5 litres

420 g (15 oz) tinned condensed tomato soup (a cheaper one works best)
½ cup white vinegar
½ cup sugar (or artificial sweetener)
½ cup oil
2–3 ham steaks, diced
1 onion, diced
1 tablespoon mustard powder
500 g (1 lb 2 oz) pasta shells or spirals, cooked
2–3 celery stalks, diced (optional)
Parsley, chopped (optional)

1. Put all of the ingredients except the pasta, celery and parsley into a slow cooker, season with salt and pepper and stir well to combine.

2. Cover and cook on LOW for 1 hour.

3. Once cooled, stir in the celery and parsley, if using.

4. Store in glass jars in the fridge and pour over cooked pasta as required.

Penelope Rieschiek

Homemade Slow-Cooker Apple Sauce

I tried making apple sauce to serve with pork and my daughter loved it, so I've kept making it for her.

Makes 1.35 kg (3 lb) • Preparation 5–10 mins • Cook 6 hours • Cooker capacity 6 litres

1.5 kg (3 lb 5 oz) Fuji apples

1. Prepare the apples by coring and slicing them (you don't have to peel them unless you want to). Put the apples in a slow cooker with ½ cup of water.

2. Cover and cook on LOW for 6 hours, or until the apples are soft.

3. In batches, transfer the sauce to a blender and blend. Be careful not to over-blend as the sauce becomes smooth very quickly.

4. Store in a sterilised jar in the fridge for up to 1 month.

Trinity Simmons

Aunty Bess's Tomato Relish

Every Christmas we would all receive a jar of relish from Aunty Bess or my mother-in-law for us all to enjoy, so I'm sharing their memory by recreating this sauce. Enjoy with roast meat or in sandwiches.

Makes 6 large (500 ml) jars • **Preparation** 20 mins • **Cook** 4 hours plus 10 mins • **Cooker capacity** 5 litres

5 kg (11 lb) tomatoes (can be over-ripe), diced
2 large brown onions, diced
1 cucumber or zucchini (courgette), diced
1 red capsicum (pepper), diced
1 cup sugar
1 cup white or apple cider vinegar plus around 2 tablespoons
2 tablespoons yellow mustard seeds
1½ tablespoons turmeric
1 tablespoon curry powder
2 tablespoons cornflour (cornstarch)

1. Put all of the ingredients except the extra vinegar and the cornflour into a slow cooker and stir well to combine.

2. Cover and cook on HIGH for 4 hours.

3. In a small bowl, mix the cornflour with the extra vinegar to form a runny paste, then stir into the cooked relish to thicken. Cook on HIGH for another 10 minutes.

4. Leave the ingredients chunky or blitz in a blender for a smoother relish. Pour into sterilised jars while still warm and set aside to cool.

5. Store in a cupboard up to 6 months. Once opened, refrigerate and use within a month.

Jackie Chalwell

Gooseberry Sauce

Another family favourite made for years on the stovetop that I have adapted for slow-cooking, for convenience. It is yummy served with meats or added to a marinade or sauce.

Makes 3 litres (approximately) • Preparation 10–15 mins • Cook 5–6 hours • Cooker capacity 5.5 litres

1.4 kg (3lb) gooseberries
1.4 kg (3 lb) sugar
1 litre (34 fl oz/4 cups) malt vinegar
250 g (9 oz) onions, chopped
45 g (1½ oz) cloves (either whole or ground)
25 g (1 oz) salt

1. Put all of the ingredients in a slow cooker and stir to combine.

2. Bring to the boil, stirring occasionally. Cover and cook on HIGH for 5–6 hours.

3. Once cool, push the reduced sauce and the fruit through a sieve. Transfer to bottles or jars and store. Best consumed within 12 months but will keep longer.

Nikki Willis

SOUP

Cream of Cauliflower Soup

I cook a lot of soups but my granddaughter loves this one.

Serves 8 • Preparation 5 mins • Cook 4–6 hours • Cooker capacity 4.5 litres

1 litre (34 fl oz/4 cups) chicken stock
1 head cauliflower, broken into florets
1 leek, chopped
4 rashers bacon, diced
600 ml thin (pouring) cream, to serve
Chopped flat-leaf (Italian) parsley, to garnish
Crusty bread, to serve

1. Put the chicken stock, cauliflower, leek and bacon into a slow cooker and mix well.

2. Cover and cook on LOW for 4–6 hours.

3. Transfer to a blender and purée until smooth.

4. Stir the cream through, add salt and pepper to taste, and serve with a sprinkle of parsley and some crusty bread.

Laura Carolan

Minestrone soup

I always love soup during the winter. Having two small children, I need a soup that is chunky – so that they can eat it without making a huge mess – as well as healthy and filling.

Serves 6–8 • Preparation 15 mins • Cook 3½–4½ hours • Cooker capacity 6.5 litres

4 cups vegetable stock
800 g (1 lb 12 oz) tinned diced tomatoes
1½ cups diced brown onion
1¼ cups diced celery
1 cup diced carrot
¼ cup sun-dried tomato pesto
2 tablespoons tomato paste (concentrated purée)
1 piece parmesan cheese rind
4–5 garlic cloves, chopped
1 teaspoon oregano
2 bay leaves
½ teaspoon rosemary
400 g (14 oz) tinned kidney beans, rinsed and drained
400 g (14 oz) tinned cannellini beans, rinsed and drained
1½ cups diced zucchini (courgette)
1½ cups ditalini or other soup pasta
2½ cups baby spinach leaves
1 cup frozen green beans
Grated parmesan cheese, to serve
Toasted Turkish bread, to serve

1. Put the stock, tinned tomatoes, onion, celery, carrots, pesto, tomato paste, parmesan rind, garlic, oregano, bay leaves and rosemary in a slow cooker with 2 cups of water. Stir well to combine.

2. Cover and cook on HIGH for 3–4 hours.

3. Add the kidney and cannellini beans, zucchini and pasta, and continue cooking for 20–25 minutes until the pasta is tender.

4. Stir in the baby spinach and green beans and cook for another 5 minutes until heated through.

5. Serve with parmesan cheese and some Turkish bread.

NOTE: This recipe can be cooked on LOW for 6–8 hours before you add the beans and pasta. Turn up to HIGH to finish cooking.

Zoe Grey

Nanna's Pumpkin Soup

This is an old pumpkin (squash) soup recipe handed down through my family. I decided to give it a whirl in the slow cooker and it came out tasting as though Nanna had just made it herself.

Serves 4–6 • Preparation 30 mins • Cook 4–6 hours • Cooker capacity 6.5 litres

1 litre (34 fl oz/4 cups) chicken stock
1 medium pumpkin (squash), peeled and chopped
4 large potatoes, peeled and chopped
3 large carrots, peeled and chopped
2 sweet potatoes, peeled and chopped
3 onions, chopped
2–4 garlic cloves
Cracked black pepper and sour cream, to serve

1. Put all the ingredients into the slow cooker and stir well to combine.

2. Cover and cook on HIGH for 4 hours or LOW for 6 hours.

3. Purée with a stick blender until smooth.

4. Serve with a sprinkle of cracked pepper and dollop of sour cream.

Nicole Williams

Easy Spicy Pumpkin Soup

My hubby wanted me to make pumpkin (squash) soup for him 'with a kick' as he had a cold. I hate pumpkin so I didn't taste test along the way at all. My hubby LOVES this! So does my mum, who always said she would never find better than my nan's. I hope you enjoy it too!

Serves 10 • Preparation 30 mins • Cook 7 hours • Cooker capacity 5.5 litres

1 litre (34 fl oz/4 cups) vegetable stock
1 bunch celery, roughly chopped
½ jap pumpkin (squash), peeled and roughly chopped
2 large red potatoes, roughly chopped
1 sweet potato, roughly chopped
1 bunch spring onions (scallions), roughly chopped
1 large onion, sliced
3 teaspoons cumin powder
2 teaspoons ground coriander
½ teaspoon turmeric powder
½ teaspoon chilli flakes
1½ small avocadoes per litre (34 fl oz/4 cups)

1. Put the vegetable stock and vegetables in a slow cooker.

2. Cover and cook on HIGH for 2 hours then LOW for 5 hours.

3. At the end of cooking, add the spices and stir.

4. Blend in 1 litre (34 fl oz/4 cups) batches, with the avocado.

Tabatha Wendell

Classic Creamy Pumpkin Soup

This was my first ever attempt at cooking a pumpkin (squash) soup, let alone a slow-cooker version. I was thrilled to be given a rousing 'hoorah' from seasoned pumpkin soup lovers for this version. The toasted pumpkin seeds on top are optional. Serve with crusty bread rolls and a dollop of cream stirred through.

Serves 12 • Preparation 20 mins • Cook 6 hours • Cooker capacity 6 litres

1 large jarrahdale or butternut pumpkin (squash), peeled and chopped
1 large potato, peeled and chopped
2 carrots, peeled and chopped
2 onions, peeled and chopped
2 garlic cloves, crushed
3 cups chicken stock

GARNISH
½ teaspoon olive oil
2 tablespoons dried pumpkin seeds
Garlic chives
Cream or sour cream

1. Put all of the ingredients for the soup in a slow cooker.

2. Cover and cook on LOW for 6 hours.

3. Using a hand-held blender, purée the soup to a smooth consistency.

4. Heat the olive oil in a small frying pan over medium heat. Add the pumpkin seeds and lightly toast, stirring constantly so they don't burn, for 3–5 minutes, or until golden.

5. Serve the pumpkin soup with a dollop of cream or sour cream, scatter with chives and toasted pumpkin seeds.

Paulene Christie

━ 'Meaty' Mushroom Soup ━●

I love mushrooms in any form and wanted to make a simple mushroom soup that wasn't cream based. I threw this in the slow cooker and was extremely happy with the result.

Serves 3 • Preparation 10–15 mins • Cook 2 hours • Cooker capacity 1.5 litres

250 g (9 oz) mushrooms
25 g (1 oz) butter
1 garlic clove, crushed
450 ml (15 fl oz) chicken stock
1–2 teaspoons arrowroot (optional)
Cream or sour cream, to serve

1. Peel and slice the mushrooms then gently sauté in a frying pan over medium heat with the butter and the garlic, until just starting to colour. Transfer to a slow cooker and add the chicken stock.

2. Cook on HIGH for 1 hour then on LOW for 1 hour.

3. Season with salt and pepper. If you want a thicker soup, mix the arrowroot with enough water to make a paste and stir into the soup to thicken.

4. Serve with a swirl of cream or with a dollop of sour cream.

Nikki Willis

Moroccan Lentil Soup

I started making this soup because I wanted to add more pulses to my diet. I regularly make it for lunch in winter and find it delicious and also filling.

Serves 6 • Preparation 15 mins • Cook 6 hours • Cooker capacity 3.5 litres

1 tablespoon oil
1 onion, finely chopped
1 garlic clove, crushed
2 tablespoons ground cumin
1 tablespoon ground coriander
1 teaspoon paprika
½ teaspoon chilli powder
½ teaspoon ground cinnamon
4 cups reduced-salt chicken stock
800 g (1 lb 12 oz) tinned crushed tomatoes
375 g (13 oz) red lentils

1. Heat the oil in a frying pan over medium–high heat. Add the onion and garlic and cook until the onion softens. Add the spices and cook for 1 minute. Add the stock and bring to a simmer.

2. Transfer to a slow cooker with 3 cups of water and the tomatoes and lentils.

3. Cover and cook on HIGH for 6 hours.

Lorna Bateman

Chicken Broth with Corn Dumplings

This is my go-to recipe when I feel like eating something fresh and light or when my family are sick with colds. I came up with this when I was experimenting with making chicken soup in my slow cooker. While searching around for ingredients to add, I came across some frozen wonton wrappers in my freezer and had the idea of a chicken and corn soup with a twist. Since then, this recipe has become a family favourite.

Serves 4–6 • Preparation 20 mins • Cook 8½ hours • Cooker capacity 6.5 litres

1 kg (2 lb 3 oz) chicken necks
2 carrots, cut in half
4 celery stalks, roughly chopped
1 unpeeled onion, halved
1 long red chilli, seeds removed and halved lengthways
6 cm (2½ in) piece ginger, 4 cm (1½ in) sliced into rounds, 2 cm (¾ in) grated
4 garlic cloves, roughly chopped
2 litres boiling water
¼ cup soy sauce
3 tablespoons fish sauce

DUMPLINGS
250 g (9 oz) minced (ground) chicken
3 tablespoons oyster sauce
¼ cup frozen corn kernels
Store-bought wonton wrappers

TO SERVE
Cooked rice noodles
Boiled eggs
Coriander leaves
Long red chilli
Cabbage
Pak choy
Bean sprouts

1. Put the chicken necks, carrot, celery, onion, chilli, sliced ginger and garlic into a slow cooker. Cover with the boiling water.

2. Cover and cook on LOW for 8 hours.

3. Strain the broth through a tea towel (dish towel) set in a colander and discard the solids. Return the broth to the slow cooker, add the soy sauce, fish sauce and grated ginger, and continue cooking for 10 minutes.

4. Meanwhile, make the dumplings. In a bowl, combine the chicken, oyster sauce and corn. Lay the wonton wrappers on a benchtop, place a teaspoon of chicken mixture in the centre of each wrapper, brush a little water around the edges of each wrapper, bring the sides up together and pinch them tightly to seal. They should resemble little money bags. Don't worry if they split a little, they will be fine. Pop them into the hot broth; once they float, they're cooked.

5. To serve, I like to add some cooked rice noodles, boiled egg, coriander, chopped fresh chilli, raw cabbage, shredded pak choy and bean sprouts to a bowl, then pour over the hot broth and cooked dumplings.

Alanna Williams

Mamma's Chicken Soup

I first made this recipe when my family and I were very sick. I had lots of vegetables in the fridge and wanted to make something that would help us get better. We all had sore throats, so I decided to make this soup. My kids generally hate soup, but after some encouragement they tried it and loved it and licked their bowls clean. It is now their favourite soup and they named it Mama's sick soup!

Serves 6 • Preparation 20 mins • Cook 6 hours • Cooker capacity 6.5 litres

- 2 chicken breasts
- 1 litre (34 fl oz/4 cups) vegetable stock
- 2 potatoes, peeled and chopped
- 1 onion, chopped
- 4 carrots, peeled and chopped
- 1 cup chopped sweet potato
- 2 celery stalks, chopped
- 1 large parsnip, peeled and chopped
- 1 turnip, peeled and chopped
- 1 swede, peeled and chopped
- 2 teaspoons crushed garlic
- 1½ teaspoons curry powder
- 1 teaspoon ground pepper
- 1 cup broken-up spaghetti

1. Heat a large frying pan sprayed with cooking oil over medium–high heat. Briefly brown the chicken on both sides and transfer to a slow cooker. Add 500 ml (17 fl oz/2 cups) of water along with all of the remaining ingredients except the spaghetti.

2. Cover and cook on low for about 4 hours.

3. Using tongs or a fork, break up the chicken and continue cooking for 1 hour.

4. Add the spaghetti and continue cooking for 1 hour. Add ½ a cup of water at this stage if the soup is a little thick.

5. Serve with fresh crusty bread.

Kara Johnson

My Version of Avgolemono
(Greek Egg and Lemon Soup)

This is by no means a traditional version of avgolemono, but in the spirit of the dish as a restorative for people with colds etc, I think the extra goodness of the chicken makes it even better!

Serves 6 • Preparation 5 mins • Cook 6–8 hours • Cooker capacity 5.5 litres

1 litre (34 fl oz/4 cups) chicken stock
6 chicken drumsticks
3 teaspoons lemon juice
2 teaspoons crushed garlic
1 teaspoon lemon rind
1 teaspoon oregano
1 teaspoon salt
1 teaspoon freshly ground black pepper
2 eggs, beaten
Crusty bread, to serve

1. Put all of the ingredients except the eggs in a slow cooker and stir well to combine.

2. Cover and cook on LOW for 6–8 hours.

3. Remove the chicken and shred the meat off the bones.

4. Pour the beaten egg into the slow cooker and quickly stir through to help thicken the soup.

5. Return the chicken to the soup and serve immediately with crusty bread.

Fiona Masters

Creamy Chicken & Rice Soup

I first made this to use up leftover soup-mix vegetables in my fridge. My children and husband absolutely love it.

Serves 4–6 • Preparation 20 min • Cook 7 hours • Cooker capacity 5 litres

500 g (1 lb 2 oz) chicken thigh fillets, sliced
2 cups chicken stock
2 celery stalks, sliced
1 large onion, sliced
½ cup peas
½ parsnip, diced
½ red capsicum (pepper), diced
½ green capsicum (pepper), diced
2 garlic cloves, minced
2 tablespoons mixed herbs
2 cups cooked rice
¼ cup shallots, diced, plus extra to garnish
150 ml (5 fl oz) cream
100 ml (3½ fl oz) sour cream
2 tablespoons sweet chilli sauce, plus extra to serve
1 tablespoon Worcestershire sauce
1 tablespoon butter
Crusty bread, to serve

1. Put the chicken, chicken stock, vegetables, garlic and mixed herbs in a slow cooker and stir well to combine.

2. Cook on LOW for 6 hours.

3. One hour before serving, add the cooked rice, cream, sour cream and shallots. Season with salt and pepper. Stir thoroughly and continue cooking for 1 hour.

4. Ten minutes before serving add sweet chilli sauce, Worcestershire sauce and butter.

5. Serve garnished with shallots, with a dash of sweet chilli sauce and crusty bread.

NOTE: If you would like a thicker soup, add 1–2 tablespoons cornflour (cornstarch) per litre of soup.

Kassandra Carter

Easy Chicken & Corn Noodle Soup

Want a no-fuss easy soup recipe? Time poor? Not feeling well? Then this is the soup for you! It's one the whole family will love.

Serves 4 • Preparation 5 mins • Cook 4 hours • Cooker capacity 6 litres

1 roast chicken, meat shredded
1 litre (34 fl oz/4 cups) chicken stock
420 g (15 oz) tinned corn kernels, drained
420 g (15 oz) tinned creamed corn
2 x 80 g (2¾ oz) packets 2-minute noodles
Sliced spring onions (scallions), to garnish

1. Put the chicken, chicken stock, corn kernels and creamed corn in a slow cooker.

2. Cover and cook on HIGH for 4 hours.

3. Add the noodles 15 minutes before the end of cooking. If you would like more flavour, you can add the flavour sachets from the noodle packets. Serve garnished with spring onion.

Amanda Kenwright

Chicken & Vegie Soup

This soup is a nice hearty winter meal. Serve it with some fresh bread.

Serves 6–8 • Preparation 20 mins • Cook 4½–6½ hours • Cooker capacity 5 litres

6 chicken drumsticks
1 litre (34 fl oz/4 cups) chicken stock
400 g (14 oz) tinned chicken noodle soup or 45 g (1½ oz) dry chicken noodle
    soup mix
100 g (3½ oz) split peas
1 onion, diced
4 celery stalks, chopped
3 carrots, peeled and grated
3 potatoes, peeled and grated
1 swede, peeled and grated
1 sweet potato, peeled and grated
1 turnip, peeled and grated

1. Put the drumsticks into a slow cooker. Add 1 litre (34 fl oz/4 cups) of water, the chicken stock, soup and split peas. Stir well to combine. Add the remaining ingredients.

2. Cover and cook on LOW for 4–6 hours (or until chicken is falling off the bone).

3. Remove the chicken and shred the meat from the bones. Discard the bones and add the chicken back into the soup. Continue cooking for another 30 minutes or until ready to serve.

Beverley Hansen

⇒— Mediterranean Seafood Soup —●

I have always loved seafood, so I decided to make a healthy family meal that would keep us full and is jam-packed with flavour.

Serves 6 • Preparation 15 mins • Cook 2¼–4½ hours • Cooker capacity 6 litres

1 leek, sliced
1 onion, roughly chopped
2 garlic cloves, finely chopped
1 chilli, deseeded and finely diced
1 litre (34 fl oz/4 cups) fish stock
400 g (14 oz) tinned diced tomatoes
2 strips lemon rind, white pith removed
Pinch of saffron
Mixed seafood of your choice (see note)
Crusty bread, to serve

1. Heat a large frying pan sprayed with cooking oil over medium–high heat. Add the leek, onion, garlic and chilli and cook, stirring occasionally, until soft. Transfer to a slow cooker.

2. Add the stock, tomatoes, lemon rind and saffron and cook on HIGH for 2 hours or on LOW for 4 hours.

3. Add the seafood and continue cooking for 15 minutes on HIGH or 30 minutes on LOW.

4. Remove the lemon rind and discard.

5. Serve the soup with crusty bread.

NOTE: You can add as much or as little seafood as you like to this recipe. I use prawns (shrimp), mussels, white fish fillets (such as pink ling), salmon and squid rings

Cheree Bone

Ham & Potato Soup

My mum used to make a soup similar to this when I was young. I've adapted it to suit my taste and for the slow cooker. It's very filling and is a meal in itself.

Serves 4 • Preparation 20 mins • Cook 4 hours • Cooker capacity 3 litres

4 large potatoes, peeled and diced
4 teaspoons chicken stock powder
4 rashers bacon, finely diced
2 onions, finely diced
Knob of butter
½ cup sour cream
Crusty bread, to serve

1. Put potatoes and stock powder in a slow cooker with 4 cups of water.

2. Cover and cook on HIGH for 4 hours.

3. Shortly before serving, fry the bacon and onion in the butter in a small frying pan with a lid, over medium heat. Put the lid on and allow the onions to sweat for about 10 minutes, or until soft.

4. Purée the potatoes and stock using a hand-held blender. When smooth, add the bacon and onion then stir through the sour cream. Season with salt and pepper.

5. Serve with fresh crusty bread.

Kylie Walford

Pea & Ham Soup

This is a great winter soup that's best served with a buttered crusty baguette.

Serves 20 • Preparation 5 min • Cook 10 hours • Cooker capacity 7 litres

1 ham hock
1 rack smoked pork bones
2 carrots, roughly chopped
2 onions, chopped
500 g (1 lb 2 oz) split peas, rinsed
4 celery stalks
1 litre (34 fl oz/4 cups) chicken, beef or vegetable stock
1 garlic clove, roughly chopped
1 teaspoon cracked black pepper
1 teaspoon salt
Baguette, to serve

1. Add all of the ingredients to a slow cooker, along with enough water to fill the slow cooker most of the way.

2. Cover and cook on LOW for 10 hours, adding a little more water from time to time if the soup becomes too thick.

3. One hour before serving, remove the ham hock and pork and shred the meat. Discard the skin and bones.

4. Blend the soup with a hand-held blender (or you can leave it chunky), and return the shredded meat to the soup.

5. Serve with a crusty baguette.

Melodie Tapp

Bacon & Vegetable Soup

This is a favourite in our household during winter, especially on the weekends as it's so easy to make. I just chuck it on and walk away, giving us more family time without worrying about what to cook for dinner.

Serves 6 • Preparation 10 mins • Cook 8 hours • Cooker capacity 5.5 litres

1 kg (2 lb 3 oz) bacon bones
250 g (9 oz) dried barley soup mix
2 potatoes, chopped
2 carrots, chopped
200 g (7 oz) pumpkin (squash), chopped
4 celery stalks, chopped
1 parsnip, chopped
½ head cauliflower, broken into florets
1 head broccoli, broken into florets

1. Put all of the ingredients in a slow cooker with 3½ cups of water and stir well to combine.
2. Cover and cook on LOW for 8 hours.

Stacey Goodall

Dannelle's Oxtail Soup

My mum would cook oxtail soup when I was growing up and it has always been a favourite of mine on a cold winter's night. I modified my mother's recipe a little to my liking and I now cook it for my family. This soup is delish!!

Serves 6 • Preparation 15 mins • Cook 6–8 hours • Cooker capacity 6 litres

1 oxtail
1 onion, diced
3 celery stalks, chopped
1 large carrot, peeled and chopped
1 turnip, peeled and chopped
1 parsnip, peeled and chopped
1 swede, peeled and chopped
¼ head cauliflower, broken into florets
1 potato, chopped into large cubes
400 g (14 oz) tinned chopped tomatoes
1 beef stock cube
1 crusty loaf, to serve
Dash soy sauce, to serve (optional)

1. Put the oxtail, vegetables and tinned tomatoes in a slow cooker. Add enough water to cover and add the beef stock cube.

2. Cover and cook on LOW for 6–8 hours.

3. Season with salt to taste and serve with crusty bread and a dash of soy sauce (if using). Pull the meat off the bones as you eat. (Alternatively, you can remove the oxtail before serving, discard the bones then return the shredded meat to the soup.)

Dannelle Quemard

Bean Soup

My mother used to make this soup for me and my siblings when we were growing up, and now I make it for my kids. It's a huge winter favourite in my house.

Serves 6 • Preparation 15 mins • Cook 6–7 hours • Cooker capacity 6 litres

1 litre (34 fl oz/4 cups) beef stock
400 g (14 oz) tinned diced tomatoes
400 g (14 oz) tinned borlotti beans, drained and rinsed
4 large potatoes, peeled and diced
1 large carrot, grated
1 zucchini, grated (optional)
500 g (1 lb 2 oz) diced beef steak or other meat suitable for soup
Dash of garlic salt
Bread rolls, to serve

1. Pour the beef stock and 1 litre (34 fl oz/4 cups) of water into a slow cooker. Add the tinned tomatoes and borlotti beans along with the vegetables. Finally, add the diced steak and garlic salt. Stir well.

2. Cover and cook on LOW for about 6–7 hours. Stir occasionally.

3. In the final hour of cooking, use a hand-held blender to blend the soup a little – this will help thicken it. If the tomato hasn't broken down and is floating on the surface, you can whizz it using the blender, too.

4. Serve hot with bread rolls.

Karen Vickers

Taco Soup

This recipe is foolproof – everyone who eats it loves it. The best part is that it is even better the next day as leftovers.

Serves 6–8 • Preparation 10 mins • Cook 4–8 Hours • Cooker capacity 5 litres

500 g (1 lb 2 oz) minced (ground) beef
800 g (1 lb 12 oz) tinned diced tomatoes
400 g (14 oz) tinned kidney beans, drained and rinsed
400 g (14 oz) tinned corn kernels, drained
1 cup tomato paste (concentrated purée)
1 small onion, chopped
1 packet taco seasoning mix
Grated cheese, to serve
Corn chips, to serve

1. Heat a large frying pan sprayed with cooking oil over medium–high heat. Add the mince in batches, breaking it up with a wooden spoon and cooking until the mince is browned.

2. Transfer the browned mince to a slow cooker. Add the tinned tomatoes, kidney beans, corn kernels, tomato paste, onion, taco seasoning mix and 1–2 cups of water (depending on how thin you like your soup). Season with salt and pepper.

3. Cover and cook on HIGH for 4 hours or on LOW for 8 hours.

4. Serve topped with grated cheese, with corn chips to the side.

Lauren Del Valle

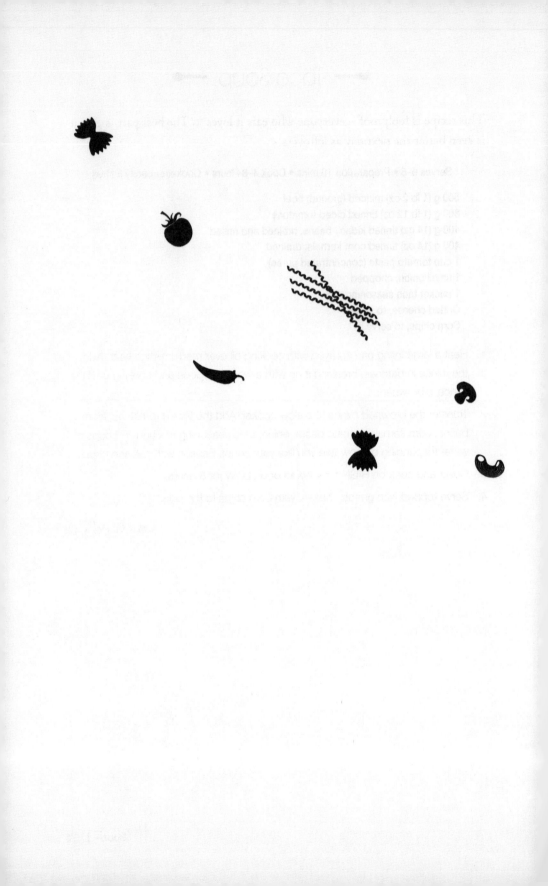

PASTA & NOODLES

Vegetarian Tomato & Basil Pasta

With the growing number of families turning to vegetarian alternatives for health benefits, I designed this full-flavoured dish to delight the taste buds. This is great for all ages and is sure to please the fussiest eaters.

Serves 4–6 • Preparation 20 mins • Cook 2½ hours • Cooker capacity 6 litres

300 g (10½ oz) farfalle (bowtie pasta)
3 tomatoes, diced
1 cup vegetable stock
1 onion
4 garlic cloves, crushed
1 tablespoon olive oil
20 g (¾ oz) basil leaves
2 teaspoons salt
1 teaspoon oregano
120 g (4½ oz) baby spinach
Parmesan cheese, to serve (optional)

1. Put all of the ingredients except the spinach and parmesan into a slow cooker. Mix gently to combine.

2. Cover and cook on HIGH for 2¼ hours, stirring occasionally.

3. Add the spinach and stir gently to combine. Continue cooking for 15 minutes.

4. Serve by itself or with a sprinkle of grated parmesan.

Simon Christie

Sausage & Vegetable Pasta

I have a 2-year-old daughter who refuses to eat vegetables. But if I use the vegetables as a sauce for the pasta she eats them every time! We eat this dish at least once a week in our household and my daughter eats two serves.

Serves 4 • Preparation 20 min • Cook 4¼ hours • Cooker capacity 4.5 litres

½ Jap pumpkin (squash), peeled and diced
2 cups stock
2 brown onions, diced
2 carrots, peeled and diced
½ sweet potato, peeled and diced
2 rashers bacon, diced
2 tablespoons crushed garlic
1 tablespoon minced ginger
6 sausages (chicken, beef or pork)
3 cups cooked pasta spirals

1. Put all the ingredients except the sausages and pasta into a slow cooker and stir well.

2. Lay the sausages flat over the diced vegetables.

3. Cover and cook on HIGH for 4 hours.

4. Remove the sausages and cut into slices.

5. Blend the pasta sauce using a hand-held blender, until you have a soup-like consistency with no lumps.

6. Add the cooked pasta and sliced sausage to the slow cooker and stir to combine. Continue cooking for 10 minutes.

Nikki Taylor

Parmesan Sausage Pasta

This simple one-pot blend of sausage, pasta and flavour is just the thing for filling empty bellies – a perfect family meal.

Serves 6 • Preparation 15 mins • Cook 3¼ hours • Cooker capacity 6 litres

1 teaspoon olive oil
12 thin barbecue beef sausages
1 small onion, diced
3 teaspoons crushed garlic
2 cups curly pasta
2 potatoes, peeled and cubed
1 cup beef stock
⅓ cup grated parmesan cheese
½ teaspoon dried Italian herbs

1. Heat the olive oil in a large frying pan over medium heat. Add the sausages, onion and garlic and cook until the sausages are well-browned.

2. Meanwhile, cook the pasta in salted boiling water until al dente. Drain, and transfer to a slow cooker.

3. Slice the sausages into bite-sized pieces and transfer to the slow cooker along with the onion and garlic from the pan, and the potatoes, beef stock and grated parmesan. Mix well to combine.

4. Cover and cook on HIGH for 2 hours.

5. Add the Italian herbs and gently stir. Continue cooking for 1 hour.

6. Season to taste and serve.

Simon Christie

➤— Hidden Veg Spaghetti Sauce —●

I love making this recipe because it can be used for so many different meals: spaghetti bolognese, pasta bake, vol-au-vents and individual shepherd's pies using taco boats. It also freezes well, so if you need a quick meal, just defrost a portion of the sauce, cook up some pasta or vegies and dinner is done.

Serves 6–8 • Preparation 30 mins • Cook 6–7½ hours • Cooker capacity 5.5 litres

1 kg (2 lb 3 oz) minced (ground) beef
1½ cups beef stock
400 g (14 oz) tinned diced tomatoes
2 tablespoons tomato sauce (ketchup)
2 tablespoons Worcestershire sauce
1 tablespoon tomato paste (concentrated purée)
1 large onion, grated
2 carrots, grated
1 zucchini (courgette), grated
2 celery stalks, grated
2 teaspoons crushed garlic
1 teaspoon mild chilli sauce
2 tablespoons cornflour (cornstarch)

1. Heat a large frying pan over medium–high heat. Brown the mince and drain off the excess fat. Transfer to a slow cooker.

2. Add the beef stock, diced tomatoes, tomato sauce, Worcestershire sauce and tomato paste and stir well to combine. Add the grated vegies and mix well.

3. Add the garlic and chilli sauce along with a little salt and pepper. Stir well to combine.

4. Cover and cook on HIGH for 2 hours and then on LOW for 4–5 hours, stirring occasionally.

5. Check the seasoning and add a little more salt and pepper if required.

6. Mix the cornflour with enough water to make a paste, stir into the sauce and continue cooking for 10–15 minutes to thicken.

Kriss Dainer

Saucy Steak Pasta

I wanted to create a meaty pasta with lots of flavour using what I could find in the pantry and it turned out amazing! Children won't be able to detect the grated vegetables – they just melt into the sauce.

Serves 4–6 • Preparation 20 mins • Cook 8+ hours • Cooker capacity 5 litres

Plain (all-purpose) flour, for dusting
1 kg (2 lb 3 oz) chuck steak, diced
1 teaspoon margarine
1 onion, sliced
1 carrot, grated
1 cup beef stock
2 tablespoons gravy powder
2 tablespoons tomato sauce (ketchup)
50 g (1¾ oz) tomato paste (concentrated purée)
1 tablespoon sweet chilli sauce
1 teaspoon raw sugar
1 teaspoon crushed garlic
Mixed herbs, to taste
375 g (13 oz) cooked penne pasta
Grated parmesan cheese, to serve

1. Put the flour in a medium-sized bowl and season well with salt and pepper. Add the beef and toss to coat.

2. Melt the margarine in a large pan over medium–high heat. Add the beef and cook, stirring constantly, for five minutes to sear the beef. Add the onion and carrot and cook until soft. Add the remaining ingredients except the pasta and stir until well combined. Transfer the mixture to a slow cooker.

3. Cover and cook on LOW for 8 or more hours. Stir the sauce a few times towards the end of cooking, as the mixture will start to stick to the sides. Add a little water if it gets too dry.

4. Stir through the pasta and serve with grated parmesan, if using.

Shaya Wright

Garlic & Bacon Mac 'n' Cheese

I like to make this as an easy weekend lunch for the grandkids while I do the housework. It's great on a cold winter's day to warm their little bellies up.

Serves 4 as a side dish • Preparation 5 mins • Cook 1¼–1½ hours • Cooker capacity 1.5 litres

1 cup diced bacon
1½ cups grated cheese
1 cup macaroni
1 cup warm water
1 cup milk
20 g (¾ oz) butter
2 garlic cloves, crushed
½ teaspoon salt

1. Heat a large frying pan sprayed with cooking oil over medium–high heat. Fry the bacon until crisp then transfer to a slow cooker.

2. Add the remaining ingredients and stir well to combine.

3. Cover and cook on HIGH for 45 minutes, stirring every 15 minutes or so.

4. Turn to LOW, remove the lid and continue cooking for 30–45 minutes until the macaroni is cooked and the sauce has thickened.

Roselyn Chrisp

Creamy Chicken & Bacon Pasta

This is my family's favourite pasta dish. I've tried to make creamy pasta on the stove before and it's never worked out. I tried this in the slow cooker and the flavours were amazing and so easy. Just chop everything up, into the slow cooker it goes – and at the other end there's a delicious creamy pasta. I also love this recipe as you can put heaps of different vegetables into it and the kids will hardly notice. An easy way to cook a yummy meal with hidden goodness.

Serves 4–6 • Preparation 20 mins • Cook 6 hours • Cooker capacity 6 litres

600 ml (20½ fl oz) cooking cream
650 g (1 lb 7 oz) chicken breast or thigh fillets, cubed
Vegetables of your choice (see note)
420 g (15 oz) tinned cream of chicken condensed soup
300 g (10½ oz) pasta
200 g (7 oz) bacon, diced
3 teaspoons crushed garlic
1 chicken stock cube

1. Put 400 ml (13½ fl oz) of the cream along with all of the remaining ingredients except for the pasta into a slow cooker and stir well to combine.

2. Cover and cook on LOW for 5½ hours.

3. Add the remaining cream and the pasta and continue cooking for 30 minutes. (The mixture may look quite runny, but the pasta will absorb most of the liquid leaving a thick creamy sauce at the end.)

NOTE: You can use whatever vegetables you like, in whatever quantity you want. I usually add beans, corn, baby spinach, mushrooms, peas and capsicum.

Andrea Bricknell

Chicken, Leek & Bacon Pasta

I was at the end of my pay week, so I looked at what I had left in the freezer and fridge and came up with this. It is now one of our regular meals as it is so yummy. I have also made the leftovers into pies.

Serves 6 • Preparation 15 mins • Cook 5–6 hours • Cooker capacity 3–5 litres

1 onion, diced
1 leek, sliced
2 garlic cloves, finely diced
1 teaspoon finely chopped ginger
2 chicken breast fillets
4 rashers bacon, diced
1½ tablespoons wholegrain mustard
1½ cups dry white wine
1½ cups chicken stock
1 cup sour cream
Cooked pasta, to serve

1. Heat a little oil in a frying pan over medium heat. Add the onion, leek, garlic and ginger and cook until soft. Add the chicken, bacon, mustard, wine and stock, and stir well to combine. Transfer the mixture to a slow cooker.

2. Cover and cook on HIGH for 5–6 hours.

3. Remove the chicken and shred the meat. Return the shredded meat to the slow cooker, add the sour cream and stir through.

4. Serve with the cooked pasta.

Cheree Bone

Honey Mustard Cauliflower & Chicken Supreme

I wanted my young child to eat cauliflower, so I decided to incorporate it with child-friendly favourites chicken and pasta.

Serves 4–6 • Preparation 15 mins • Cook 5¼ hours • Cooker capacity 4 litres

1 kg (2 lb 3 oz) chicken thigh fillets, cut into 3 cm (1¼ in) pieces
375 ml (12½ fl oz/1½ cups) evaporated milk
1 small head cauliflower, broken into florets
1 cup vegetable stock
1 onion, finely chopped
100 g (3½ oz) ham or rindless bacon, shredded
½ cup shredded mozzarella
2 tablespoons honey
1 tablespoon dijon mustard
1 garlic clove, crushed
1 teaspoon mild paprika
1 teaspoon za'atar
500 g (1 lb 2 oz) penne pasta

1. Put all of the ingredients except the pasta in a slow cooker. Stir gently to combine.

2. Cook on LOW for 5 hours, or until the cauliflower is soft and the chicken is cooked through.

3. Cook the pasta in a large saucepan of salted boiling water until al dente. Drain the pasta and add to the slow cooker. Stir gently to combine and serve.

Juny Lucin

One-Pot Creamy Chicken Pasta

This would have to be one of my favourite homemade meals, and it's all done in one pot. With chicken, vegies, pasta and BACON involved, you know it's going be a hit in your family!

Serves 4–6 • Preparation 15 mins • Cook 4 hours • Cooker capacity 6 litres

1 kg (2 lb 3 oz) chicken thigh fillets, cut into strips
1 onion, sliced
1 tablespoon crushed garlic
150 g (5½ oz) diced bacon
1 cup sliced spring onions (scallions)
1 tomato, diced
½ teaspoon paprika
¼ teaspoon freshly ground black pepper
200 g (7 oz) thin spaghetti
1 cup cooking cream
50 g (1¾ oz) butter
250 g (9 oz) broccoli florets

1. Heat a little oil in the searing insert of a slow cooker or a frying pan over medium–high heat. Add the chicken with the onion and garlic and cook until browned. Transfer to the slow cooker.

2. Add the bacon, spring onion, tomato, paprika and pepper and mix to combine.

3. Cover and cook on LOW for 2 hours.

4. Add the pasta, cream and butter and stir well to combine. Continue cooking for 1 hour, stirring occasionally.

5. Stir in the broccoli and continue cooking for 1 hour.

6. Serve by itself or with a selection of fresh vegetables on the side.

Simon Christie

Cannelloni with Chicken Mince

This recipe came to me one day while I was trying to choose something for dinner that was a little different. My family and I love pasta so this is a huge hit in our house. Sometimes I add grated vegies such as sweet potato or even carrot, for my fussy veggie eaters.

Serves 4–6 • Preparation 30 mins • Cook 3 hours • Cooker capacity 5–6 litres

800 g (1 lb 12 oz) tomato-based pasta sauce
200 g (7 oz) cannelloni
500 g (1 lb 2 oz) minced (ground) chicken
200 g (7 oz) cream cheese
3 spring onions (scallions), sliced
1 tablespoon dijon mustard
Handful of baby spinach
2 teaspoons garlic salt
400 g (14 oz) tinned diced tomatoes
1 cup grated cheese
Garlic bread, to serve

1. Put the pasta sauce in a slow cooker.
2. In a large bowl, combine the chicken mince, cream cheese, spring onion, dijon mustard, baby spinach and garlic salt. Season with pepper and mix well.
3. With a piping bag or using your hands, fill the cannelloni with the chicken mixture.
4. Arrange the cannelloni in two layers in the pasta sauce. Add the tinned tomatoes.
5. Cover and cook on HIGH for 2½ hours.
6. Add the grated cheese and continue cooking for 30 minutes.
7. Serve with garlic bread.

Lisa Casey

Swiss Chicken Pasta

My mother-in-law has always cooked an awesome Swiss chicken recipe, so I thought I would experiment and try to make my own.

Serves 6 • Preparation 10 mins • Cook 5½–6½ hours • Cooker capacity 6 litres

Plain (all-purpose) flour, for dusting
2 chicken breast fillets
2 garlic cloves, finely diced
1 cup dry white wine
Mushrooms (as many as you want), sliced
Spring onions (scallions), to taste, sliced
1 cup cream
1½ tablespoons French mustard
Cooked pasta, to serve
Grated parmesan cheese, to serve

1. Season the flour with salt and pepper, then dust the chicken with the seasoned flour to coat.

2. Heat a little oil in a frying pan over medium–high heat. Add the chicken breasts and diced garlic and cook until the chicken is browned on all sides. Transfer to a slow cooker. Add the wine and the sliced mushrooms.

3. Cover and cook on LOW for 5–6 hours.

4. Remove the chicken breasts and shred the meat.

5. Add the spring onions, cream and mustard to the slow cooker and stir to mix well. Return the chicken to the slow cooker and stir through the sauce.

6. Cook, uncovered, for 30 minutes to help thicken the sauce.

7. To serve, stir through the cooked pasta and sprinkle with parmesan cheese.

Cheree Bone

Chicken Fettuccine

I love a good pasta dish and love making this one as it's so tasty. I used to make it on the stovetop but now I make it in my slow cooker.

Serves 6–8 • Preparation 10–15 mins • Cook 5 hours • Cooker capacity 5.5 litres

800 g (1 lb 12 oz) chicken breast or thigh fillets, diced
1 onion, chopped
1 capsicum (pepper), diced
3 cups chopped mushrooms
3 garlic cloves
400 g (14 oz) tinned diced tomatoes
4 tablespoons tomato paste (concentrated purée)
250 g (9 oz) chopped bacon
200 g (7 oz) broccoli or cauliflower
1 cup chicken stock
½–¾ cup cooking cream
Cooked fettuccine, to serve

1. Put all of the ingredients except the cream and fettuccine into a slow cooker with 1 cup of water and stir well to combine.

2. Cover and cook on LOW for 5 hours.

3. Add the cream and stir the cooked fettuccine through. Season with salt and pepper and serve.

Lynda Eagleson

Easy Chow Mein

This is a great dish to cook at the end of the pay week – it's cheap and so easy to prepare, even the kids can do it!

Serves 4 • Preparation 10 mins • Cook 5 hours • Cooker capacity 3 litres

500 g (1 lb 2 oz) minced (ground) beef
1 onion, diced
250 g (9 oz) frozen stir-fry vegetables
¼ cabbage, shredded
2 x 80 g (2¾ oz) packets chicken-flavoured 2-minute noodles
1 tablespoon mild curry powder

1. In a frying pan, brown the mince and the onion.

2. Put everything but the noodles in a slow cooker, including the flavour sachets from both packets of noodles.

3. Cover and cook on LOW for 5 hours.

4. 5 minutes before serving, cook the noodles in the microwave as per the packet instructions, drain and add to the cooker. Mix through and serve.

Jaime Caillot de Chadbannes

Chicken Chow Mein

I was looking for an easy chow mein recipe that could be converted for the slow cooker. The flavours in this version blew me away and this has now become an absolute favourite of mine.

Serves 3–4 • Preparation 20 mins • Cook 4 hours • Cooker capacity 5.5 litres

400 g (14 oz) chicken thigh fillets, thinly sliced
1 small wombok (Chinese cabbage), trimmed and roughly shredded
425 g (15 oz) tinned whole baby corn spears, drained and corn halved
    lengthways
1 onion, cut into wedges
1 small carrot, sliced
3 spring onions (scallions), cut into 5 cm (2 in) lengths
2 tablespoons soy sauce
2 tablespoons oyster sauce
1½ tablespoons peanut oil
2 teaspoons cornflour (cornstarch)
1 cm (½ in) piece fresh ginger, peeled and grated
1 garlic clove, crushed
½ teaspoon sesame oil
100 g (3½ oz) cup mushrooms, sliced
350 g (12½ oz) fresh chow mein (or hokkien) noodles

1. Put the chicken, wombok, corn, carrot, onion and spring onion into a slow cooker.

2. In a bowl, combine the soy sauce, oyster sauce, peanut oil, cornflour, ginger, garlic and sesame oil.

3. Pour the sauce over the chicken and stir.

4. Cover and cook for 3 hours on LOW.

5. Stir in the mushrooms and continue cooking for the final 1 hour on LOW.

6. 10 minutes before serving, prepare the noodles as directed on the packet, and divide between three or four bowls.

7. Serve the chicken and sauce over the top of the noodles.

NOTE: I cook this in a Contempo slow cooker, which cooks at a higher heat than most models. Times may vary in other slow cookers.

Denise Roberts

▬ My Own Chicken Noodle Stir-fry ▬

Absolutely love this stuff! It's so delicious and filling too. I'll cook this any time of the week for our dinner – it's just something I whipped up one day and have been making ever since.

Serves 4–6 • Preparation 1 hour • Cook 1½–2 hours • Cooker capacity 6 litres

3–4 x 80 g (2¾ oz) packets 2-minute noodles
2 tablespoons sesame oil
1 barbecue chicken, meat shredded
1½ capsicums (peppers), sliced (I use a combination of red, yellow and green)
1 cup cauliflower florets
1 cup broccoli florets
1 stalk celery, sliced
½ leek, sliced
½ cup frozen peas
½ cup frozen corn
1 carrot, grated
1 zucchini (courgette), grated
1 onion, sliced
1 yellow squash, grated
½ tablespoon soy sauce
½ tablespoon hoisin sauce
½ tablespoon oyster sauce
1 red chilli, diced (optional)
1 green chilli, diced (optional)
1 teaspoon sweet chilli sauce
1 teaspoon chicken stock powder
½ teaspoon fish sauce

1. Prepare the noodles according to the packet instructions but leave out the flavour sachets. Drain.

2. Add the sesame oil to a slow cooker. Add all of the remaining ingredients and the noodles, and stir well to combine.

3. Cover, putting a tea towel (dish towel) under the lid, and cook on LOW for 1½–2 hours until the vegetables are cooked to your liking.

Judith Clark

Pad Thai Noodles

This is one of my all-time favourite recipes. I have cooked it for years – and converted it from the stovetop to the slow cooker. I find it has much more intense flavours! We love this recipe in our house – I hope your house can enjoy it just as much!

Serves 4–6 • Preparation 20 mins • Cook 1½ hours • Cooker capacity 6 litres

½ cup light brown sugar
½ cup mild chilli sauce
½ cup fish sauce
2 tablespoons tomato sauce (ketchup)
4 teaspoons soy sauce
4 garlic cloves, crushed (or 2 heaped tablespoons crushed garlic from a jar)
2 tablespoons minced ginger
400–500 g (14 oz–1 lb 2 oz) chicken thigh fillets, diced
2 eggs, lightly beaten
1 cup chicken stock
800 g (1 lb 12 oz) egg or rice noodles
1 bunch spring onions (scallions), chopped
300 g (10½ oz) bean sprouts
1 handful chopped coriander (cilantro)
½–1 cup chopped peanuts

1. Combine the brown sugar and the sauces in a slow cooker and cook on HIGH, stirring occasionally, until the sugar is dissolved. Stir in the garlic and ginger, then add the chicken pieces and stir to coat.

2. Pour the beaten egg over the top and leave it to set for about 25–35 minutes. Once the egg starts to set, stir it through. Continue cooking for 25–35 minutes, to make up 1 hour of cooking time.

3. Stir in the chicken stock and top with the noodles and spring onion. Continue cooking for 20 minutes.

4. Stir the noodles through, top with the bean sprouts and continue cooking for 10 minutes.

5. Stir, and serve topped with coriander and peanuts.

NOTE: This is delicious with prawns (shrimp); just add them before you add the noodles, at the 1 hour 20 minute mark. This is a mild pad Thai, so add some extra chilli for extra spice!

Suscha Benson

MINCE

Stuffed Capsicums
with Chicken Mince

A healthy yummy recipe full of deliciousness. I prepare this while my husband is home in the morning and pop it in the cooker at midday to be ready for dinnertime. Even our 18-month-old son enjoys this dish, and I'm looking forward to making it for our daughter, too. The recipe is easily adaptable and you can precook the mince if you prefer. Ensure you buy capsicums (peppers) that are wide and can stand upright.

Serves 4 • Preparation 15 mins • Cook 5 hours • Cooker capacity 3.5 litres

500 g (1 lb 2 oz) minced (ground) chicken
¼ cabbage, thinly sliced
2 carrots, grated
1 onion, grated
3 tablespoons sweet soy sauce
1 tablespoon crushed garlic
1 teaspoon minced ginger
1 teaspoon mustard powder
1 teaspoon curry powder
4 large red capsicums (peppers)

1. In a bowl, mix together all the ingredients except the capsicums.
2. Cut out the stem and core from each capsicum and stuff with the mince mixture.
3. Place the filled capsicums into a slow cooker, standing upright.
4. Add 1 cup of water around the capsicums.
5. Cover and cook on LOW for 5 hours.

Jodi Kemp

Sweet & Sour Chicken Meatballs

I created this recipe when I had chicken mince to use up. It's a hit with my children.

Serves 4–6 • Preparation 20 mins • Cook 6½–7 hours • Cooker capacity 3.5 litres

500 g (1 lb 2 oz) minced (ground) chicken
1 cup breadcrumbs
1 spring onion (scallion), finely sliced
1 carrot, grated and excess liquid squeezed out
1 egg
Mixed herbs, to taste
440 g (15½ oz) tinned pineapple pieces in juice, drained and juice reserved
½ red capsicum (pepper), thinly sliced
2 heaped tablespoons cornflour (cornstarch)
50 ml (1¾ fl oz) soy sauce
¼ cup white vinegar
¼ cup light brown sugar
Broccoli (as much as you want), sliced
1 zucchini, cut into matchsticks

1. In a large bowl, combine the mince, breadcrumbs, spring onion, carrot, egg and mixed herbs. Roll into 24 balls.

2. Heat a large frying pan sprayed with cooking oil over medium–high heat. Fry the meatballs, in batches, until lightly browned, then transfer to a slow cooker along with the pineapple pieces and capsicum.

3. In a bowl, mix the cornflour with the soy sauce to make a paste. Mix in the vinegar, sugar and reserved pineapple juice. Pour over the meatballs.

4. Cover and cook on LOW for 5½–6 hours.

5. Remove the meatballs with a slotted spoon and set aside. Stir the sauce well, add the broccoli and zucchini and stir well to combine. Return the meatballs to the sauce and continue cooking for 45 minutes.

Narelle Youngs

Chicken & Broccoli Meatloaf

I love the chicken and broccoli duets that you get from takeaway shops, so I wanted to try and make something similar for my family.

Serves 4 • Preparation 10 mins • Cook 3 hours • Cooker capacity 5 litres

500 g (1 lb 2 oz) minced (ground) chicken
1 cup grated tasty cheese, plus extra for topping
½ cup grated parmesan cheese
2 tablespoons breadcrumbs
1 egg
3–4 garlic cloves, crushed
125 g (4½ oz) cream cheese, softened
½ head broccoli, finely chopped
Chips or hasselback potatoes and vegetables, to serve

1. In a large bowl, combine the mince, half of the tasty cheese, half of the parmesan, the breadcrumbs, the egg and half of the garlic.

2. Lay out two sheets of aluminium foil, overlapping the long edges and folding to make a join. At one end of the foil, pat the mince mixture out into a rectangle about 1.5 cm (½ in) thick.

3. In a bowl, combine the cream cheese, broccoli, remaining cheeses and remaining garlic. Spread the cream cheese mixture along one end of the flattened mince, then, using the foil to help you, roll the mince into a log. Wrap in the foil and place in a slow cooker.

4. Cover and cook on HIGH for about 2¾ hours.

5. Carefully unwrap the meatloaf and top with grated cheese. Continue cooking for 20 minutes.

6. Serve with chips or hasselback potatoes and vegetables.

NOTE: You can transfer the meatloaf to a preheated oven and bake for 15–20 minutes to make the cheese golden and crispy.

Brodie Lucciannio

Lamb Meatballs
with Minted Yoghurt Dressing

I've found that the number-one rule for slow-cooking meatballs is to resist all urges to touch or turn them until they are firm. Then you can do so without them breaking. The minted yoghurt dressing is the perfect accompaniment to this dish for a fresh zingy touch. These are also great as a filling party-food option.

Makes 25 meatballs • Preparation 15 mins • Cook 3 hours • Cooker capacity 5 litres

500 g (1 lb 2 oz) minced (ground) lamb
¾ cup fine breadcrumbs
1 tablespoon finely chopped mint
1 egg
½ onion, grated
2 teaspoons crushed garlic
1 teaspoon minced ginger
1 vegetable stock cube
1 cup boiling water

MINTED YOGHURT DRESSING
200 g (7 oz) natural yoghurt
1 tablespoon finely chopped mint
2 teaspoons lemon juice

1. Grease the bowl of a slow cooker.

2. In a large bowl, combine the mince, breadcrumbs, onion, egg, mint, garlic and ginger. Season with salt and pepper. With clean hands, form into golf-ball-sized balls and gently place into a slow cooker in a single layer.

3. Dissolve the stock cube in the water, then carefully pour into the slow cooker.

4. Cover and cook on LOW for 3 hours. Try not to move or turn the meatballs, until they are fully sealed, if at all so as not to break them. I turn my meatballs gently after 2 hours and the finished meatballs stay firm and intact.

5. To make the dressing, combine the ingredients in a small bowl. Drizzle over the meatballs or serve on the side as a dipping sauce.

NOTE: Uncooked meatballs can be prepared the night before and stored in the fridge in a single layer in a sealed container.

Paulene Christie

Vicki's Chilli

I love a hot chilli and have been making this recipe for many years. It can be served with rice or mashed potato, on toast, with pasta as a spicy spaghetti sauce, or on its own in a bowl.

Serves 6 • Preparation 5 mins • Cook 7–8 hours • Cooker capacity 5.5 litres

1 tablespoon olive oil
500 g (1 lb 2 oz) minced (ground) beef
420 g (15 oz) tinned tomato soup
400 g (14 oz) tinned diced tomatoes
400 g (14 oz) tinned red kidney beans, drained
2 onions, roughly chopped
1 carrot, thinly sliced
1 capsicum (pepper), diced
4 tablespoons chilli powder
3 tablespoons chilli flakes

1. Grease the base of a slow cooker with the olive oil. Add all of the other ingredients and stir well to combine.

2. Cover and cook on LOW for 7–8 hours.

3. Stir and serve.

Vicki Gray

Beanz Mince

I first made this recipe when I had some thawed mince to use and I wanted a change from meatballs and savoury mince. The beans make this meal very hearty and healthy. It has a fabulous flavour.

Serves 4–6 • Preparation 10 mins • Cook 4–8 hours • Cooker capacity 6 litres

1 kg (2 lb 3 oz) minced (ground) beef
800 g (1 lb 12 oz) tinned diced tomatoes
750 ml (25½ fl oz/3 cups) beef stock
500 g (1 lb 2 oz) tomato-based pasta sauce
400 g (14 oz) tinned red kidney beans, drained
400 g (14 oz) tinned cannellini beans, drained
1 onion, diced
1 carrot, grated
5 teaspoons dried parsley
2 teaspoons oregano
1 teaspoon freshly ground black pepper
250 g (9 oz) pasta of choice
Steamed green vegetables (such as broccoli or cabbage), to serve

1. Heat a large frying pan sprayed with cooking oil over medium–high heat. Add the mince in batches, breaking it up with a wooden spoon and cooking until the mince is browned.

2. Put the mince in a slow cooker with all the other ingredients except the pasta and steamed vegetables.

3. Cover and cook on LOW for 7–8 hours or HIGH for 4–5 hours.

4. At the last hour (30 minutes if cooking on HIGH) add the pasta.

5. Serve with steamed green vegetables.

Carolyn Tolley

Mexican Beef Tortilla Stack

Think of this dish as a Mexican-style lasagne, where the pasta is replaced with tortillas. It's so easy to prepare and so easy to serve directly from the slow cooker. I like to add a side salad and garlic bread.

Serves 6 • Preparation 20 mins • Cook 4¾ hours • Cooker capacity 3 litres

500 g (1 lb 2 oz) minced (ground) beef
435 g (5½ oz) tinned refried beans
4 ripe tomatoes, diced
35 g packet taco seasoning mix
5 tortilla wraps
2 cups grated tasty cheese
Paprika, to garnish

1. Combine the mince, beans, tomato and seasoning in a slow cooker and mix well.

2. Cover and cook on LOW for about 4 hours.

3. Transfer the mince mixture to a bowl and clean the slow cooker insert.

4. Lay a tortilla wrap flat in the bowl of the slow cooker. Top with a fifth of the meat mixture and sprinkle with ⅓ cup of grated cheese. Lay another tortilla wrap over the top and press down. Repeat the meat, cheese and tortilla layering until you've used up the meat and tortillas. Top the stack with grated cheese and garnish with paprika (it will give the cheese a nice browned look).

5. Cover and cook on HIGH for 45 minutes or until the stack is heated through and the cheese has melted.

NOTE: If you don't have the right-sized slow cooker, you can assemble the stack in a baking dish and cook in a moderate oven for about 30 minutes until heated through.

Paulene Christie

Loaded Nachos

This was made at the end of the pay week, when the cupboard was looking pretty sorry for itself. Now it's one of the kids' favourite meals to make!

Serves 4 • Preparation 10 min • Cook 4 hours • Cooker capacity 3 litres

250 g (9 oz) minced (ground) beef
1 onion, diced
1 teaspoon crushed garlic
420 g (15 oz) tinned 4-bean mix (drained and rinsed) or baked beans
420 g (15 oz) tinned corn kernels, drained
125 g (4½ oz) cherry tomatoes, quartered
1 carrot, grated
½–2 tablespoons curry powder
½ cup tomato paste (concentrated purée)
2 tablespoons dried Italian mixed herbs
300 g (10½ oz) grated cheese
170 g (6 oz) corn chips

1. Heat a large frying pan sprayed with cooking oil over medium–high heat. Add the mince, breaking it up with a wooden spoon and cooking until browned. Drain any fat and transfer the mince to a slow cooker. Fry the onion and garlic for a couple of minutes until soft. Transfer to the slow cooker.

2. Add the beans, corn, tomatoes, carrot amd curry powder. Stir well to combine.

3. Cover and cook on LOW for 4 hours or on HIGH for 2 hours.

4. Meanwhile, preheat the oven to 200°C (400°F).

5. In a small bowl, combine the tomato paste with the herbs. (Dilute with a tablespoon of BBQ sauce if it's too thick.)

6. In an ovenproof dish, layer half the chips, half the meat and bean mix and half the cheese. Then layer the rest of the chips, the rest of the meat and bean mix, the tomato paste mix and the rest of the cheese.

7. Bake in the oven for 5–10 minutes, until the cheese is melted and browned.

Jaime Caillot de Chadbannes

Slow-cooked Mexican Taco Mince

This recipe was created for those who like to avoid packets and pre-made ingredients. Why buy taco seasoning when you can make your own with just a simple mix of spices at home? This recipe will create a flavour-packed mince to serve with tacos, burritos or any other Mexican dish you like. Use lean mince for a low-fat option.

Serves 8 • Preparation 10 mins • Cook 2 hours • Cooker capacity 1.5 litres

1 kg (2 lb 3 oz) lean minced (ground) beef
¼ cup hot water
1½ teaspoon chilli flakes
1 teaspoon ground cumin
1 teaspoon paprika
1 teaspoon garlic powder
½ teaspoon onion powder
½ teaspoon dried oregano

1. Heat a little oil in the searing insert of a slow cooker or a frying pan over medium–high heat. Add the mince and cook until browned. Transfer to the slow cooker.

2. Add the remaining ingredients and stir to combine.

3. Cook on HIGH for 2 hours or on LOW for 4 hours. Stir occasionally if nearby.

NOTE: This is about as spicy as regular store-bought taco seasoning, so it is child-friendly for our family. Increase the chilli if you like more heat.

Paulene Christie

# Meatballs

I love this recipe because it is easy and my children love it.

Serves 4 • Preparation 15 mins • Cook 6 hours • Cooker capacity 5 litres

500 g (1 lb 2 oz) minced (ground) beef
⅓ cup grated parmesan
¼ cup breadcrumbs
3 garlic cloves, crushed
1 tablespoon oil
1 onion, chopped
500 g (1 lb 2 oz) passata
1 cup uncooked pasta rinsed under cold water

1. In a bowl, mix together the mince, breadcrumbs, parmesan and garlic then form into balls.

2. Heat the oil in a large frying pan over medium–high heat. Fry the onion until it's clear then stir in the tomato paste. Cook until heated through then transfer to a slow cooker along with the meatballs.

3. Cover and cook on LOW for 6 hours.

4. Stir in the pasta and continue cooking for 45 minutes or until the pasta is cooked and the sauce is thick.

Ariella Tairea

Spicy Meatballs

A friend gave me a basic meatballs recipe that uses a frying pan. I decided to try a version of it in the slow cooker one day when I was going to work.

Serves 4 • Preparation 20 mins • Cook 6 hours • Cooker capacity 3.5 litres

12 store-bought or homemade meatballs
500 ml (17 fl oz/2 cups) passata (puréed tomato)
2 large carrots, grated
1 large leek, finely chopped
1 tablespoon Worcestershire sauce
2 garlic cloves, crushed
2 teaspoon Chinese five-spice
1 teaspoon soy sauce
Pasta and grated cheese, to serve

1. Put all of the ingredients into a slow cooker and stir well to combine.

2. Cover and cook on LOW for 6 hours.

3. Serve with pasta and grated cheese.

Natalie Liquorish

Italian Meatballs

I came up with this recipe because my family and I love the meatball subs from Subway and I wanted to try and replicate that taste. This is the result – and we haven't had to go back to Subway for a while now!

Serves 4–6 • Preparation 20–30 min • Cook 4–5 hours • Cooker capacity 5 litres

2 eggs, lightly beaten
¼ cup milk
½ cup dry breadcrumbs
2 tablespoons grated cheese
1 teaspoon crushed garlic
1 teaspoon salt
¼ teaspoon freshly ground black pepper
1 kg (2 lb 3 oz) minced (ground) beef
500 g (1 lb 2 oz) sausage mince
445 ml (15 fl oz) tomato sauce (ketchup)
175 ml (6 fl oz) tomato paste (concentrated purée)
1 small onion, diced (optional)
½ cup beef stock
Dried parsley, to taste
Steamed rice or rolls filled with grated cheese, to serve

1. In a large bowl, combine the eggs and milk. Add the breadcrumbs, cheese, garlic, salt and pepper. Add the beef mince and sausage mince and mix well. Shape into 2.5 cm (1 in) balls (about the size of a ping pong ball).

2. Heat a large frying pan sprayed with cooking oil over medium–high heat. Fry the meatballs, in batches, until lightly browned, then transfer to a slow cooker.

3. In another bowl, combine the tomato sauce, tomato paste, onion (if using), beef stock, and parsley with ⅓ cup water. Season with salt and pepper. Stir until combined and pour over the meatballs.

4. Cook on HIGH for 4–5 hours.

5. Serve on a bed of rice or in rolls with grated cheese.

Trudi Derbyshire

Devilled Meatballs

A light fresh sauce over meatballs, this is great with sausages as well.

Serves 3–4 • Preparation 15 mins • Cook 6 hours • Cooker capacity 3.5 litres

500 g (1 lb 2 oz) minced (ground) beef
½ cup cornflake crumbs
2 onions, diced
3 tablespoons curry powder
1 egg
420 g (15 oz) tinned tomato soup
2 tablespoons light brown sugar
1 tablespoon vinegar
1 teaspoon mustard

1. Combine the mince, cornflake crumbs, half the onion, 2 tablespoons of the curry powder and the egg in a bowl. Form into meatballs.

2. Heat a large frying pan sprayed with cooking oil over medium–high heat. Fry the meatballs, in batches, until lightly browned, then transfer to a slow cooker. Turn the heat down and fry the remaining onion until caramelised. Transfer to the slow cooker.

3. Combine the remaining tablespoon of curry powder with the other remaining ingredients in the slow cooker. Mix well to combine.

4. Cover and cook on LOW for 6 hours.

5. Serve with mashed potatoes and steamed vegetables.

NOTE: You can substitute sausages for the meatballs.

Dianna Cutting

Beef Meatballs in Tomato Mushroom Sauce

As a busy mother with a newborn, I don't have a lot of time to make complex dinners. I wanted a delicious, easy and quick recipe that I could chuck together. This is perfect on a cold night served with rice, mash and vegies, or for lunch on a slice of crusty bread.

Serves 4 • Preparation 20 mins • Cook 3½–4 hours • Cooker capacity 6.5 litres

420 g (15 oz) tinned cream of mushroom condensed soup
250 g (9 oz) shredded bacon
3–4 tablespoons tomato paste (concentrated purée)
¼ cup grated cheese
1 handful baby spinach leaves
Rice, mashed potato and vegetables or crusty bread, to serve

MEATBALLS
500 g (1 lb 2 oz) minced (ground) beef
½ cup breadcrumbs
1 egg
1 tablespoon mixed dried herbs
1 tablespoon paprika
1 tablespoon onion powder
3 garlic cloves, crushed

1. To make the meatballs, mix all the ingredients together in a medium-sized bowl. Season with salt and pepper. Roll into golf ball-sized balls and place into a slow cooker.

2. In a bowl, combine the soup, bacon and tomato paste. Mix well and pour over the meatballs. Top with the cheese and spinach.

3. Cover and cook on HIGH for 3½–4 hours.

4. Serve with rice, mash and vegies or on bread.

Sandra Stocker

Porcupines in Barbecue Sauce

Porcupines were my first-ever slow-cooker fail, back in the day. But I'm nothing if not determined! Regular porcupines are popular, but I'm a barbecue sauce girl through and through so I knew I had to make a barbecue version if I was going to love them. It turned out even better than I'd hoped and the whole family loved this one. Serve over pasta or on their own with a side of seasonal vegetables.

Makes 24 large meatballs • **Preparation** 15 mins • **Cook** 6 hours • **Cooker capacity** 5 litres

500 g (1 lb 2 oz) lean minced (ground) beef
½ cup uncooked long grain white rice
1 large onion, grated
1–2 garlic cloves, crushed
Plain (all-purpose) flour, for dusting
420 g (15 oz) tinned cream of tomato condensed soup
400 g (14 oz) tinned diced or crushed tomatoes
½ cup barbecue sauce
1 packed tablespoon light brown sugar

1. In a large bowl, combine the mince, rice, onion, and garlic. Season with salt and pepper. With clean hands, form into golf-ball sized balls. Roll each ball lightly in flour to coat and gently place into a slow cooker in a single layer.

2. Combine the soup, tomatoes, barbecue sauce and sugar in a bowl and mix well. Pour gently over the meatballs.

3. Cover and cook on LOW for 6 hours. If you wish to stir, wait until the meatballs are cooked through and firm.

Paulene Christie

➤ Pum-cupines ➤

I always liked to make stuffed pumpkins (squash) and I had never tried
a porcupines recipe before so I thought, why not add the two together?
It worked brilliantly! For an alternative, wrap the meat mixture around
small cubes of cheese.

Serves 4 • Preparation 20 mins • Cook 8 hours • Cooker capacity 5 litres

500 g (1 lb 2 oz) minced (ground) beef
1 onion, diced
½ cup rice
1 handful baby spinach leaves, chopped
1 garlic clove, crushed
Spices of your choice (I use chilli, paprika and pepper), to taste
840 g (1 lb 14 oz) tinned tomato soup
1 jap pumpkin (squash) (whatever size will fit in your slow cooker)
1 handful finely chopped parsley

1. In a bowl, combine the beef, onion, rice, spinach, garlic and spices. Mix
   thoroughly.

2. Cut the top off the pumpkin and scoop out all of the seeds and the stringy flesh.
   Roll the meat into balls and place inside the pumpkin (you may have some
   meatballs left over). Put the pumpkin inside a slow cooker.

3. Pour half the tomato soup into the pumpkin and the other half into the slow
   cooker along with ½ cup of water. Sprinkle the parsley over the pumpkin.

4. Cook on LOW for 8 hours or until the rice is cooked and the pumpkin is soft.

Sam Williams

⌗— Budget Mince & Vegetable Stew —●

I grew up eating this meal (I'm now in my 50s). When I was a small child on my grandparents' dairy farm, Grandma never knew how many might be coming to any meal, so she had to be prepared. Grandpa grew most vegetables and had an extremely large patch near the chook pen. Grandma and Mum always cooked this with dough boys (dumplings) added to the casserole in the last 30 minutes. Sadly, my slow cooker is not big enough, so I serve the stew with warm crusty bread instead. The beef mince can be replaced with any other type of mince or any diced meat, so this is a handy recipe for taking advantage of meat specials.

Serves 8+ • Preparation 15–20 mins • Cook 8 hours • Cooker capacity 5.5 litres

600 g (1 lb 5 oz) minced (ground) beef
3 tablespoons tomato paste (concentrated purée)
2 tablespoons Worcestershire sauce
3 teaspoons stock powder (or 3 stock cubes)
1–3 teaspoons curry powder (optional)
2 large potatoes, diced
1 large sweet potato, diced
½ butternut pumpkin (squash), diced
2 onions, diced
¼ cabbage, shredded
½ cup peas
½ cup corn kernels
3–4 heaped tablespoons cornflour (cornstarch)

1. Grease the bowl of a slow cooker.

2. Combine the mince with 1 litre (34 fl oz/4 cups) of water in the slow cooker. Add the tomato paste, Worcestershire sauce, stock powder and curry powder. Season with salt and pepper and stir well to combine. Stir in the potato, sweet potato, pumpkin, onion and cabbage.

3. Cover and cook on HIGH for 1 hour, then reduce temperature and cook on LOW for 6 hours.

4. Mix the cornflour with enough water to make a paste and stir into the stew. Add the peas and corn, increase the temperature to HIGH and continue cooking for 1 hour.

NOTE: This meal freezes and reheats extremely well.

Vicky Kemp

Sloppy Joes

When you feel like burgers but can't be bothered making them, this is perfect!

Serves 6 • Preparation 15 mins • Cook 3–4 hours • Cooker capacity 5 litres

500 g (1 lb 2 oz) minced (ground) beef
1 onion, chopped
¾ cup tomato sauce (ketchup)
¼ cup barbecue sauce
1 tablespoon Worcestershire sauce
1 tablespoon crushed garlic
1 tablespoon vinegar
1–2 tablespoons light brown sugar
1 teaspoon mustard
6 hamburger buns
1–2 tablespoons cornflour (cornstarch), if required
Pickles, tomato and cheese, or coleslaw, to serve

1. Heat a large frying pan sprayed with cooking oil over medium–high heat. Add the mince and onion and fry until browned. Transfer to a slow cooker.

2. In a bowl, combine the sauces, garlic, vinegar, sugar and mustard, then pour into the slow cooker. Cover and cook on LOW for 3–4 hours.

3. When 30 minutes from cooked, check the mince. If it's too watery, mix the cornflour with enough water to make a paste and stir it through the sauce.

4. Serve in hamburger buns with pickles, tomato and cheese, or coleslaw.

Kimberlee Webb

Shepherd's Pie Loaded Meatloaf

We love this recipe; it's great for winter or in summer with a salad. And it's a good way to use up vegetables – hide them in the meatloaf. I love how the slow cooker keeps the meatloaf moist.

Serves 4 • Preparation 20 mins • Cook 4 hours • Cooker capacity 6 litres

Butter, for mashing
Cream, for mashing
3–4 cups cooked mashed potato
⅓ cup diced bacon
500 g (1 lb 2 oz) minced (ground) beef
1 onion, chopped
¼ cup grated zucchini
¼ cup grated carrot
1 egg
1–2 packets taco seasoning mix
1 teaspoon crushed garlic
⅓ cup grated cheese
½ –1 red capsicum (pepper), diced
1–2 tomatoes, diced
Potato wedges and homemade gravy, to serve

1. Grease a slow cooker and line it with baking paper. If desired, grease and line a loaf tin that fits in your slow cooker (see page 15 for hints on using cake tins in your slow cooker).

2. Add as much butter and cream as you want to the mashed potato and mash to combine.

3. Heat a frying pan sprayed with cooking oil over medium–high heat. Add the bacon and fry until cooked. Mix through the mashed potato.

4. In a bowl, combine the mince, onion, zucchini, carrot, egg, taco mix and garlic. Press the mixture into the slow cooker or into the loaf tin if using.

5. Spread the mashed potato over the mince and sprinkle with half the grated cheese. Top the potato with the capsicum and tomato and season with salt and pepper. Top with the remaining cheese.

6. Cover, putting a tea towel (dish towel) under the lid, and cook on LOW for 4 hours.

7. Use the baking paper to lift the meatloaf out of the slow cooker. Serve with potato wedges and some homemade gravy.

Robyn Clark

Slow-cooked Shepherd's or Cottage Pie

Traditionally, shepherd's pie is cooked with lamb mince and cottage pie is cooked with beef. This recipe can be made with either to make whichever pie you want. You can also create a dairy-free version of this dish by leaving out the cheese, milk and butter from the potato mash. Serve with steamed broccoli or broccolini.

Serves 6+ • Preparation 15 mins • Cook 4 hours • Cooker capacity 5 litres

700 g (1 lb 9 oz) lean minced (ground) beef or lamb
1 onion, diced
420 g (14 oz) tinned diced tomatoes
2 large carrots, grated
2 stalks celery, sliced
½ cup dried green peas
½ cup beef stock
1 tablespoon Worcestershire sauce
1 heaped tablespoon tomato paste (concentrated purée)
2 garlic cloves, crushed
1 teaspoon dried thyme
6 large potatoes (I like golden delight potatoes for mashing), peeled and cut into
      large pieces
60 ml (¼ cup) milk
1 tablespoons butter
150 g (5½ oz) grated tasty cheese
Paprika, to garnish

1. Heat a large frying pan sprayed with cooking oil over medium–high heat. Add the mince and onion in batches, breaking it up with a wooden spoon and cooking until the mince is browned. Transfer the browned mince and onion to a slow cooker.

2. Add the tomato, carrot, celery, peas, beef stock, Worcestershire sauce, tomato paste, garlic, and thyme to slow cooker and stir to combine.

3. Cover and cook on HIGH for 1 hour.

4. Meanwhile, cook the potato in a large saucepan of boiling salted water until tender. Drain. Add milk and butter and mash to a smooth consistency.

5. Use the back of a large wooden spoon or a ladle to press the meat mixture flat into the slow cooker. Spoon the mashed potato over the top and smooth out with a metal spoon.

6. Cover and cook on LOW for 3½ hours.

7. Sprinkle grated cheese over the top of the potato and garnish with paprika (it will give the pie a nice browned look). Cover, putting a tea towel (dish towel) under the lid, and continue cooking for 30 minutes.

Paulene Christie

Bobotie (South African Spiced Mince Pie)

I first made this in an oven when I cooked in a daycare centre and all the children loved it. I tried it in a slow cooker and it was just as good!

Serves 6–8 • Preparation 15 mins • Cook 4½–5 hours • Cooker capacity 6 litres

1 egg
¼ cup milk
3 slices bread, roughly torn
1 kg (2 lb 3 oz) minced (ground) beef
2 onions, diced
3 teaspoons crushed garlic
2 tablespoons light brown sugar
2 teaspoons ground ginger
3 tablespoons curry powder
1½ tablespoons turmeric
2 tablespoons Worcestershire sauce
½ cup beef stock

CUSTARD TOPPING
6 eggs
2 cups milk

1. Combine the egg and milk in a mixing bowl. Mix in the torn bread and leave to soak for 5–10 minutes.

2. Heat a little oil in a large frying pan over medium–high heat. Brown the mince, onion and garlic then add the sugar and spices and fry until fragrant. Add the sauce, stock and soaked bread and stir until combined. Pour into a slow cooker and pat down.

3. Cover and cook on LOW for 4 hours.

4. Combine the custard topping ingredients and pour over the top of the mince. Continue cooking on LOW for 1 hour or increase temperature to HIGH and cook for 30 minutes, until the custard has set.

Lynda Eagleson

Aussie Meat Pie Filling

My three children are very fussy eaters and don't like frozen party pies. I first made this recipe for my son's birthday when we wanted to do pies, sausages rolls and other finger foods. I played around with the recipe many times as the sauce wasn't as thick as I liked, and then it had too much tomato flavour – eventually, it was the addition of Vegemite that gave it the little bit of saltiness it needed.

Makes 16 small pies or 2–3 family-sized pies • **Preparation** 10 mins • **Cook** 2–5 hours • Cooker capacity 5–6 litres

500 g (1 lb 2 oz) minced (ground) beef
1 onion, diced
1 tablespoon cornflour (cornstarch)
¾ cup beef stock
¾ cup tomato sauce (ketchup)
2 tablespoons Worcestershire sauce
1 tablespoon barbecue sauce
1 teaspoon Vegemite

1. Heat a large frying pan sprayed with cooking oil over medium–high heat. Add the mince in batches, breaking it up with a wooden spoon and cooking until the mince is browned. Transfer the browned mince to a slow cooker along with the onion.

2. In a bowl, mix the cornflour with 1 tablespoon of the stock to make a paste.

3. Add the remaining ingredients to the slow cooker and stir well to combine. Mix in the cornflour paste (this will help to thicken the sauce as it cooks).

4. Cover and cook on HIGH for 2–3 hours.

NOTE: You can skip the meat-browning step if you want – just put the raw mince into the slow cooker along with the other ingredients. You will need to increase the cooking time to 3–5 hours. Once you've made the filling, you can then make it into pies using a pie maker or a pie dish in the oven. It can also be frozen for future use.

Alycia Park

SAUSAGES

Sausage & Potato Casserole

I love this recipe as I can prepare all the ingredients the night before, store them in containers in the fridge overnight and then just pour everything into the slow cooker the next morning. The potatoes in this recipe mean you don't need to prepare a side dish, which means less washing up too! This is my go-to meal when I'm working longer days as the flavours just get better the longer you cook it. I've cooked this dish for 12 hours and it was delicious. My young kids devour it and usually go back for seconds. Definitely a winner in our household!

Serves 4–6 • Preparation 20 mins • Cook 8–12 hours • Cooker capacity 6 litres

8–12 sausages, cut into bite-sized pieces
4–5 potatoes, cubed
2–3 carrots, chopped
¼ cup barbecue sauce
¼ cup tomato sauce (ketchup)
2–3 tablespoons gravy powder
1 tablespoon Worcestershire sauce
2–3 teaspoons Vegemite

1. Put the sausages, potato and carrot into a slow cooker.
2. In a jug, combine the remaining ingredients with 1 cup of water and pour over the sausages. Mix to combine well. (Don't worry if the liquid doesn't cover everything.)
3. Cover and cook on LOW for 8–12 hours.

NOTE: You can also add sweet potato, corn, peas, mushrooms or any other vegetable you can think of as well.

Andrea Bricknell

Saucy Snag Casserole

This is a family favourite that pleases the fussiest of eaters in my house.

Serves 5 • Preparation 5 mins • Cook 6 hours • Cooker capacity 6 litres

750 g (1 lb 11 oz) sausages
500 g (1 lb 2 oz) frozen mixed vegetables
400 g (14 oz) tinned crushed tomatoes
2 carrots, sliced
1 potato, diced
1 brown onion, sliced
¼ cup tomato sauce (ketchup)
¼ cup barbecue sauce
2 tablespoons Worcestershire sauce
35 g French onion soup mix, dry
1 tablespoon plain (all-purpose) flour, if required
Mashed potato or steamed rice, to serve

1. Put all of the ingredients into a slow cooker and stir well to combine.

2. Cover and cook on LOW for 5½ hours.

3. Remove the sausages and cut into bite-sized pieces. Return to the slow cooker. If the sauce is too runny, mix the flour with enough water to make a paste and stir through the sauce. Continue cooking for 30 minutes.

4. Serve with mashed potatoes or rice.

Melissa Negus

Tomato Sausage Casserole

This is a quick throw-together I made one evening – it turned out to be a success!

Serves 4–6 • Preparation 15 mins • Cook 4–8 hours • Cooker capacity 8 litres

1 red capsicum (pepper), deseeded and chopped
1 large onion, chopped
2 stalks celery, chopped
8 sausages (chopped or left whole)
400 g (14 oz) tinned chopped tomatoes
250 ml (8½ fl oz/1 cup) vegetable stock
Steamed rice, mashed potato or steamed vegetables, to serve

1. Heat a large frying pan sprayed with cooking oil over medium–high heat. Sauté the capsicum, onion and celery and transfer to a slow cooker. Fry the sausages in the same pan until browned. Transfer to the slow cooker either whole or cut up.

2. Pour the tinned tomatoes and the stock over the sausages.

3. Cover and cook on LOW for 8 hours or on HIGH for 4 hours.

4. Serve with rice, mash, or vegetables, and enjoy!

Caitlyn Muller

Sausage & Potato Bake

No mess. No fuss. A meal for the whole family using one pot. Simplicity and taste all with ease.

Serves 4–6 • Preparation 15 mins • Cook 5 hours • Cooker capacity 5 litres

12 thin beef sausages
1 teaspoon all-purpose seasoning
Small piece pumpkin (squash), thinly sliced (optional)
3 large potatoes, thinly sliced
1 onion, sliced
250 ml (8½ fl oz/1 cup) light cooking cream
2 tablespoons crushed garlic
2 cups grated tasty cheese
Vegetables, to serve

1. Heat a large frying pan sprayed with cooking oil over medium–high heat. Fry the sausages, cooking for 2–3 minutes until browned. Set aside to cool a little then cut into bite-sized pieces and transfer to a slow cooker. (You can skip this browning step and just cut the raw sausages and put them straight into the slow cooker if you wish.)

2. Sprinkle the seasoning over the sausages, then layer the sliced pumpkin on top, if using, followed by the potato and then the onions.

3. Mix the garlic into the cream and then pour over the top of the onions, spreading the cream evenly with a spoon.

4. Cover and cook on HIGH for 4 hours or until the potato has softened.

5. Top with the grated cheese, then cover, putting a tea towel (dish towel) under the lid, and continue cooking for 1 hour.

6. Serve as is or with a variety of vegetables to suit.

Simon Christie

Sweet & Sour Sausages

I've made sweet and sour sauce from scratch many times but never in the slow cooker. We were heading out for a long day at our son's soccer carnival and thought what a great idea it would be to have dinner cooked when we got home. I had everything out to make sweet and sour sausages on the stovetop but threw it all in the slow cooker instead and I'm glad I did!

Serves 4–6 • Preparation 15–20 mins • Cook 6–7 hours • Cooker capacity 5–6 litres

2 teaspoons cornflour (cornstarch)
225 g (8 oz) tinned pineapple pieces in juice, drained
200 ml (7 fl oz) vegetable stock
1 kg (2 lb 3 oz) sausages
⅓ cup rice vinegar
4 tablespoons light brown sugar
1 tablespoon tomato sauce (ketchup)
1 teaspoon soy sauce
1 carrot, sliced
1 onion, sliced
1 red capsicum (pepper), cut into large pieces
Steamed rice, to serve

1. In a bowl, mix the cornflour with enough water to make a paste.

2. Put the pineapple, stock, vinegar, sugar, tomato sauce, soy sauce and cornflour paste into a slow cooker and stir well to combine.

3. Add the sausages, carrot and onion.

4. Cover and cook on LOW for 5 hours.

5. Add the capsicum and continue cooking for 1 hour.

6. Before serving, strain the sauce from the other ingredients, transfer to a saucepan and heat on the stovetop on HIGH for 2–3 minutes. Alternatively, remove the lid and cook on HIGH for a further 30–60 minutes.

7. Serve with rice.

Alycia Park

Creamy Satay Sausages

I created this recipe because I noticed a gap in the available satay recipes I'd seen. Satay beef, satay chicken, satay everything except satay sausages! So, I decided to make them myself and they turned out great. The same recipe can, of course, be used for other meats if you prefer. It's a thick, almost fluffy (for lack of a better word) satay sauce that isn't spicy – suitable for children and adults alike. Note the recipe uses cooking cream, which is less prone to splitting than regular cream.

Serves 6 • Preparation 5 mins • Cook 4–5 hours • Cooker capacity 5 litres

12 thin beef sausages, cut into thirds
300 ml (10 fl oz) reduced-fat cooking cream
1 cup peanut butter (smooth or crunchy)
1 teaspoon curry powder
2 tablespoons sweet chilli sauce

1. Put the sausages into a slow cooker.
2. Combine the remaining ingredients in a bowl with 1 cup of water, then pour into the slow cooker.
3. Cover and cook on LOW for 4–5 hours.

NOTE: Some slow cookers that cook 'hotter' may benefit from 1–2 cups of water added during the cooking process to maintain the saucy finish. Just check as you go along, and if it's drying out, add water.

NOTE: You can brown or pre-cook the sausages before adding to the slow cooker, but I don't find it necessary.

Paulene Christie

Simple Curried Snags

This recipe is a favourite of the whole family. The kids even eat the vegetables in this mild and smooth curry.

Serves 4 • Preparation 10 mins • Cook 3 hours • Cooker capacity 5.5 litres

8 chicken sausages, skin removed
Your choice of diced vegetables (I use 3 carrots and a few stalks of celery)
1 onion, diced
1 cup chicken stock
½ tablespoon curry powder (or to taste)
375 ml (12½ fl oz/1½ cups) tinned light coconut-flavoured evaporated milk, or light coconut milk
2 tablespoons cornflour (cornstarch)
Boiled rice, to serve

1. Put the sausages, vegetables, stock and curry powder in a slow cooker and stir well to combine.
2. Cover and cook on HIGH for 3 hours.
3. When 30 minutes from cooked, mix the coconut milk and cornflour together to make a paste. Stir through the curry to thicken.
4. Serve with boiled rice.

NOTE: Removing the skin from the sausages is easy if you sear them lightly in a frying pan first, then slice them into bite-sized pieces.

Lynne Johnstone

Creamy Curried Sausages with Quinoa

I first made this dish about six months ago because I needed to use up some sausages and cream left over from a barbecue. I wanted a one-pot dish that didn't require having to cook extra pasta or mashed potato to serve. It is super yummy and very filling. I like to cook this once a fortnight and freeze the leftovers for lunches.

Serves 8 • Preparation 10 min • Cook 5–7 hours • Cooker capacity 6 litres

8–10 sausages, sliced into chunks
3 cups beef stock
4 potatoes, chopped
3 carrots, chopped
400 g (14 oz) tinned diced tomatoes
1 large onion, chopped
1 cup frozen peas
1 tablespoon curry powder, or to taste
½ cup cooking or thickened cream
½ cup quinoa

1. Heat a large frying pan sprayed with cooking oil over medium–high heat. Add the sausages in batches, cooking for 2–3 minutes until browned. Transfer to a slow cooker. (You can skip this step and put the sausages straight into the slow cooker if you wish.)

2. Put the stock, potato, carrot, tomato onion, peas and curry powder into the slow cooker and stir well to combine.

3. Cover and cook on LOW for 4–6 hours.

4. Stir in the cream and quinoa and continue cooking for 1 hour.

Vanessa Pardy

➤— Nana's Curried Sausages —●

This is an old-fashioned recipe that's been handed down. It's great on toast and in pies or jaffles. My family's favourite.

Serves 8 • Preparation 30 mins • Cook 6½ hours • Cooker capacity 6.5 litres

24 sausages
4 potatoes, cut into chunks
1 large onion, diced
1 turnip, diced
1 swede (rutabaga), diced
1 parsnip, diced
3 carrots, sliced
2 stalks celery, sliced
1 zucchini, diced
1 red capsicum (pepper), diced
1 cup peas
125 g (4½ oz) tinned corn kernels (optional)
1 handful sultanas (golden raisins) (optional)
3 tablespoons curry powder, or to taste
1 cup plain (all-purpose) flour, plus extra if needed
Lemon wedges, to serve (optional)

1. Bring a large saucepan of water to the boil. Add the sausages and boil for about 15 minutes or until skins shrink. Drain and set aside to cool. Once cool, remove and discard the skins, slice the sausages and put in a slow cooker. (You can skip the pre-boiling if you want and just slice the raw sausages and put them straight into the slow cooker.)

2. Add all of the vegetables, the sultanas and the curry powder along with a pinch of salt and 4 cups of water.

3. Cover and cook on LOW for about 6 hours, until the vegetables are tender.

4. In a bowl, mix the flour with some water to make a runny paste. Stir into the curry. If the sauce is still very runny, make more flour paste and stir in (the sauce will thicken when it cooks).

5. Continue cooking for 30 minutes (the mixture should be very thick).

6. If you like, serve with a squeeze of lemon over the top.

NOTE: For a sweeter curry add 1 diced green apple and 1 diced banana to the vegetables.

Karen Schreck

Sausage Stroganoff

I needed to make something for the husband for his lunch at work, so I quickly grabbed these few ingredients and made this dish. He doesn't eat mushrooms but couldn't even tell I used mushroom soup. Something easy and budget-friendly for the whole family to enjoy.

Serves 4 • Preparation 30 mins • Cook 3–6 hours • Cooker capacity 5 litres

8 thin sausages
420 g (15 oz) tinned cream of mushroom condensed soup
2 tablespoons tomato paste (concentrated purée)
1 tablespoon Worcestershire sauce
1 tablespoon sweet chilli sauce (optional)
1 tablespoon tomato sauce (ketchup)
1 onion, diced
2 carrots, diced
½ cup frozen peas
½ cup frozen corn kernels
2 tablespoons sour cream
Mashed potatoes or pasta, to serve

1. Heat a large frying pan sprayed with cooking oil over medium–high heat. Add the sausages and fry until browned. Set aside to cool slightly. (You can skip this frying step if you wish.)

2. In a bowl, combine the soup, tomato paste and sauces.

3. Put the onion and carrot into a slow cooker. Cut the sausages into bite-sized pieces and add to the slow cooker. Pour the soup mix over and stir to combine.

4. Cover and cook on LOW for 6 hours or on HIGH for 3 hours.

5. When 30–45 minutes from cooked, add the peas, corn and sour cream.

6. Serve with mashed potatoes or pasta.

Leah Shrubb

Spicy BBQ Sausages

This is such a yummy recipe I threw together one day. I cook it quite often, as everybody enjoys it. It's a bit like a slow-cooked stir-fry.

Serves 4–6 • Preparation 5 mins • Cook 4 hours • Cooker capacity 4 litres

6–8 sausages, chopped
220 g (8 oz) tinned crushed pineapple in juice (half a tin)
1 large brown onion, sliced
2 carrots, julienned
½ red capsicum (pepper), julienned
¼ cup tomato sauce (ketchup)
¼ cup barbecue sauce
2–4 tablespoons sweet chilli sauce
Steamed rice, to serve

1. Put all of the ingredients into a slow cooker, season with salt and pepper and stir well to combine.

2. Cover and cook on LOW for 4 hours or until the carrot and onion are cooked but still have texture.

3. Serve with rice.

sam schmaling

Smoky Bacon and BBQ Sausages

Barbecue-flavoured sausages and bacon are the perfect match. The flavours blend during cooking to produce a delicious finished dish. No need to brown your sausages, I cook mine from raw. We like to serve ours with creamy mashed potato, fresh corn on the cob and steamed greens.

Serves 6 • Preparation 5 mins • Cook 4 hours • Cooker capacity 5 litres

12 thin beef sausages
2 small onions, diced
200 g (7 oz) diced bacon
1 cup smoky barbecue sauce (salt-reduced if you prefer)
1 tablespoon Worcestershire Sauce
¼ teaspoon paprika

1. Put the sausages into a slow cooker and top with the onion and bacon.

2. Combine the remaining ingredients in a bowl with 1 cup of water, then pour into the slow cooker.

3. Cover and cook on LOW for 4 hours.

Paulene Christie

Sausage Sensation

This is a great budget bulk meal for larger families, or for smaller families who like to freeze one portion for another day. You can halve the number of sausages for a smaller recipe but leave the other ingredient quantities for a lovely saucy finish.

Serves 10–12 • Preparation 5 mins • Cook 6 hours • Cooker capacity 6 litres

24 thin beef sausages
2 small onions, diced
100 g (3½ oz) diced bacon
Pepper
420 g (15 oz) tinned condensed tomato soup
½ cup barbecue sauce
4 garlic cloves, crushed
2 teaspoons mustard powder

1. Put the sausages into a slow cooker. Add the onion and bacon.
2. Combine the remaining ingredients in a bowl, season with pepper and pour over the sausages.
3. Cover and cook on LOW for 6 hours (although you can cook for longer if you need to).

NOTE: Some slow cookers that cook 'hotter' may benefit from 1–2 cups of water added during the cooking process to maintain the saucy finish. Just check as you go along, and if it's drying out, add water.

Paulene Christie

⊨━ Slow Cooker Hot Dogs ━●

The hot dog needs no formal introduction but these little beauties make my mouth water every time I think about them. From this basic recipe you can add any topping that tickles your fancy to start a mouth party of your very own.

Serves 6 • Preparation 10 mins • Cook 1 hour • Cooker capacity 7 litres

6 long bread rolls
Butter, for spreading
6 wieners or frankfurts
Handful diced bacon
½ red onion, diced
Grated cheese, for topping
Ranch dressing or other sauce, for topping
Dried Italian herbs, for sprinkling

1. Cut a slit lengthways down the middle of each roll and butter the inside. Place a hot dog in each roll and top with bacon, onion, cheese, dressing and herbs. Carefully place the rolls into a slow cooker.

2. Cover, putting a tea towel (dish towel) under the lid, and cook on HIGH for 1 hour.

Simon Christie

BEEF

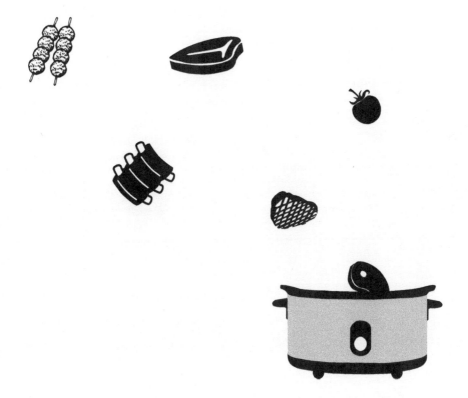

Blackberry Sweet & Savoury Steak

I first made this when we had nothing in the cupboard. It was an experiment, which I hoped would work. I had heard that using jam in the slow cooker can give amazing flavour so I wanted to give it a go. It's a very simple recipe which can be adjusted to anyone's taste. My husband was really impressed and has asked me to make it almost every week since!

Serves 4–6 • Preparation 10–15 mins • Cook 3–6 hours • Cooker capacity 5–6 litres

1–1.5 kg (2 lb 3 oz–3 lb 5 oz) rump steak, or steak of choice
¾ cup tomato sauce (ketchup)
½ cup blackberry jam, or to taste
40 g (1½ oz) French onion soup mix, dry
1 teaspoon cracked black pepper

1. Put the steak in a slow cooker and put the remaining ingredients on top (no need to stir).

2. Cover and cook on LOW for 6 hours or on HIGH for 3 hours.

3. Taste the sauce about 1 hour before serving. If it is too savoury, add another tablespoon of jam.

Alycia Park

Slow-cooked Steak with Creamy Mushroom Sauce

I am married to a steak-lover, and he loves my creamy mushroom stovetop sauce. So naturally I wanted to try the combination in the slow cooker. The results were a smashing success! Serve with crunchy chips and salad for a home-cooked meal the steak-lover in your life is bound to love. Who says you can't slow-cook steak? Not us! The steak is fall-apart, melt-in-your-mouth tender. 2 – 4 – 6 – 8, dig in, don't wait!

Serves 4 • Preparation 5 mins • Cook 5½ hours • Cooker capacity 7 litres

1 kg (2 lb 3 oz) beef chuck or rump steaks
2 teaspoons beef stock powder
500 ml (17 fl oz/2 cups) cooking cream
300 g (10½ oz) mushrooms, quartered
2 tablespoons cornflour (cornstarch)

1. Put the steaks into a slow cooker and top with the mushrooms.

2. In a bowl, whisk together the cream and stock powder, then pour into the slow cooker.

3. Cover and cook on LOW for 5 hours.

4. Carefully remove the steaks onto a serving plate (I use two egg flips, to stop them falling apart).

5. Mix the cornflour with enough water to make a paste and whisk into the mushroom sauce. Gently return the steaks to the slow cooker.

6. Cover, putting a tea towel (dish towel) under the lid, and cook on HIGH for 30 minutes.

7. Gently lift the steaks out onto a plate and serve with lots of the creamy mushroom sauce.

Paulene Christie

⋑— Easy Steak Diane —●

I first tried this recipe when I wanted to cook steak Diane for my husband, as it's his favourite. Dinner times are so busy for me so I thought I'd give it a go in the slow cooker. It's very flavoursome and so easy!

Serves 4 • Preparation 5 mins • Cook 4 hours • Cooker capacity 5.5 litres

1 kg (2 lb 3 oz) piece chuck steak
320 ml (11 fl oz/1⅓ cup) cooking cream
4 tablespoons Worcestershire sauce
4 tablespoons tomato sauce (ketchup)
1 brown onion, finely chopped
2 tablespoons olive oil
Mushrooms, sliced (optional – use as many as you like)
2 garlic cloves, crushed
Chopped parsley, to garnish

1. If desired, heat a large frying pan sprayed with cooking oil over medium–high heat. Add the beef and sear quickly on all sides to brown. Transfer to a slow cooker. (You can skip this step and put the steak straight into the slow cooker if you wish.)

2. In a bowl, combine the remaining ingredients, then pour into the slow cooker.

3. Cover and cook on LOW for 4 hours.

4. If desired, remove the steak from the slow cooker and simmer the sauce, uncovered, on HIGH to thicken.

Katrina Renwick

Heavenly Steak Temptation

We love to cook this, as it's a very easy go-to recipe made with ingredients that are all staples in our household. It can easily be doubled or tripled if you have guests.

Serves 2 • Preparation 10 mins • Cook 3–6 hours • Cooker capacity 1.5 litres

250 g (9 oz) steak, cut into 6 pieces
½ cup smoky barbecue sauce
⅓ cup tomato sauce (ketchup)
¼ cup soy sauce
¼ cup honey
2 garlic cloves, crushed
1 tablespoon sesame seeds
1 tablespoon smoked paprika
1 large onion, sliced
100 g (3½ oz) button mushrooms, sliced
10 kalamata olives, sliced (optional)
Steamed rice and green beans, to serve

1. In a bowl, mix together the sauces, honey, garlic, sesame seeds and paprika and set aside.

2. Spread half the onion in a layer over the base of a slow cooker. Top with half the mushrooms, half the olives, if using, and half the steak. Top with half the sauce mixture. Repeat with the remaining ingredients.

3. Cover and cook on LOW for 6 hours, or on HIGH for 3 hours.

4. Serve with rice and green beans for a great combination.

Louanne & John Callaghan

Mindy's Yummy Steak

I just made this up as I went along with things my family likes – and it was a HIT!

Serves 6 • Preparation 10 mins • Cook 6 hours • Cooker capacity 7 litres

300 ml (10 fl oz) thickened (whipping) cream
¾–1 cup Worcestershire sauce
½ cup tomato sauce (ketchup)
3 tablespoons gravy powder or instant mashed potato powder
2 tablespoons paprika
2–6 garlic cloves, crushed (use as much garlic as you like – we like lots)
6 steaks (I use blade)
1 large onion, chopped
1 large capsicum (pepper), chopped
5 really big field mushrooms, cut into chunks
3 spring onions (scallions), chopped

1. In a bowl, combine the cream, sauces, gravy powder (if using; if using potato powder add later), paprika and garlic.

2. Put the steaks into the bowl of a slow cooker and cover with the onion, capsicum, mushroom and spring onion. Pour the sauce mix over the top.

3. Cover and cook on HIGH for 1 hour, then reduce to LOW and cook for 4½ hours.

4. Remove the lid and stir in the potato powder, if using. Cook, uncovered, for 30 minutes to thicken.

Merinda Haydon

Steak & Bacon Roll-ups

We love fancy, light steak meals. This one hits the spot!

Serves 2 • Preparation 15 mins • Cook 2+ hours • Cooker capacity 6 litres

5 beef sizzle steaks (or other thin-cut beef steaks)
Cream cheese, for spreading
Garlic flakes, for sprinkling
Chilli powder, for sprinkling
Handful baby spinach leaves
5 semi-dried tomatoes
5 rashers shortcut bacon
1 tablespoon plain (all-purpose) flour
1 tablespoon soy sauce
½ teaspoon beef stock powder

1. Lay the steaks onto a clean work surface. Spread each steak with cream cheese and sprinkle with garlic flakes and chilli powder. Top with spinach leaves and place a semi-dried tomato at one end of each steak. Roll the steaks up tightly and wrap each roll with a piece of bacon. Secure each with two toothpicks. Place into a slow cooker.

2. Cover and cook on HIGH for 2 hours.

3. Carefully remove the steak rolls and set aside to keep warm. Combine the flour with ⅓ cup of water to make a paste. Add to the slow cooker along with the soy sauce and stock. Mix well to combine.

4. Return the steaks to the slow cooker and cook on LOW for 10 minutes or until the sauce has thickened.

Deb Harrison

━ Tender Roast Beef ━

After careful consideration I decided I would try a roast beef specifically designed to be family-friendly. Trying to keep the salt down and using natural ingredients I came up with this melt-in-your-mouth roast beef recipe. This is a sure-fire winner!

Serves 4 • Preparation 10 mins • Cook 5 hours LOW • Cooker capacity 6 litres

1 kg (2 lb 3 oz) beef blade roast
1 tablespoon crushed garlic
1½ teaspoon seeded mustard
1 teaspoon olive oil
¼ cup Worcestershire sauce
1 teaspoon oregano
½ teaspoon cracked black pepper
Roast vegetables, to serve

1. Heat a little oil in the searing insert of a slow cooker or a frying pan over medium-high heat. Add the beef, garlic, mustard and oil and brown the beef on all sides. Transfer to the slow cooker.

2. Combine the Worcestershire sauce, oregano and pepper and pour over the beef.

3. Cover and cook on LOW for 5 hours, turning the beef after 2 hours.

4. Serve with a selection of roast vegetables.

Simon Christie

Fall-apart Mustard Crust Roast Beef

My husband used to cook this recipe in our barbecue, and when we got the slow cooker, he decided to give it a go in there. He's never gone back to cooking it in the barbecue again! This is a never-fail dish for us – our guests always ask us for the recipe.

Serves 6–8 • Preparation 15 mins • Cook 8 hours • Cooker capacity 6 litres

2 large onions, thickly sliced
1–1.5 kg (2 lb 3 oz–3 lb 5 oz) topside roast beef (or any roast beef cut you prefer)
100 g (3½ oz) button mushrooms, sliced
10 black kalamata olives, sliced (optional)
¼ cup red wine
Roast vegetables, beans and peas, to serve

CRUST
3 tablespoons wholegrain mustard
3 tablespoons red wine
2 tablespoons hot English mustard (or whatever mustard you prefer)
1 tablespoon smoked paprika
1 tablespoon vegetable oil
2 teaspoons crushed garlic

1. In a bowl, combine the crust ingredients.

2. Spread the onions in the bowl of a slow cooker. Brush the bottom of the beef with a small amount of the crust mixture and then place on top of the onions (crust-side down). Brush the remaining sides of the beef with the rest of the crust mixture.

3. Add the mushrooms and olives (if using) to the slow cooker. Gently pour the red wine over the onions.

4. Cover and cook on HIGH for 2 hours, then reduce the temperature and cook on LOW for 6–8 hours until the meat is falling apart.

5. Serve with roast vegetables, beans and peas.

Louanne & John Callaghan

⚏— BBQ Beef Brisket —●

I love to cook for family and friends and this recipe is just perfect for
entertaining. I pop the brisket on the table with lots of fresh salads and bread
and let everyone tuck in!

Serves 3–4 • Preparation 15 mins + marinating time • Cook 6–8 hours
• Cooker capacity 5 litres

1 kg (2 lb 3 oz) beef brisket
Salads, tacos or vegetables, to serve

RUB
2 teaspoons smoked paprika
2 teaspoons crushed garlic
1 teaspoon dried thyme
1 teaspoon dried parsley
1 teaspoon mustard powder
Pinch of cayenne pepper

SAUCE
2 cups barbecue sauce
1 cup beef stock
1 onion, sliced
⅓ cup apple cider vinegar
2 teaspoons smoked paprika
2 teaspoons crushed garlic
1 teaspoon light brown sugar
1 teaspoon dried thyme

1. Combine the rub ingredients in a bowl. Coat the beef in the rub and set aside for
   at least 30 minutes.

2. Put all of the sauce ingredients into a slow cooker and stir well to combine.
   Season with pepper and add the beef.

3. Cover and cook on LOW for 6–8 hours.

4. Serve with fresh salad, in tacos with coleslaw, or with new potatoes and
   seasonal vegetables.

Jarrah King

Korean Beef Bulgogi

Bulgogi is a Korean classic of marinated grilled beef and I am very excited to share this dish with you. It is very tasty and pretty easy to make. You can add more vegetables such as mushroom and broccoli, and serve with steamed rice.

Serves 4 • Preparation 10 mins • Cook 3–7 hours. • Cooker capacity 3 litres

600 g (1 lb 5 oz) beef sirloin, very thinly sliced across the grain
1 large onion, thinly sliced
1 carrot, thinly sliced

SAUCE
6 tablespoons light soy sauce (or 3 tablespoons regular soy sauce)
3 tablespoons sugar
½ pear or apple, grated (about 3–4 tablespoons)
3 tablespoons rice wine (or mirin)
3 tablespoons chopped spring onions (scallions)
1½ tablespoons crushed garlic
1 tablespoon sesame seeds
1 tablespoon sesame oil
⅛ teaspoon minced ginger
⅛ teaspoon freshly ground black pepper

1. In a bowl, combine all of the sauce ingredients. Put the sauce and the remaining ingredients into a slow cooker and mix well to combine.

2. Cover and cook on HIGH for 3–4 hours or LOW for 6–7 hours.

3. Serve with steamed rice.

NOTE: Sirloin beef is usually used but you can also use eye fillet, T-bone, tenderloin, or chuck steak.

NOTE: Tiffany Southam also has a fantastic beef bulgogi recipe which she came up with for her eldest son, who loves slow cooker meals! To make Tiffany's recipe, marinate 1 kg (2 lb 3 oz) sliced flank steak overnight with 4 tablespoons tamarind, 2 tablespoons sesame oil, 2 tablespoons white vinegar, 1 tablespoon honey, 4 crushed garlic cloves and ⅓ teaspoon white sugar. Brown the steak and ½ a sliced onion then put them into the slow cooker with the marinade on LOW for 6–8 hours. Serve garnished with spring onions (scallions) and sesame seeds.

Juyea Choi

Marinated Beef & Capsicum

This is a recipe I created for my hubby and me – we absolutely love it. You can add whatever vegies you like. It goes beautifully with fried rice.

Serves 4–6 • Preparation 30 mins + marinating time • Cook 4 hours
• Cooker capacity 5 litres

500 g (1 lb 2 oz) rump or topside steak, sliced
2 large onions, cut into wedges
1 red capsicum (pepper), cut into wedges
1 green capsicum (pepper), cut into wedges
2 teaspoons cornflour (cornstarch)
Fried or boiled rice, to serve

MARINADE
2 tablespoons soy sauce
1 teaspoon crushed garlic
½ teaspoon minced ginger

SAUCE
1 cup beef stock
1 tablespoon soy sauce
2 teaspoons black bean sauce
2 teaspoons hoisin sauce
2 teaspoons crushed garlic
1 teaspoon sugar
½ teaspoon minced ginger
¼ teaspoon Chinese five-spice

1. In a large bowl, combine the marinade ingredients. Add the steak and set aside for at least 40 minutes.

2. In a bowl, combine the sauce ingredients.

3. Put the beef and onion in a slow cooker and pour the sauce over the top.

4. Cover, putting a tea towel (dish towel) under the lid, and cook on LOW for 4 hours.

5. Put the capsicum in for the last 30 minutes.

6. In a bowl, mix the cornflour with enough water to make a paste. Stir into the beef and continue to cook for 10 minutes to thicken.

7. Serve with fried or boiled rice.

Carol Wilkinson

⊨━ Asian-style Beef ━●

We love Asian-style food and I was experimenting without the wok as I wanted something I could just throw into the slow cooker.

Serves 3–4 • Preparation 10–15 mins • Cook 3 hours • Cooker capacity 3.5 litres

500–750 g (1 lb 2 oz–1 lb 11 oz) beef (such as chuck or rump steak),
    cut into strips
1 cup beef stock
3 tablespoons soy sauce
2 tablespoons light brown sugar
2 tablespoons garlic sauce or 2 teaspoons crushed garlic
2 tablespoons sherry or brandy
1 teaspoon sesame oil
1 teaspoon Chinese five-spice
2 cups frozen stir-fry vegetable mix
1 x 80 g (2¾ oz) packet 2-minute noodles (optional)

1. Heat a large frying pan sprayed with cooking oil over medium–high heat. Brown the beef then transfer to a slow cooker. (You can skip this step and put the steak straight into the slow cooker if you wish.)

2. Combine the stock, soy sauce, sugar, garlic, sherry or brandy, oil and five-spice and add to slow cooker.

3. Cover and cook on HIGH for 1 hour, then reduce the temperature and cook on LOW for 1 hour.

4. Add the vegetables and continue cooking for 1 hour. If using the noodles, add the noodles and flavouring 30 minutes before serving.

NOTE: You can use fresh vegetables; just cut them into small pieces and add them at the start (except for broccoli, which should be added 30–45 minutes before serving).

Nikki Willis

Beef Strips in Sweet Soy Sauce

A tender Asian-style stir-fry in your slow cooker? It can be done. I use inexpensive cuts of beef and still it comes out absolutely tender. The sauce is superb. Be sure to use the sweet kecap manis soy sauce, not the regular soy sauce. Serve with brown rice and Asian vegetables.

Serves 6 • Preparation 15 mins • Cook 3 hours • Cooker capacity 5 lites

1 kg (2 lb 3 oz) gravy beef or chuck steak, sliced into strips
2–3 tablespoons plain (all-purpose) flour
1 onion, thinly sliced
1 cup hot water
½ cup kecap manis (sweet soy sauce)
2 beef stock cubes
2 garlic cloves, finely diced
Sliced spring onions (scallions) and sesame seeds, to garnish

1. Place the beef in a plastic bag with the flour and shake well to coat.
2. Heat a little oil in the searing insert of a slow cooker or a frying pan over medium–high heat. Add the beef and onion and cook until browned. Transfer to the slow cooker.
3. In a bowl, combine the water, kecap manis, stock cubes and garlic, then pour into the slow cooker.
4. Cover and cook on LOW for 3 hours, stirring once after 2 hours (if possible).
5. Serve garnished with spring onions and sesame seeds.

Paulene Christie

Beef & Broccoli

A popular recipe that I adapted and made my own.

Serves 3 • Preparation 10–15 mins • Cook 3½ hours • Cooker capacity 1.5 litres

1 cup beef stock
¼ cup soy sauce or kecap manis (sweet soy sauce)
¼ cup light brown sugar, lightly packed
1 tablespoon hoisin sauce
2 teaspoons sesame oil
2 large garlic cloves, crushed
500 g (1 lb 2 oz) beef (such as chuck or rump steak), thinly sliced
As much broccoli as you want, cut into florets
1 tablespoon cornflour (cornstarch)

1. Combine the stock, soy sauce, sugar, hoisin sauce, sesame oil and garlic and add to a slow cooker. Add the beef and coat well in the sauce.

2. Cover and cook on LOW for 3 hours.

3. Mix the cornflour with enough water to make a paste, then stir into the sauce. Gently stir in the broccoli and continue cooking for 30 minutes.

Nikki Willis

Burmese Curry

This is one of our family favourites. The original recipe was given to us by a friend and I have converted it for the slow cooker. My kids absolutely love this so it's always a winner in our house, full of spice and flavour. Don't forget to mop up the beautiful sauce with some crusty bread. Enjoy!

Serves 4–6 • Preparation 20 mins • Cook 4–8 hours • Cooker capacity 6 litres

2 tablespoons olive oil
2 large onions, cut into medium-sized pieces
3 garlic cloves, crushed
3 teaspoons yellow mustard seeds
750 g–1 kg (1 lb 11 oz–2 lb 3 oz) chuck steak, cut into cubes
2–4 potatoes, cut into medium pieces
400 g (14 oz) tinned chopped tomatoes
Juice of 1 lemon
1 tablespoon tomato paste (concentrated purée)
Crusty bread, to serve

SPICE MIX
3 teaspoons sweet paprika
3 teaspoons ground coriander
3 teaspoons ground cumin
2 teaspoons garam masala
1 teaspoon ground ginger
1 teaspoon turmeric
1 teaspoon salt
1 teaspoon chilli powder, or 2 chillies, deseeded and finely chopped

1. Heat the oil in the searing insert of a slow cooker, or in a frying pan on the stove. Add the onions, garlic and mustard seeds and cook until soft. If cooking on a stovetop, transfer the onion mixture to the slow cooker at this point.

2. In a bowl, combine all of the spice mix ingredients with about ¾ cup of water. Add to the onion mixture along with the steak and stir well to combine. Add ¼–½ cup water and the remaining ingredients, season with salt and pepper and combine well.

3. Cover and cook on LOW for 6–8 hours or on HIGH for 4–6 hours.

4. Serve with crusty bread.

Terri Donnarumma

⚡ Beef with a Twist ⚫

This beef dish uses plum jam, which some might find a bit unusual! My youngest was helping me to make it one time and kept asking me, 'Are you sure that it has plum jam in it Mum?'

Serves 4 • Preparation 15 mins • Cook 6 hours • Cooker capacity 5.5 litres

1 kg (2 lb 3 oz) beef (chuck or rump steak works best), cut into strips
3 tablespoons plain (all-purpose) flour
½–1 teaspoon chilli powder
2 tablespoons oil
1 tablespoon butter
2 onions, diced
3 garlic cloves, finely chopped
1 cup chicken stock
2 tablespoons plum jam
1 handful slivered almonds
Juice and zest of 2 lemons
1 teaspoon salt
Mashed potatoes, steamed rice, steamed vegies or crusty bread, to serve

1. Place the beef in a plastic bag with 2 tablespoons of the flour and the chilli powder and shake well to coat.

2. Heat the oil and butter in a large frying pan over medium–high heat. Add the onions, garlic and beef and cook until the meat is lightly browned and the onions and garlic are fragrant. Transfer to a slow cooker.

3. Add all the remaining ingredients. Cover and cook on LOW for 6 hours or until meat is tender.

4. When 30 minutes from cooked, check the thickness of the sauce. If it is too watery, mix the remaining 1 tablespoon of flour with enough water to make a paste, and stir through the stew to thicken.

5. Serve with mashed potatoes, steamed rice, steamed vegies or crusty bread rolls.

NOTE: This dish makes a great meat pie filling.

Cassandra Van Breugel

Traditional Beef & Vegetable Hot Pot

Who doesn't love an old-style beef and vegetable casserole-style dish in a slow cooker? I love that it's a complete meal in one bowl and packed with vegetables, ready to serve garnished with fresh parsley and with a crusty bread roll if you choose. Feel free to change up the vegetables for whatever you have on hand.

Serves 6+ • Preparation 15 mins • Cook 9 hours • Cooker capacity 7 litres

1 kg (2 lb 3 oz) gravy beef, diced
2 tablespoons plain (all-purpose) flour
2 tablespoons oil
420 g (14 oz) tinned diced tomatoes
1 cup beef stock
1 large onion, cut into thin wedges
4 celery stalks, sliced
3 small carrots, sliced
4 small red potatoes, unpeeled and diced
4 tablespoons fruit chutney
2 tablespoons Worcestershire sauce
1 tablespoon crushed garlic
1 tablespoon finely chopped parsley
2 teaspoons dried oregano
3 bay leaves
1 cup frozen mixed peas and corn

1. Place the beef in a plastic bag with the flour and shake well to coat.

2. Heat the oil in the searing insert of a slow cooker or a frying pan over medium–high heat. Add the beef and cook until browned. Transfer to the slow cooker along with all the remaining ingredients except the peas and corn.

3. Cover and cook on LOW for 8 hours.

4. Add the peas and corn and continue cooking for 1 hour.

5. Remove the bay leaves before serving.

NOTE: Some cookers will cook slower or faster, so be sure your potato and carrot are tender before serving.

NOTE: You can double the beef stock if you like more liquid in your finished dish.

Paulene Christie

Pink Stew

This has been a family favourite for generations. I just reduced the liquid to convert the recipe for the slow cooker. The name comes from the pinkish colour created by the bacon. We usually serve this with mashed potato.

Serves 6–8 • Preparation 10 mins • Cook 8 hours • Cooker capacity 5 litres

1 kg (2 lb 3 oz) beef (gravy beef, chuck or similar), sliced
500 g (1 lb 2 oz) bacon, diced
1 large onion
2 beef stock cubes

1. Put all of the ingredients into a slow cooker with 125 ml (½ cup) water and stir well to combine.
2. Cover and cook on LOW for 8 hours.

Heather Seccull

Slow Cooker Beef Stew

This is a fantastic and filling meal for cold winter nights, great served with some warm fresh bread with a bit of butter.

Serves 4–6 • Preparation 20 mins • Cook 8–10 Hours • Cooker capacity 5.5 litres

800 g (1 lb 12 oz) tinned whole tomatoes
6 potatoes, cut into cubes (can leave skins on)
4 carrots, peeled and chopped
2 onions, chopped into large pieces
2 stalks celery, chopped
1 tablespoon olive oil
900 g (2 lb) stewing beef, trimmed and cut into cubes
1 tablespoon dried Italian herbs
3 cups beef stock
3 bay leaves
1 cup frozen peas
¼ cup plain (all-purpose) flour

1. Pour the tomatoes into a slow cooker (juice and all). Crush them with a potato masher or the back of a spoon. Add the potato, carrot, onion and celery.

2. Heat the oil in large frying pan over medium–high heat. Fry the beef in batches until browned, then transfer to the slow cooker, along with any juices in the pan.

3. Sprinkle the Italian herbs over the beef and vegies and then add 2½ cups of the beef stock. Give the mixture a quick stir then add the bay leaves.

4. Cover and cook on LOW for 8–10 hours.

5. About 20 minutes before serving, add the peas and season with salt and pepper. In a small bowl, whisk together the flour and the remaining beef stock to make a smooth paste. Stir into the stew. Continue cooking for 15–20 minutes, until the sauce has thickened.

6. Remove and discard bay leaves before serving.

Melissa Hansen

Mirella's Meat & Potato Stew

This is my mother's recipe but made in my slow cooker. My mum passed away last year, and on the first anniversary of her passing, I cooked this in memory of her. It brought me great comfort. This is a hearty family meal, best served with crusty bread, or you can serve up some buttered fettuccine as a base. I hope you enjoy this dish as much as I do.

Serves 4–6 • Preparation 10 mins • Cook 6 hours • Cooker capacity 6 litres

500 g stewing steak, cut into 6–8 pieces
800 g (1 lb 12 oz) tinned diced tomatoes
4 potatoes, peeled and cut into large pieces
250 g (9 oz) green beans (optional)
1 onion, diced
½ cup white wine (optional)
4 garlic cloves, chopped finely
Crusty bread or buttered fettuccine, to serve

1. Put all of the ingredients into a slow cooker and stir well to combine.

2. Cover and cook on HIGH for 6 hours.

3. Serve with crusty bread or some fettuccine tossed with butter.

Paula Cappelletto

Ashy's Easy Casserole

This recipe was handed down through generations in my family as a cheap, easy and tasty meal. Each generation has tweaked it in their own way. This recipe is a favourite winter warmer in my family. Leftovers make a great pie filling.

Serves 6–8 • Preparation 20 mins • Cook 6–8 hours • Cooker capacity 4 litres

500 g (1 lb 2 oz) gravy beef, diced
1 onion, thickly sliced
1 swede (rutabaga), diced
2 parsnips, diced
3 carrots, diced
3 celery stalks, diced
1 cup diced pumpkin (squash)
200 g (7 oz) button mushrooms, quartered
3 bay leaves
¼ cup Worcestershire sauce
¼ cup tomato sauce (ketchup)
¼ cup gravy powder
¼ cup fruit chutney or jam
Handful of sultanas (golden raisins)
Mashed potato or fresh bread, to serve

1. Put all of the ingredients into a slow cooker and stir well to combine.

2. Cover and cook on LOW for 6–8 hours.

3. Serve with mashed potato or fresh bread.

NOTE: Don't add any water to this. The meat and vegetables release enough liquid as they cook.

Ashley Polachek

Cheesy Tuscan Dinner

This easy pasta meal just needs a side salad to set it off. Leftovers are great reheated for lunch the next day.

Serves 4 • Preparation 15 mins • Cook 3½ hours • Cooker capacity 5 litres

500 g (1 lb 2 oz) minced (ground) beef
½ teaspoon wholegrain mustard
1 cup macaroni
½ teaspoon salt
1 onion, diced
1 carrot, grated
100 g (3½ oz) diced bacon
1 teaspoon Tuscan seasoning
2 cups grated cheese (such as tasty cheese)

1. Heat a large frying pan sprayed with cooking oil over medium–high heat. Add the mince and the mustard and fry until browned. Transfer to a slow cooker. (You can skip this frying step and put the mince and mustard straight into the slow cooker if you wish.)

2. Bring a pot of water to the boil. Add the macaroni and the salt and boil for 5 minutes. Drain and add to the slow cooker.

3. Put all the remaining ingredients except the cheese into the slow cooker. Stir well to combine.

4. Cover and cook on LOW for 3 hours.

5. Stir in the cheese and continue cooking for 30 minutes.

Simon Christie

Hearty Beef Goulash with Cheese Dumplings

My family enjoys beef goulash but I wanted to make it a bit more substantial and didn't want to have to worry about cooking extra vegetables when I got home for work. I added the cheese dumplings to make this dish even heartier for those cold winter nights.

Serves 4–6 • Preparation 10 mins • Cook 7½–8¼ hours • Cooker capacity 5.5 litres

1.5 kg (3 lb 5 oz) rump steak, diced
400 g (14 oz) button mushrooms, halved
2 brown onions, thinly sliced
2 large potatoes, diced
300 g (10½ oz) pumpkin (squash), diced
2 carrots, diced
1 cup frozen mixed peas and corn
2 cups beef stock
400 g (14 oz) tinned diced tomatoes
3 garlic cloves, crushed
2 tablespoons tomato paste (concentrated purée)
1½ tablespoons paprika

CHEESE DUMPLINGS
1 cup self-raising flour
30 g (1 oz) butter, cubed
⅓ cup grated cheese
5 tablespoons milk

1. Put the beef and vegetables into a slow cooker. Combine the stock, tinned tomato, garlic, tomato paste and paprika in a bowl and pour into the slow cooker. Stir well to combine.

2. Cover and cook on LOW for 7–7½ hours.

3. Meanwhile, make the dumplings. In a large bowl, rub the flour and butter together until it's the texture of fine breadcrumbs. Stir in the cheese and milk, mixing with your hands until a dough forms. Turn out onto a floured work surface and knead until smooth.

4. Roll into balls and add to the goulash. Continue cooking for 40 minutes.

Stacey Goodall

Mum's Beef Casserole with Dumplings

I grew up eating this casserole. My mother would make it regularly, and I now make it for my family. It is very simple to make. The baked beans break down and help to thicken the juices into a very tasty gravy – you don't even know they are there. This casserole has a rich, meaty flavour and uses only a few ingredients – which most people would already have in their pantry or fridge. Other vegetables can be added to suit your family's taste.

Serves 6–8 • Preparation 10 mins • Cook 8 hours • Cooker capacity 6 litres

1 kg (2 lb 3 oz) chuck, blade or oyster steak, cut into cubes
2 rashers bacon, cut into pieces
2 onions, diced
1 cup beef stock or water
420 g (15 oz) tinned baked beans, roughly mashed
4 carrots, sliced
2 tablespoons gravy powder
Mashed potato, to serve

DUMPLINGS
1 cup self-raising flour
¼ teaspoon salt

1. Heat a little oil in a frying pan over medium–high heat. Brown the beef, bacon and onion in batches and transfer to a slow cooker. Add the beef stock or water to the pan and bring to a simmer, scraping the bottom of the pan to get all of the cooking juices. Add to the slow cooker.

2. Add the baked beans and carrots to the slow cooker and stir well to combine.

3. Cover and cook on LOW for 7 hours.

4. Meanwhile, make the dumplings. In a mixing bowl, combine the flour and salt with ¼ cup of water and season with pepper. Mix together to make a sticky dough.

5. Mix the gravy powder with enough water to make a paste then stir into the sauce. Drop spoonfuls of the dumpling mixture into the casserole. Continue cooking for 1 hour.

6. Serve with mashed potato.

Ellie Kerr

Beef Casserole & Ground Almond Dumplings

This is a hearty winter stew that I adapted from an oven recipe I've been using for a couple of years. I came up with these dumplings when I once purchased a discounted bag only to realise I had no idea what to make with 500 g (1 lb 2 oz) of ground almonds! These dumplings turned out to be my partner's favourite and are requested whenever I mention I might make dumplings.

Serves 6 • Preparation 15 mins • Cook 8–9 hours • Cooker capacity 5 litres

1 kg (2 lb 3 oz) gravy or stewing beef
2 tablespoons plain (all-purpose) flour
2 cups beef stock
400 g (14 oz) mushrooms, sliced
200 g (7 oz) bacon, diced
½ cup red wine
1 onion, diced
2 tablespoons chopped fresh thyme
1 tablespoon crushed garlic
Mashed potato and steamed vegetables, to serve

GROUND ALMOND DUMPLINGS
1 cup ground almonds
1 cup plain (all-purpose) flour
2 teaspoons baking powder
4 tablespoons milk, plus extra if necessary
50 g (1¾ oz) butter, softened

1. Toss the beef in the flour to coat.
2. Heat a large frying pan sprayed with cooking oil over medium–high heat. Brown the beef then transfer to a slow cooker. (You can skip this step and put the steak straight into the slow cooker if you wish.)
3. Put the remaining ingredients into the slow cooker, season with salt and pepper and stir well to combine.
4. Cover and cook on LOW for 7–8 hours.
5. Meanwhile, make the dumplings. Combine the dry ingredients in a bowl and season with salt and pepper. Add the milk and butter and mix to form a soft dough, adding more milk if necessary. Roll into eight equal-sized balls.
6. Place the dumplings on top of the casserole and cook on HIGH for 1 hour.
7. Serve with mashed potato and steamed vegetables.

Teresa McNab

Oxtail Stew with Dumplings

I grew up making this stew with my mum. It is definitely a winter favourite in our house.

Serves 6 • Preparation 10 mins • Cook 6 hours • Cooker capacity 6 litres

1 oxtail
500 g (1 lb 2 oz) beef (such as chuck steak or stewing beef), cubed
1 onion, diced
Mixed vegies of your choice, cut into bite-sized pieces
3 potatoes, cubed
1 piece pumpkin (squash), cubed
2 beef stock cubes or 1 package concentrated beef stock
½ cup gravy powder

DUMPLINGS
2 cups self–raising flour
Pinch of salt
2 tablespoons butter
About ¾ cup cold water

1. Heat a large frying pan sprayed with cooking oil over medium–high heat. Add the oxtail and sear quickly on all sides to brown. Transfer to a slow cooker. Add the beef and fry until browned all over then transfer to the slow cooker.

2. Add the onion, mixed vegies, potatoes and pumpkin to the slow cooker.

3. Mix the stock with a little hot water to dissolve then add to slow cooker along with enough water to fill to about level with the meat and vegetables.

4. Cover and cook on HIGH for 4½ hours.

5. Meanwhile, make the dumplings. In a bowl, combine the flour and salt. Rub in the butter until it's the texture of fine breadcrumbs. Mix in enough water to form a slightly dry dough. Roll into 12 even balls.

6. Mix the gravy powder with enough water to make a paste then stir through the stew. Place the dumplings on top and continue cooking for 1½ hours.

Jamie–Lea McConachy

Mushroom Meatballs

I came up with this dish when I had some meatballs I wanted to use up.

Serves 8 • Preparation 20 mins • Cook 6½ hours • Cooker capacity Any

800 g–1 kg (1 lb 12 oz–2 lb 3 oz) store-bought or homemade meatballs
420 g (15 oz) tinned cream of mushroom condensed soup
400 g (14 oz) tinned mushrooms in sauce
1 onion, chopped
40 g (1½ oz) French onion soup mix, dry
1 tablespoon Worcestershire sauce
Rice and garlic bread, to serve

1. Put all of the ingredients into a slow cooker and stir well to combine.

2. Cover and cook on LOW for 6 or more hours.

3. Turn up to HIGH and cook, uncovered, for about 30 minutes, until the sauce has thickened.

4. Serve with rice and garlic bread.

Lana Devonshire

Chunky Steak Pie

I invented this one for my lovely partner, Matt. We now have it on a weekly basis. There are so many things you can add to the recipe – curry, extra pepper, bacon and cheese, vegetables. It never gets boring.

Serves 4–6 • Preparation 20 mins • Cook 8½ hours • Cooker capacity 5 litres

420 g (15 oz) tinned cream of chicken condensed soup
3 tablespoons gravy powder
2 tablespoons tomato sauce (ketchup)
1 beef stock cube
1 teaspoon crushed garlic
½ teaspoon pepper
Splash of Worcestershire sauce
1 kg (2 lb 3 oz) chuck steak, diced
Plain (all-purpose) flour, to coat
1 tablespoon butter
1 onion, diced
2–4 sheets puff pastry

1. Combine the soup, gravy powder, sauces, stock cube, garlic and pepper in a slow cooker.
2. Toss the beef in a little bit of flour, to coat.
3. Heat the butter in a frying pan over medium–high heat. Add the beef and onion and cook until browned. Transfer to the slow cooker.
4. Cover and cook on LOW for 8 hours. If the mixture starts to get dry, add a little bit of water.
5. Meanwhile, preheat the oven to 170°C (340°F). Grease a pie dish or baking dish.
6. Line the dish with puff pastry, scoop the beef mixture in and top with pastry, trimming to fit the dish if necessary.
7. Bake for about 20–30 minutes or until the pastry is a nice golden colour.

NOTE: There's no need to blind bake the pie base.

Shaya Wright

Loaded Steak, Bacon, Cheese & Potato Pie

My partner and I wanted something different from store-bought pies. I've always made chicken pie and thought I would give a steak pie a go. Then all at once ideas started flowing through our heads. He said to put potato on top instead of pastry, to make it like a shepherd's pie, and I thought to add cheese sauce to the middle because I had some left over from lasagne the night before. Then he suggested bacon on top! It sounded like the perfect pie and it really is. A household favourite here.

Serves 4 • Preparation 15–30 mins • Cook 8½ hours • Cooker capacity 6.5 litres

2–3 potatoes, cut into quarters
Butter or milk, for mashing (optional)
1 sheet puff pastry
2 rashers bacon, diced

PIE FILLING
Plain (all-purpose) flour, for coating
All-purpose seasoning, to taste
Garlic powder, to taste
1 kg (2 lb 3 oz) chuck steak, diced
1 onion, diced
2 garlic cloves, diced
420 g (15 oz) tinned cream of chicken condensed soup
4–5 tablespoon tomato sauce (ketchup)
4 tablespoons gravy powder
4 rashers bacon, diced
1 beef stock cube, crushed
Generous splash of Worcestershire sauce

CHEESE SAUCE
1 tablespoon butter
1 tablespoon plain (all-purpose) flour
1 cup milk
1 cup grated cheese

1. To make the pie filling, mix together the flour, seasoning and garlic powder. Add the steak and toss to combine. Heat a little oil in a frying pan over medium–high heat. Add the beef, onion and garlic and cook until browned. Transfer to the slow cooker along with the remaining ingredients. Mix well to combine.

2. Cover and cook on LOW for 8 hours.

3. Preheat the oven to 200°C (400°F). Grease a pie dish.

4. Boil the potato in salted water until cooked. Mash with a little butter or milk (if using) and set aside.

5. To make the cheese sauce, melt the butter in a saucepan over medium heat. Add the flour, mix until combined and fry for 1–2 minutes. Add the milk and stir continuously until the sauce has thickened. Remove from the heat, add the cheese and stir until melted and smooth. Season with salt and pepper.

6. Line the pie dish with puff pastry. Fill most of the way with the pie filling, spread with the cheese sauce and top with mashed potato. Sprinkle with diced bacon.

7. Bake in the oven for about 30 minutes, until golden.

Jessica Trew

CHICKEN

Creamy Chicken Fajitas

This is a quick-prep dish perfect for a casual meal in any season. I offer it on hectic weekday evenings, allowing my teens to serve themselves as they come in from their various activities at staggered times. And if they bring a friend home with no warning – no problem! The recipe is also easy to adjust to suit individual tastes, it uses ingredients most people have on hand and diners can choose their own toppings. Leftovers are perfect for lunch the next day.

Serves 6–8 • Preparation 10 mins • Cook 4–5 hours • Cooker capacity 5.5–7 litres

4–6 chicken breasts (about 1–1.5 kg/2 lb 3 oz–3 lb 5 oz)
400 g (14 oz) tinned crushed tomatoes
1 red capsicum (pepper), thinly sliced
1 yellow capsicum (pepper), thinly sliced
1 large onion, sliced
150 g (5½ oz) cream cheese
Tortilla wraps, to serve
Shredded lettuce, to serve
Quartered cherry or grape tomatoes, to serve
Grated cheese, to serve

SEASONING
1½ tablespoons cornflour (cornstarch)
1 tablespoon chilli powder
1½ teaspoons paprika
1½ teaspoons sugar
1 chicken stock cube
½ teaspoon salt
½ teaspoon onion powder
¼ teaspoon garlic powder
¼ teaspoon cayenne pepper
¼ teaspoon ground cumin
Pinch of crushed red pepper flakes

1. Grease the bowl of a slow cooker and add the chicken breasts.

2. In a bowl, combine the seasoning ingredients and then sprinkle over the chicken. Add the tinned tomato, capcisum and onion.

3. Cook on LOW for 4–5 hours, until the chicken can be easily shredded with two forks.

4. Shred the chicken in the slow cooker bowl and add the cream cheese. Allow to soften (this will take about 10 minutes) and then stir through the shredded chicken.

5. To serve, spoon the chicken onto tortillas, add your choice of toppings, roll up and enjoy.

NOTE: The seasoning is quite mild – increase the chilli, cayenne or red pepper flakes to taste.

shelleyrae Cusbert

Mexican Chicken Drummies

This is the ultimate cheat's recipe – it's so quick and easy and my family of six love it. While you get a hint of heat it's not so spicy that my children turn their noses up at it – winner, winner, Mexican chicken dinner!

Serves 6 • Preparation 5 mins • Cook 6–8 hours • Cooker capacity 5 litres

2 kg (4 lb 6 oz) chicken drumsticks
800 g (1 lb 12 oz) tinned diced tomatoes
400 g (14 oz) tinned kidney beans or 4-bean mix, drained
400 g (14 oz) tinned corn kernels, drained
1 onion, diced
1 packet salt-reduced taco seasoning mix
Brown rice and salad or steamed greens, to serve

1. Put all of the ingredients except the brown rice or greens into a slow cooker and stir well to combine.

2. Cover and cook on LOW for 6–8 hours.

3. Serve with brown rice and salad or steamed greens.

NOTE: The chicken will be very tender and falling off the bone when cooked so make sure you get all of the small bones out of the slow cooker before serving up the delicious sauce!

Fiona Masters

Spicy Shredded Mexican Chicken

This recipe does have a bit of a bite to it, so beware. Perfect for those who like a bit of heat in their meals. We serve ours on tortilla wraps with avocado, lettuce, tomato, cucumber, cheese and sour cream for a Mexican night!

Serves 6 • Preparation 15 mins • Cook 5 hours • Cooker capacity 3 litres

1 kg (2 lb 3 oz) skinless chicken thigh fillets
435 g (5½ oz) tinned refried beans
1½ teaspoon chilli flakes
1 teaspoon ground cumin
1 teaspoon paprika
1 teaspoon garlic powder
½ teaspoon onion powder
½ teaspoon oregano

1. Put the chicken in a slow cooker.
2. Combine the remaining ingredients in a bowl, then pour into the slow cooker. Stir well to combine.
3. Cover and cook on LOW for about 5 hours (the chicken will release enough juices to keep the meat moist).
4. When cooked, use two forks to shred the meat.

Paulene Christie

Salsa Chicken

We love this recipe as it is so quick and easy to prepare on a busy workday morning. It is so tasty. The kids love it as much as the adults.

Serves 4–6 • Preparation 5 mins • Cook 6–8 hours • Cooker capacity 6 litres

8 chicken thigh fillets
1 packet taco seasoning mix
300 g (10½ oz) tomato salsa
200 g (7 oz) light sour cream
Salad or vegetables, to serve

1. Put the chicken into a slow cooker. Sprinkle with the seasoning and cover with salsa.

2. Cook on LOW 6–8 hours.

3. Stir in the sour cream and continue cooking for 15 minutes.

4. Serve with salad or vegetables.

Deb Cross

◂━ Lemon & Coriander Chicken ━●

This is a recipe that my mother has made for many years. Our family loved it so much that my mother used to double the sauce and still it wasn't enough. So when I make it I triple the amount of sauce and that seems to be just perfect. What's nice about using boneless chicken cut into bite-sized pieces is that when the cream is stirred in, some of the chicken breaks up a little and thickens the sauce a bit more. Yum!

Serves 4 • Preparation 15–20 mins • Cook 4¼–4¼ hours • Cooker capacity 3.5 litres

1 kg (2 lb 3 oz) bone-in chicken pieces of your choice or 500 g (1 lb 2 oz) chicken breast or thigh fillets, cut into bite-sized pieces
2 tablespoons plain (all-purpose) flour
2 tablespoons oil
1½ cups hot water
½ cup lemon juice
3–6 tablespoons chopped fresh coriander (cilantro) or 3–6 teaspoons dried coriander
3 garlic cloves, crushed
1½ chicken stock cubes
3 tablespoons cooking cream
Fettuccine and salad, to serve

1. Place the chicken in a plastic bag with the flour, season with salt and pepper, and shake well to coat.

2. Heat the oil in a frying pan over medium–high heat. Add the chicken in batches and cook until browned. Transfer the browned chicken to a slow cooker.

3. Put all the remaining ingredients except the cream into the slow cooker and stir well to combine.

4. Cover and cook on LOW for 4–6 hours.

5. If using bone-in chicken pieces, remove these from the slow cooker and set aside while you stir in the cream. Add the cream to the slow cooker and stir well. Return the chicken to the sauce and continue cooking for 15 minutes.

6. Serve the chicken and sauce on fettuccine with salad.

Teresa McNab

Thai Pineapple Curry

This recipe is our family favourite – it's easy to make and super tasty! You can adjust the heat by using more or less red curry paste. After discovering the wonders of pineapple curries while on our honeymoon in Thailand, we arrived home and immediately looked up recipes. After some trial and error, we came up with this winning recipe for delicious Thai pineapple curry!

Serves 4–6 people • Preparation 10 mins • Cook 4–8 hours • Cooker capacity 5 litres

800 ml (27 fl oz) tinned coconut cream
3 skinless chicken breast fillets, cut into strips
250 g (9 oz) tinned pineapple pieces in juice, drained
200 g (7 oz) tinned sliced bamboo shoots, drained
1 red capsicum (pepper), finely sliced
1 yellow capsicum (pepper), finely sliced
1 onion, sliced
¼ cup Thai red curry paste
¼ cup white sugar
3 tablespoons fish sauce
Steamed rice, to serve

1. Put all of the ingredients into a slow cooker and stir well to combine.

2. Cover and cook on LOW for 6–8 hours or on HIGH for 4–5 hours.

3. Serve with rice.

Michele Drinnan

Thai Green Chicken Curry

My family thinks this one is a winner – apparently even better than our local takeaway's version! It is an easy and nutritious dinner.

Serves 6 • Preparation 10 mins • Cook 4½–5 hours • Cooker capacity 3.5 litres

600 g (1 lb 5 oz) chicken breast or thigh fillets, cut into cubes
½ head cauliflower, broken into florets
100 g (3½ oz) Thai green curry paste
270 ml (9 fl oz) tinned coconut milk
1 cup frozen green baby beans
Steamed basmati rice, to serve

1. Put the chicken, cauliflower and curry paste into a slow cooker and stir well to combine.

2. Cover and cook on LOW for 4 hours.

3. Stir in the coconut milk, then add the beans. Continue cooking for 30–60 minutes.

4. Serve with basmati rice.

Laurel Judd

Best-ever Thai Red Curry

This is my all-time favourite go-to curry recipe. I love the creamy texture and the spicy citrus flavours amongst the chilli in the sauce. Enjoy it as a winter curry with a nice glass of red or as a summer spice meal with a rosé. It is simple and full of flavour – sure to make a lasting impression!

Serves 4–6 • Preparation 20 mins • Cook 4½–4¾ hours • Cooker capacity 1.5–6 litres

Splash of peanut oil
3 tablespoons red curry paste
100 ml (3½ fl oz) fish sauce
80 g (2¾ oz) palm sugar (or light brown sugar)
500–750 ml (17–25½ fl oz/2–3 cups) chicken stock
500 g (1 lb 2 oz) chicken thigh fillets, trimmed
400 ml (13½ fl oz) coconut milk
230 g (8 oz) tinned bamboo shoots, drained
4 kaffir lime leaves, torn
¼ cup frozen peas
1 zucchini, diced
12 cherry tomatoes
½ red capsicum (pepper), sliced
Coriander (cilantro) leaves, to garnish
Thai basil, to garnish
Steamed jasmine rice, to serve

1. Preheat a slow cooker to HIGH.

2. Heat the peanut oil in the slow cooker, add the curry paste and fry until fragrant. Add the fish sauce and sugar and stir until combined. Add the chicken stock, chicken, coconut milk, bamboo shoots and lime leaves.

3. Cover and cook on LOW for 4 hours.

4. Add the peas, zucchini, tomatoes and capsicum and continue cooking for 30–45 minutes, until the vegetables are cooked to your liking.

5. Garnish with coriander and Thai basil, and serve with jasmine rice.

NOTE: My recipe uses chicken, but you can use any other meat you like. And all veg is optional – just use what you have!

Suscha Benson

Chicken Tikka Masala

I love Indian food. I wanted to try making it from scratch instead of using ready-made sauce – and it was delicious.

Serves 6 • Preparation 15 mins + marinating time • Cook 6 hours • Cooker capacity 5.5 litres

1 kg (2 lb 3 oz) chicken thigh fillets, diced
1 onion, diced
3 garlic cloves, crushed
4 tablespoons tomato paste (concentrated purée)
2.5 cm (1 in) piece ginger, peeled and grated
2–3 tablespoons garam masala, or to taste
2 teaspoons paprika
400 g (14 oz) tinned diced tomatoes
¾ cup cooking cream or coconut milk
1–2 tablespoons cornflour (cornstarch), if required
Steamed jasmine or basmati rice and pappadams, to serve

MARINADE
¾ cup Greek yoghurt
1½ tablespoons ground cumin
1½ tablespoons ground coriander

1. Combine the marinade ingredients in a bowl. Add the chicken, cover and refrigerate for up to 6 hours to marinate. Transfer the chicken to a slow cooker, leaving out the excess marinade.

2. Heat a little oil in a frying pan over medium–high heat. Fry the onion and garlic until soft. Add the tomato paste, ginger and spices and fry until fragrant. Transfer to the slow cooker. (You can skip this step and put all of these ingredients straight into the slow cooker if you wish.) Add the diced tomatoes.

3. Cover and cook for 5¾ hours on LOW.

4. Stir in the cream or coconut milk and add more garam masala if necessary. If the sauce is too runny, mix the cornflour with enough water to make a paste and stir it through the sauce. Continue cooking for 15 minutes.

5. Serve with rice and pappadams.

Lynda Eagleson

⚖— Butter Chicken —⬤

I love butter chicken, but after too many disappointing takeaways I decided to try and create my own at home. After much tweaking and experimenting, this recipe is the result! My family loves it and the chilli and cayenne pepper can easily be adapted or omitted to meet your family's tastes. I like the richness of the thickened (whipping) cream, but if you're watching your waistline, you can leave it out and add an extra 200 ml (7 fl oz) coconut milk instead.

Serves 6 • Preparation 15 mins • Cook 4–8 hours • Cooker capacity 5 litres

40 g (1½ oz) butter
30 ml (1¼ fl oz) vegetable oil
8 skinless chicken thigh fillets, cut into bite–sized pieces
1 onion, diced
3 garlic cloves, crushed
140 g tomato paste (concentrated purée)
1 tablespoon Indian curry paste
1 teaspoon garam masala
1 teaspoon ground cumin
½ teaspoon fenugreek powder
½ teaspoon cardamom
¼ teaspoon chilli powder
Pinch of cayenne pepper
250 ml (8½ fl oz/1 cup) natural yoghurt
200 ml (7 fl oz) coconut milk
200 ml (7 fl oz) thickened (whipping) cream
Steamed basmati rice and warm naan bread, to serve

1. Melt the butter and oil in a large frying pan over medium heat. Add the chicken, onion and garlic. Cook, stirring often, until the onion is soft and translucent (about 5–10 minutes).

2. Stir in the tomato paste, curry paste, garam masala, cumin, fenugreek, cardamom, chilli powder and cayenne pepper. Stir until well combined.

3. Pour into slow cooker and stir in the yoghurt, coconut milk and cream.

4. Cover and cook on HIGH for 4–6 hours or on LOW for 6–8 hours.

5. Serve with steamed basmati rice and warm naan bread or other accompaniments of your choice.

Kate Justelius–Wright

Chicken & Vegetable Coconut Curry

I love curries. There is a long list of ingredients here but once you buy all the spices they will make many curries. This recipe has a simple formula: choose meat, then choose vegetables, then add the coconut cream mix. The heat is medium but you can alter it to suit your taste.

Serves 6–8 • Preparation 15–20 mins • Cook 8 hours • Cooker capacity 5.5 litres

700 g (1 lb 9 oz) chicken thigh fillets, cut into bite-sized pieces
2 large potatoes, diced
1 large sweet potato, diced
½ butternut pumpkin (squash), diced
2 carrots, diced
2 onions, finely diced
¼ head cauliflower, broken into florets
1 litre (34 fl oz/4 cups) vegetable or chicken stock
400 ml (13½ fl oz) coconut cream
2 teaspoons curry powder
1 teaspoon ground garam masala
1 teaspoon ground turmeric
1 teaspoon ground cumin
1 teaspoon ground coriander
1 teaspoon paprika
1 finely chopped teaspoon chilli
1 teaspoon crushed garlic
1 teaspoon minced ginger
2–4 tablespoons cornflour (cornstarch)
½ cup peas
½ cup corn kernels
1½ cups rice, cooked, to serve

1. Grease the bowl of a slow cooker. Add the chicken, potato, sweet potato, pumpkin, carrots, onion and cauliflower and mix well.

2. In a large jug, combine the stock and coconut cream and mix well.

3. Heat a dry frying pan over medium heat. Fry the curry powder, garam masala, turmeric, cumin, coriander and paprika until fragrant, then add the chilli, garlic and ginger and fry for 1–2 minutes. Transfer to the jug and mix thoroughly. (You can skip this frying step and put the spices straight into the jug if you wish.)

4. Pour the liquid into the slow cooker and mix well.

5. Cover and cook on HIGH for 1 hour, then reduce the heat and cook on LOW for 6 hours.

6. Mix the cornflour with enough water to make a paste, then stir into the curry. Add the peas and corn, increase the temperature to HIGH and continue cooking for 1 hour.

7. Serve with rice.

NOTE: This curry freezes and reheats well. Mix the curry and rice together before dividing into containers.

Vicky Kemp

Creamy Chicken Curry

This recipe is very easy and it's so yummy. My family love it and it's my go-to meal if I can't be bothered cooking.

Serves 4 • Preparation 5 mins • Cook 3 hours • Cooker capacity 5 litres

2–3 large skinless, chicken breast fillets
500 ml (17 fl oz/2 cups) cooking cream
2 tablespoons curry powder
20 g (¾ oz) mushroom soup mix, dry
Steamed rice, to serve

1. Put all of the ingredients into a slow cooker and stir well to combine.
2. Cover and cook on LOW for 3 hours, checking and stirring about once an hour to make sure that the cream doesn't split.
3. Shred the chicken (I find using a hand-held electric mixer on low does an amazing job, but be careful not to whip the cream).
4. Serve with rice.

Kaitlyn Adams

Lazy Man's Chicken Curry

This recipe came from pure laziness and finding very few ingredients in the cupboard at the end of the week. It turned out divine and is even better reheated the following day. It goes great with pasta or rice or even turned into a pie filling.

Serves 4–5 • Preparation 10 mins • Cook 5 hours • Cooker capacity 3 litres

1 kg (2 lb 3 oz) chicken thigh fillets, cut into pieces
2 x 420 g (15 oz) tins cream of chicken soup
1 teaspoon curry powder

1. Put all of the ingredients into a slow cooker and stir well to combine.
2. Cover and cook on LOW for 5 hours.

Bea Arnel

Thai Chicken & Prawn Yellow Curry (Gaeng Karee)

I created this dish in the early days of my interest in Thai cooking, and to this day it remains hands-down my favourite Thai dish to cook! If you don't like seafood you can easily leave the prawns (shrimp) out. It's not too spicy for little ones but you can lower the heat factor by adding less curry paste. This curry is lovely served with a side of basmati rice.

Serves 6 • Preparation 10 mins • Cook 4 hours • Cooker capacity 5 litres

1 teaspoon olive oil
700 g (1 lb 9 oz) skinless chicken thigh fillets, trimmed and diced
4 tablespoons Thai yellow curry paste
400 ml (13½ fl oz) tinned light coconut milk
1 large onion, cut into thin wedges
1 red capsicum (pepper), sliced
1 heaped tablespoon light brown sugar
2 baby pak choy, base trimmed
12 snow peas (mange tout), trimmed
14 medium green prawns (shrimp), peeled and deveined with tails left on
1–2 tablespoons cornflour (cornstarch), if required

1. Heat the oil in the searing insert of a slow cooker or a frying pan over medium–high heat. Add the chicken and cook for about 5 minutes, until browned. Add the curry paste and cook, stirring, for 3 minutes, until fragrant. Transfer to the slow cooker.

2. Add the coconut milk, onion, capsicum and brown sugar and stir to combine.

3. Cover and cook on HIGH for 1 hour then on LOW for 2½ hours.

4. Add the pak choy, snow peas (mange tout) and green prawns (shrimp). Stir to combine and continue cooking for 30 minutes.

5. When 15 minutes from cooked, check the thickness of the sauce. If it is too watery, mix the cornflour with enough water to make a paste and stir into the curry to thicken.

Paulene Christie

Apricot Chicken Curry

A slight variation on the traditional apricot chicken. The curry makes a lovely flavoursome addition and goes so well with the apricot chicken flavours. I like to serve mine with creamy mashed potato and fresh steamed vegetables. You can replace the apricot nectar with mango nectar and enjoy a mango chicken curry instead, with no other changes needed.

Serves 5 • Preparation 5 mins • Cook 5 hours • Cooker capacity 5 litres

1kg chicken drumsticks
1 onion, diced
425 ml (14½ fl oz) tinned apricot nectar
40 g (1½ oz) French onion soup mix, dry
1–2 teaspoons curry powder

1. Put the chicken and onion into a slow cooker.

2. Combine the apricot nectar with the soup mix and curry powder and pour over the chicken.

3. Cover and cook on LOW for about 5 hours.

NOTE: You can substitute any cut of chicken, bone-in or fillets. Reduce the cooking time to 4 hours if using fillets.

Paulene Christie

⫶— Caz's Chicken in Chilli Sauce —●

This is a lovely dish! You can add more or less chilli depending on your taste.
I hope you enjoy.

Serves 4–6 • Preparation 30 mins • Cook 2 hours • Cooker capacity 5 litres

500 g (1 lb 2 oz) chicken breast fillets, cut into strips
1 tablespoon cornflour (cornstarch), plus extra if required
3 tablespoons olive oil
2 onions, thinly sliced
1 large carrot, julienned
Finely sliced spring onions (scallions), to garnish
Boiled or fried rice, to serve

SAUCE
¼ cup tomato sauce (ketchup)
1 tablespoon oyster sauce
1 tablespoon olive oil
1 tablespoon soy sauce
2 teaspoons sweet chilli sauce
2 teaspoons sugar
2 teaspoons crushed garlic
½ teaspoon minced ginger
¼ teaspoons chilli powder

1. Place the chicken in a plastic bag with the cornflour and shake well to coat.

2. Heat the oil in a frying pan over medium–high heat. Add the chicken in batches
   and cook until browned. Transfer the browned chicken to a slow cooker.

3. Add the onions to the frying pan and cook over low–medium heat until the
   onion is clear. Transfer to the slow cooker. Cook the carrot in the frying pan over
   medium–high heat for 2 minutes and transfer to the slow cooker.

4. In a bowl, combine the sauce ingredients with ⅓ cup of water. Pour over the
   chicken.

5. Cover, putting a tea towel (dish towel) under the lid, and cook on HIGH for
   2 hours.

6. When 30 minutes from cooked, check the thickness of the sauce. If it is too
   watery, mix 1–2 tablespoons of cornflour with enough water to make a paste and
   stir through the stew to thicken.

7. Sprinkle with spring onion and serve with boiled or fried rice.

Carol Wilkinson

Devilled Chicken

This is an old favourite recipe that my mum used to make for my dad and is now one of my husband's favourites. Loads of flavour, super easy.

Serves 4–6 • Preparation 10 mins • Cook 2–3 hours • Cooker capacity 5 litres

2 tablespoons oil, plus extra for frying
1 large onion, chopped
1.5 kg (3 lb 5 oz) chicken pieces (drumsticks or thigh fillets)
1 cup tomato sauce (ketchup)
2 tablespoons lemon juice
2 tablespoons vinegar
1 tablespoon grated lemon rind
1 tablespoon light brown sugar
1 teaspoon mustard powder
1 teaspoon curry powder
1 teaspoon soy sauce
2 garlic cloves, crushed
Steamed rice, to serve

1. Heat the 2 tablespoons of oil in a frying pan over medium–high heat. Sauté the onion and slightly brown the chicken, drain and transfer to a slow cooker.
2. Combine the remaining ingredients in a bowl, mix well and then pour the mixture over the chicken.
3. Cook on HIGH for 2–3 hours until the chicken is tender.
4. Serve with steamed rice.

Jodi Johnson

Sticky Teriyaki Chicken

Nothing gets my attention like the words 'sticky' and 'chicken' in the same sentence! You can substitute other cuts of chicken in this recipe. I love the flavours in this dish and it's great served with fried rice and steamed broccolini.

Serves 6 • Preparation 10 mins • Cook 3¼ hours • Cooker capacity 5 litres

1 kg (2 lb 3 oz) skinless chicken breast fillets, diced
2 tablespoons plain (all-purpose) flour
1 tablespoon oil
⅓ cup low-sodium soy sauce
¼ cup pineapple juice
3 tablespoons honey
2 tablespoons hoisin sauce
1 tablespoon apple cider vinegar
1½ teaspoon crushed garlic
1 teaspoon minced ginger
2 tablespoons cornflour (cornstarch)

1. Place the chicken in a plastic bag with the flour and shake well to coat.

2. Heat the oil in the searing insert of a slow cooker or a frying pan over medium–high heat. Add the chicken and fry for about 5 minutes, until browned. Transfer to the slow cooker.

3. Combine the remaining the ingredients (except the cornflour) in a bowl with ¼ cup of water, then pour into the slow cooker.

4. Cover and cook on HIGH for 3 hours.

5. Mix the cornflour with enough water to make a paste and stir into the sauce.

6. Continue cooking for 5–10 minutes until the sauce is lovely and thick.

Paulene Christie

Sticky Honey Chicken

I absolutely love Chinese food and wanted to create my own honey chicken. I did not expect it to turn out this good!

Serves 4–5 • Preparation 20 mins • Cook 2 hours • Cooker capacity 5 litres

1 kg (2 lb 3 oz) chicken breast fillets, diced
Plain (all-purpose) flour, to coat
1 tablespoon butter
1 small onion, thinly sliced
6 tablespoons honey
¼ cup light soy sauce
2 tablespoons light brown sugar
1 teaspoon crushed garlic
Rice and vegetables, to serve

1. Toss the chicken in a little bit of flour, to coat.

2. Heat the butter in a frying pan over medium–high heat. Add the chicken and cook until browned. Transfer to a slow cooker. Fry the onion until softened and transfer to the slow cooker.

3. Combine the remaining ingredients in a bowl, then pour into the slow cooker.

4. Cover and cook on HIGH for 2 hours.

5. Serve with rice and vegetables.

Shaya Wright

◗━━ Asian-inspired Whole Chicken ━◗

I love chicken, everything chicken! And Asian is my favourite international food fare, so it was only to be expected that I would try to combine the two. The result was this delicious recipe for a whole chicken that is lovely served with a crunchy Asian salad.

Serves 4–6 • **Preparation** 5 mins • **Cook** 6 hours • **Cooker capacity** 6 litres

1 large whole chicken (about 2.5 kg/5½ lb)
½ cup soy sauce
¼ cup (firmly packed) light brown sugar
3 tablespoons finely diced ginger
5 garlic cloves, crushed
2 teaspoons sesame oil
1 teaspoon cracked black pepper

1. Put the chicken into a slow cooker, breast-side down.
2. Combine the remaining ingredients in a bowl and pour over the chicken.
3. Cover and cook on LOW for 6 hours. If you are around to do so, spoon the juices over the chicken every hour or so. This will help to achieve a rich colour by the end of cooking.

NOTE: A smaller chicken will require a shorter cooking time.

Paulene Christie

Chicken Biryani

I love chicken Biryani and there are plenty of very different recipes out there for it. This is my take on it for the slow cooker. It smells absolutely delicious while cooking!

Serves 4 • Preparation 10 mins • Cook 6–8 hours • Cooker capacity 5.5 litres

2 tablespoons olive oil
500 g (1 lb 2 oz) chicken breast fillets, cubed
2 brown onions, finely chopped
½ red capsicum (pepper), chopped
2 garlic cloves, crushed
2 cm piece ginger, grated
1 teaspoon fennel seeds
1 teaspoon ground allspice
1 teaspoon garam masala
1 teaspoon ground coriander
1 teaspoon turmeric
½ teaspoon ground cumin
¼ teaspoon ground cardamom
3 cups basmati rice
1 cup sultanas (golden raisins)
2 teaspoons vegetable stock powder
2 bay leaves
Pinch of saffron
Pinch of salt

1. Heat the oil in a frying pan over medium–high heat. Add the chicken in batches and cook until browned. Transfer the browned chicken to a slow cooker. Add the onions, capsicum, garlic and ginger to the frying pan and cook for 5–10 minutes, until the onion is clear. Add the spices (except the saffron) and fry for a few minutes until aromatic.

2. Stir in the rice and fry for a minute or two, until well coated in all of the spices.

3. Transfer to the slow cooker and add the sultanas, stock powder, bay leaves, saffron, salt and 4 cups of water. Stir well to combine.

4. Cover and cook on LOW for 6–8 hours until the rice is cooked, stirring two or three times during cooking.

Sandra Rielly

⚞— Luau Chicken —●

A sweet and tasty meal perfect for balmy summer nights.

Serves 4–6 • Preparation 10 mins • Cook 3–4 hours • Cooker capacity 7 litres

1 red capsicum (pepper), sliced into strips
1.5 kg (3 lb 5 oz) chicken breast fillets, diced
½ cup cornflour (cornstarch)
1 tablespoon light brown sugar
1 teaspoon all-purpose seasoning
425 g (15 oz) tinned pineapple pieces in juice, drained
250 g (9 oz) diced bacon
425 g (15 oz) honey–barbecue sauce
Potatoes, noodles or rice and salad, to serve

1. Grease the bowl of a slow cooker. Add the capsicum.

2. Dust the chicken lightly in the cornflour and add to the slow cooker. Sprinkle with the brown sugar and seasoning and top with the pineapple and bacon. Cover evenly with the barbecue sauce.

3. Cover and cook for 2 hours on HIGH, stirring twice, and then reduce to LOW and continue cooking for 1–2 hours.

4. Serve with potatoes, noodles or rice, and salad.

shelleyrae Cusbert

More-4-Me Chicken Wings

Whether it's for the boys watching the footy, or a children's party, these treats are a great addition to any finger-food platter. Made with simple ingredients we have in our pantry, these wings will not last long on a plate.

Serves 5 • Preparation 15 mins • Cook 2½–3½ hours • Cooker capacity 7 litres

1.5 kg (3 lb 5 oz) chicken wings, tipped and sectioned
1 garlic clove, finely chopped
1 teaspoon mustard powder
1½ tablespoons tomato sauce (ketchup)
1½ tablespoons soy sauce
1½ tablespoons barbecue sauce

1. Heat a little oil in the searing insert of a slow cooker or a frying pan over medium–high heat. Add the chicken wings, garlic and mustard and cook until browned. Transfer to the slow cooker along with the remaining ingredients. Stir well to combine.

2. Cover and cook on HIGH for 2½–3½ hours.

Simon Christie

Honey BBQ Whole Chicken

A whole chicken is great done in the slow cooker. This one uses that magical combination of honey and barbecue sauce to produce a lovely sweet flavour. I like to serve this with salad, 'slaw, and potato or sweet potato wedges for a great summer meal. Or combine it with steamed or roasted vegetables in cooler weather.

Serves 6 • Preparation 5 mins • Cook 7 hours on LOW • Cooker capacity 6 litres

1 large whole chicken (about 2 kg/4 lb 6 oz)
½ cup honey
½ cup barbecue sauce
¼ cup soy sauce
2 garlic cloves, crushed
1 teaspoon mustard powder

1. Place the chicken into a slow cooker.

2. In a bowl, combine all the other ingredients. Pour over the chicken.

3. Cover and cook on LOW for 7 hours. If you are around to do so, spoon the juices over the chicken every hour or so. This will help to achieve a rich colour by the end of cooking.

NOTE: Use two utensils (such as tongs and a slotted spoon) to gently lift the chicken out of the slow cooker without it falling apart.

Paulene Christie

Smoky BBQ Chicken with Bacon

This recipe combines my two favourite flavours: chicken and barbecue- anything, and I'm there! What better to combine with these two flavour powerhouses than bacon? I serve this with mashed potato and steamed vegetables. Be sure to spoon some of the sauce over your potatoes too – so yummy!

Serves 6 • Preparation 10 mins • Cook 4 hours • Cooker capacity 7 litres

1 kg (2 lb 3 oz) chicken thigh fillets
250 g (9 oz) bacon, sliced into strips
½ cup barbecue sauce
¼ cup tomato sauce (ketchup)
2 tablespoons Worcestershire sauce
1 tablespoon light brown sugar
1 heaped teaspoon crushed garlic
¼ teaspoon paprika
½ teaspoon mustard powder

1. Heat a little oil in the searing insert of a slow cooker or a frying pan over medium–high heat. Add the chicken and bacon and cook until browned. Transfer to the slow cooker.

2. Combine the remaining ingredients in a bowl with ¼ cup water and pour over the chicken and bacon.

3. Cover and cook on LOW for 4 hours.

Paulene Christie

Honey Mustard Chicken

The traditional honey–mustard flavour pairing that goes beautifully with chicken. I like to slow cook with chicken thigh fillets but this recipe works with whatever chicken cut you like to use. I serve mine with green leafy salad and/or vegetables.

Serves 6 • Preparation 10 mins • Cook 4 hours • Cooker capacity 5 litres

1 kg (2 lb 3 oz) skinless chicken thigh fillets
4 tablespoons mild American mustard
4 tablespoons honey
1–2 tablespoons cornflour (cornstarch)

1. Put the chicken into a slow cooker (don't add anything else at this stage).

2. Cover and cook on LOW for 2 hours.

3. Remove the chicken and break into smaller pieces (or you can leave them whole if you wish). Drain all but ⅓ cup of the chicken juices from the slow cooker. Return the chicken to the slow cooker.

4. Combine the honey and mustard, pour over the chicken and continue cooking for 2 hours.

5. When 15 minutes from cooked, mix the cornflour with enough water to make a paste and stir it through the sauce.

Paulene Christie

Sweet Plum Chicken

This naturally sweetened chicken dish can be served up with rice, pasta or fresh vegetables. Healthy for all the family.

Serves 4 • Preparation 5 mins • Cook 3 hours • Cooker capacity 1.5 litres

750 g (1 lb 11 oz) chicken thigh fillets, sliced
½ cup plum jam, plus extra to serve
1 tablespoon honey, plus extra to serve
1 teaspoon finely diced ginger
1 teaspoon cracked black pepper
¼ teaspoon salt
Vegetables, to serve

1. Put all of the ingredients into a slow cooker and stir well to combine.

2. Cover and cook on LOW for 2 hours, stirring occasionally.

3. Remove the lid and continue cooking, uncovered, for 1 hour.

4. Serve with an assortment of vegetables and a dollop of jam and honey for dipping if desired.

Simon Christie

Marinated Chicken Kebabs

My kids love the marinated chicken kebabs sold at my local deli – but I don't like the price of them! To make matters worse, they almost always stuck and burn in my frying pan. The obvious solution was to make my own and slow cook them. Hey presto, my problems were solved! You can also swap this marinade for a store-bought bottled version if you prefer. Great served with garden salad and potato salad.

Make: 6 skewers • Preparation 15 mins • Cook 2 hours • Cooker capacity 7 litres

½ cup soy sauce
1 tablespoon olive oil
4 garlic cloves, crushed
500 g (1 lb 2 oz) chicken breast fillet, cut into large cubes

1. Combine the soy sauce, oil and garlic in a bowl. Add the chicken and mix well to coat. Cover and refrigerate for at least 2 hours or overnight to marinate.

2. Meanwhile, place six bamboo skewers in cold water to soak for at least 2 hours.

3. Line a slow cooker with baking paper.

4. Thread the chicken onto the skewers and gently place into the slow cooker.

5. Cover and cook on HIGH for 2 hours, turning the skewers over after 1 hour.

Paulene Christie

Vegemite Chicken

Vegemite: the flavour hit this little paste can create is phenomenal! Why should it be any different in our slow cookers? Combine Vegemite and garlic and you've got yourself a little piece of Oz on your plate.

Serves 4–6 • Preparation 5 mins • Cook 6 hours • Cooker capacity 5 litres

1 medium whole chicken (about 1.7 kg/3 lb 12 oz)
2 tablespoons butter, softened
1 tablespoon Vegemite
3 garlic cloves, crushed
Vegetables, to serve

1. Put the chicken into a slow cooker, breast-side down.
2. In a small bowl, combine the butter, Vegemite and garlic. Rub the butter mixture all over the chicken.
3. Cover and cook on LOW for 6 hours.
4. Serve with fresh vegetables of all colours.

Simon Christie

Slow-cooked Marinated Chicken Wings

So often in our Facebook group I see members asking whether they can cook pre-marinated chicken wings in their slow cooker – so I set out to find out just how to do it and for how long. The result is perfect, juicy wings every time! They're great served on their own at parties and my kids love them served with salad and chips for a fun weekend dinner.

Makes 1 kg (2 lb 3 oz) wings • **Preparation** 5 mins • **Cook** 4 hours • **Cooker capacity** 5 litres

1 kg (2 lb 3 oz) pre-marinated chicken wings

1. Put the wings into a slow cooker.
2. Cook for about 4 hours on LOW (the time varies between slow cookers).
3. Serve straight away for sticky yummy wings with zero fuss!

Paulene Christie

Man's Mix for Drumsticks

An easy chicken meal any of us guys can knock up. Packing a full-flavoured punch, this creamy dish is a perfect complement to pasta or rice.

Serves 4 • Preparation 20 mins • Cook 5 hours • Cooker capacity 6 litre

8 chicken drumsticks
1 tablespoon Moroccan seasoning
2 garlic cloves, crushed
1 large onion, roughly chopped
400 g (14 oz) tinned diced tomatoes
200 ml (7 fl oz) chicken stock
2 tablespoons Worcestershire sauce
250 ml (8½ fl oz/1 cup) thickened (whipping) cream
Pasta, to serve

1. Heat a little oil in the searing insert of a slow cooker or a frying pan over medium–high heat. Add the chicken, sprinkle with Moroccan seasoning and fry for 5 minutes. Add the garlic and fry for 5 minutes. Add the onions and fry for a final 5 minutes, until chicken is browned and onion is soft. Transfer to the slow cooker along with all the remaining ingredients except the cream and pasta.

2. Cover and cook on LOW for 4 hours, stirring and turning the chicken once after 2 hours.

3. Remove the drumsticks, shred the meat off the bones and return the chicken to the slow cooker. Stir in the cream.

4. Cover and cook on HIGH for 1 hour, stirring twice.

5. Serve on pasta, being generous with the sauce.

NOTE: You can make this recipe with boneless chicken: use 700 g (1 lb 9 oz) chicken thigh fillets, diced.

NOTE: You can make your own Moroccan seasoning with 2 crushed garlic cloves, ¼ teaspoon turmeric, ¼ teaspoon paprika, ¼ teaspoon ground cumin and a grind of black pepper.

Simon Christie

Chicken in Marinade Sauce

This is a recipe I use as a chicken marinade – I wanted to try it out in the slow cooker and it turned out to be very delicious. I have made this now several times, and my partner and I love this recipe very much.

Serves 4 • Preparation 30 mins • Cook 5 hours • Cooker capacity 5 litres

1 kg (2 lb 3 oz) chicken thigh fillets, sliced
Plain (all-purpose) flour, for dusting
1 onion, thinly sliced
4 garlic cloves, finely chopped
½–⅔ cup light brown sugar
½ cup honey
⅓ cup balsamic vinegar
¼ cup soy sauce
¼ cup sweet chilli sauce
½ teaspoon grated fresh ginger or to taste
½–1½ teaspoons chilli powder
1 teaspoon chicken stock powder
Steamed rice and vegetables, to serve

1. Toss the chicken in a little bit of flour, to coat.

2. Heat a little oil in a frying pan over medium–high heat. Add the chicken in batches and cook until browned. Transfer to a slow cooker. Fry the onion and garlic until softened, scraping up the flour left in the pan from the chicken (this will help the sauce thicken). Transfer to the slow cooker.

3. In a bowl, combine the brown sugar, honey, balsamic vinegar, soy sauce, sweet chilli sauce, ginger and chilli powder. Mix the chicken stock powder with ½ cup of water then add to the sauce. Pour into the slow cooker. Mix well.

4. Cover and cook on LOW for about 5 hours.

5. Served on rice and vegetables

Doris Kühberger

Not-roast Chicken (& Ahh-mazing Gravy)

Traditionally, roast is a Sunday meal, but once you have had this chicken you will want it every other day. The cooking juices make a gravy guaranteed to knock your socks off!

Serves 4+ • Preparation 10 mins • Cook 6 hours • Cooker capacity 5 litres

1 medium whole chicken (about 1.5 kg)
1 tomato
½ red onion
2 teaspoons crushed garlic
2 teaspoons thyme
2 teaspoons cracked black pepper
Steamed vegetable mix and mashed potatoes, to serve

GRAVY
1 cup cooking juices
1 tablespoon plain (all-purpose) flour
½ cup chicken stock
¼ cup cream
½ teaspoon dried thyme

1. Core out the top of the tomato and fill with the thyme and garlic. Stuff the tomato into the chicken cavity, and wedge it in place with the onion. Put the chicken, breast-side down, into a slow cooker. Sprinkle the pepper over the top.

2. Cover and cook on AUTO for 6 hours or on HIGH for 2 hours and then on LOW for 4 hours.

3. Remove the chicken from the slow cooker and set aside to keep warm.

4. To make the gravy, pour 1 cup of the chicken cooking juices into a small saucepan over medium heat. Whisk the flour into the chicken stock then add to the saucepan along with the cream and the thyme. Simmer until reduced to a nice gravy consistency.

5. Serve with a steamed vegetable mix and mashed potatoes.

Simon Christie

Sweet Rosy Chicken

This is a sweet chicken dish complemented by rosemary and turmeric. It will suit any chicken cuts or a whole chicken. This recipe is perfect to serve with fresh vegetables or a garden salad for a healthy family meal.

Serves 4 • Preparation 5 mins • Cook 5 hours LOW • Cooker capacity 5 litres

- 4 skin-on bone-in chicken thighs
- 3 tablespoons honey
- 2 tablespoons olive oil
- 4 cloves garlic or 4 teaspoons crushed garlic
- 1 teaspoon dried rosemary
- ½ teaspoon ground turmeric
- ¼ teaspoon freshly ground black pepper

1. Put the chicken into a slow cooker, skin-side up.
2. Mix the remaining ingredients in a bowl and pour into the slow cooker.
3. Cover and cook on LOW for 5 hours.

Simon Christie

Broccoli Cheesy Chicken

Comfort food at its finest. So simple to make and kids love it! Best of all, it will feed a family of four for next to nothing.

Serves 4 • Preparation 10 mins • Cook 5 hours • Cooker capacity 3.5 litres

2–3 chicken breasts
420 g (15 oz) tinned cream of celery or cream of chicken soup
125 g (4½ oz) cream cheese, left at room temperature to soften
¼ cup milk
2 tablespoons butter, melted
300 g (10½ oz) frozen broccoli florets
Cooked pasta or rice, to serve

1. Grease the bowl of a slow cooker and add the chicken breasts.

2. In a bowl, combine the soup, cream cheese, milk and butter. Spoon over the chicken.

3. Cover and cook on LOW for 4 hours.

4. Shred the chicken and return to the slow cooker along with the broccoli. Cover and continue cooking for 1 hour.

5. Serve over pasta or rice.

Rachael Willcox

Chicken & Asparagus

This was an experiment that worked and went down well in my house.

Serves 4 • Preparation 10 mins • Cook 4 hours • Cooker capacity 6 litres

2 bunches asparagus, trimmed and cut into thirds
4 chicken breasts, cut in half
1 onion, chopped
2 celery stalks, chopped
45 g (1½ oz) cream of chicken soup mix, dry
2 tablespoons drained green peppercorns
1 tablespoon crushed garlic
1 tablespoon mustard

1. Put the asparagus into a slow cooker. Place the chicken on top. Add the onion and celery.

2. In a bowl, combine the soup mix with 1½ cups of water and the peppercorns, garlic and mustard. Pour over the chicken.

3. Cover and cook on LOW for 4 hours.

Cath McGraw

Chicken and Pumpkin Rice

I was never really a fan of pumpkin (squash), so I first made this dish at the request of my wife. It has since become one of my favourite recipes!

Serves 6 • Preparation 15 mins • Cook 7 hours • Cooker capacity 5 litres

2 kg (4 lb 6 oz) chicken thigh or breast fillets, cut into pieces
40 g (1½ oz) French onion soup mix, dry
1 tablespoon plain (all-purpose) flour
1 large brown onion chopped
10 mushrooms, sliced
1 red capsicum (pepper), sliced
420 g (15 oz) tinned cream of pumpkin (squash) soup
1 cup brown rice

1. Place the chicken in a plastic bag with the soup mix and the flour. Shake well to coat, then transfer the chicken to a slow cooker. Add the onion, mushrooms and capsicum.

2. Pour the soup into a bowl. Half-fill the soup can with water and mix into the soup. Pour over the chicken.

3. Cover and cook on LOW for 6 hours.

4. Stir in the rice and continue to cook for 1 hour.

5. If you want to thicken the sauce a little you can leave the lid off the slow cooker for the last 30–45 minutes of cooking.

John Walter

Chicken with Creamy Mushroom Rice

I first made this because I just wanted to try something different. It's a family recipe.

Serves 4 • Preparation 20 mins • Cook 3–4 hours • Cooker capacity 6 litres

1 tablespoon oil
8 chicken drumsticks
2 tablespoons finely chopped onion
1 garlic clove, crushed
2 cups milk
420 g (15 oz) tinned cream of mushroom condensed soup
¾ cup jasmine rice
¼ cup grated parmesan cheese
2 teaspoon salt
1 teaspoon pepper

1. Heat the oil in large frying pan over medium–high heat. Brown the chicken drumsticks on all sides, remove from the pan and set aside. Add the onion and garlic and fry until softened.

2. Remove from the heat and mix in the milk and the soup, stirring until smooth. Add the rice, cheese, salt and pepper. Stir to combine, then transfer to a slow cooker. Place the browned chicken on top (I can do this in a single layer with my rectangular cooker, but you may have to layer depending on the shape of your slow cooker).

3. Cover and cook on HIGH for 3–4 hours, until the chicken is done and the rice is tender and creamy.

Trinity Simmons

Angie's Italian Chicken Mignons

I was experimenting with flavours that my family enjoys and came up with this dish. It's a winner!

Serves 2 • Preparation 10 mins • Cook 3–6 hours • Cooker capacity Any

2 rashers bacon
1 chicken breast, sliced in half horizontally to make it thinner and easier to roll
4 slices salami
½ red capsicum (pepper), sliced
1 small handful sliced olives
1 small handful crumbled feta
A few sundried tomatoes, sliced
A few basil leaves

1. On a clean work surface, layer the bacon, chicken breast, salami, capsicum, olives, feta, sundried tomatoes and basil, in that order. Roll up and secure with a toothpick. Carefully place in a slow cooker.

2. Cover and cook on HIGH for 3 hours or on LOW for 5–6 hours.

Samantha Steele

Chicken Parmigiana

A family favourite made so tender in the slow cooker. These do not turn out super crisp, like the fried version, but this way is much more healthier!

Serves 2 • Preparation 10 mins • Cook 2 hours • Cooker capacity Any

1 egg, lightly beaten
1–2 tablespoons milk or water
Flour, for coating
Breadcrumbs, for crumbing
2 chicken breasts
1–2 tablespoons tomato-based sauce
1 large handful grated cheese

1. Grease the bowl of a slow cooker.

2. Mix the egg with the milk or water in a bowl to make an egg wash. Pour the flour and breadcrumbs into separate dishes for coating and crumbing. Dip the chicken breasts in the flour, egg and then crumbs to coat well. Transfer to the slow cooker.

3. Cover, putting a tea towel (dish towel) under the lid, and cook on HIGH for 1 hour.

4. Top the chicken with the sauce and cheese and continue cooking for 1 hour.

Samantha Steele

Pizza Pocket-Stuffed Chicken

Chicken fillets are easy to stuff with anything you like simply by cutting a little pocket in the chicken. And what better to match with chicken than pizza flavours? You could change your fillings to anything you like. I serve mine with garden salad, coleslaw and sweet potato wedges.

Serves 3–4 • Preparation 10 mins • Cook 4 hours • Cooker capacity 5 litres

3 large skinless chicken breast fillets
3 slices mozzarella cheese
9 slices mild pepperoni
3 tablespoons pizza sauce

1. Line the bowl of a slow cooker with baking paper.
2. Carefully cut a pocket into each chicken breast, ensuring that you don't cut all the way through.
3. Cut each slice of cheese into two and lay one of these halves inside the pocket. Top the cheese with 3 slices of pepperoni. Cover with the second half of the cheese.
4. Tuck as much of the filling as you can into the pocket and push to close.
5. Spread a dollop of pizza sauce on top of each breast. Carefully put the chicken into the slow cooker.
6. Cover and cook on LOW for 4 hours.

NOTE: Chicken breast fillets tend to be large, so I serve one per adult, and my two children share one. You can alter this recipe to serve any number of adults by allowing 1 breast, 1 cheese slice, 3 pepperoni slices and 1 tablespoon of pizza sauce per person.

Paulene Christie

Poached Chicken Breast

I first made this because I wanted chopped chicken on hand for sandwiches and school lunches. Ready-cooked chicken meat is expensive and I didn't like using a whole chicken because that meant removing the skin and the bones. This recipe produces moist, tender 100% chicken breast. You can easily vary the flavour with additional herbs and spices – I kept this one generic for use in other dishes and sandwiches.

Serves 8–10 • Preparation 5 mins • Cook 2 hours • Cooker capacity 5 litres

4 skinless chicken breast fillets
Pinch of garlic salt
Pinch of onion powder
1 teaspoon chicken stock powder
1 cup hot water

7. Put the chicken breasts into a slow cooker. Sprinkle with the garlic salt, onion powder and stock. Season with pepper and pour in the hot water.

8. Cover and cook on HIGH for 2 hours.

9. Remove and dice or shred chicken to desired size.

NOTE: The chicken can be frozen in bags for smaller serves. Perfect for use on sandwiches, wraps and other dishes requiring cooked chicken.

Paulene Christie

Chicken Pie Filling

This was just a trial to begin with but now I cook it regularly. I mainly use this filling for pies.

Serves 4–6 • Preparation 5 mins • Cook 4 hours • Cooker capacity 5 litres

1 large chicken breast fillet
1 large onion, sliced into rings
45 g (1½ oz) salt-reduced chicken noodle soup mix, dry
½ teaspoon vegetable stock powder (optional)

1. Put all of the ingredients into a slow cooker with 1½–2 cups water and stir well to combine.

2. Cover and cook on HIGH for 4 hours, checking and turning the chicken every now and then. Add more water if the liquid starts to dry out.

3. Shred the chicken and stir it back into the sauce.

NOTE: If making pie, I line a pie dish with puff pastry, fill with the cooled chicken and top with more puff pastry. Bake in a 170°C (340°F) oven for about 30 minutes. You can also add the shredded chicken to cooked pasta for an easy meal or add extra water and vegetables to make a chicken soup.

Kelly Sinclair

French Island Chicken

A friend gave me this recipe years ago. I love it and use the leftover sauce for a potato-bake base the next day. It's a budget-friendly meal.

Serves 4–6 • Preparation 5 mins • Cook 2–5 hours • Cooker capacity 5.5–6.5 litres

2 kg (4 lb 6 oz) chicken pieces
2 tablespoons plain (all-purpose) flour
40 g (1½ oz) salt-reduced French onion soup mix, dry
300 ml (10 fl oz) bottled thousand island dressing

1. Place the chicken in a plastic bag with the flour and soup mix and shake well to coat.
2. Transfer the chicken to a slow cooker and pour the dressing over the top. Quarter-fill the dressing bottle with water, shake to rinse, then pour into the slow cooker.
3. Cover and cook on LOW for 4–5 hours or on HIGH for 2 hours.
4. To thicken the sauce, cook uncovered for the final 30 minutes to reduce

NOTE: Just halve all of the ingredients if you only have 1 kg (2 lb 3 oz) of chicken.

Robyn Clark

⚏— Creamy Bacon Chicken —●

This is a very simple creamy chicken recipe. It can be served with rice, pasta, or vegies. I love it with rich and creamy mashed potato.

Serves 4 • Preparation 30 mins • Cook 6 hours • Cooker capacity 6 litres

1 kg (2 lb 3 oz) chicken thigh fillets
500 g (1 lb 2 oz) diced bacon
420 g (15 oz) tinned cream of chicken soup
1 onion, diced
1 tablespoon crushed garlic
250 ml (8½ fl oz/1 cup) cooking cream

1. Put all of the ingredients except the cream into a slow cooker with 50 ml (1¾ fl oz) of water and stir well to combine. Season with salt and pepper.

2. Cover and cook on LOW for 6 hours.

3. When ready to serve, stir the cream through.

Duane Rasmussen

Hearty Chicken Casserole

This recipe was an accidental creation when I had some leftover wine that no-one wanted to drink and some veggies that needed to be used. This recipe has become a family favourite (even my teenager loves it) and it's gluten and dairy free!

Serves 6 • Preparation 15 mins • Cook 6–8 hours • Cooker capacity 6 litres

2 bunches Dutch carrots, cut at both ends, or 3 large carrots cut into chunks
300 g (10½ oz) green beans, trimmed and cut in half
2 small bouquet garni of thyme, parsley and rosemary
1 large green or red capsicum (pepper), cut into medium-sized pieces
700 g (1 lb 9 oz) chicken thigh fillets or breast, diced
250 g mushrooms, quartered
3 large garlic cloves, crushed
1 large onion, cut into quarters
5 rashes unsmoked gluten-free bacon, diced
3 teaspoons gluten-free chicken stock powder
500 ml (17 fl oz/2 cups) dry or semi-dry white wine
2 small punnets of cherry tomatoes, whole
1–2 tablespoons gluten-free cornflour (cornstarch), if required
½ sour cream (optional)
Mashed potato, to serve

1. Place the carrots and beans in a slow cooker along with one bouquet garni. Add capsicum followed by chicken and mushrooms on top.

2. Heat 1–2 tablespoons of oil in a frying pan and fry the garlic and onion until fragrant. Add the bacon and fry until it starts to turn brown. Add the second bouquet garni and chicken stockpowder and cook for 30 seconds.

3. Add the wine and cook for a minute to burn alcohol off. Pour the hot mixture over the ingredients in the slow cooker. Cover and cook on LOW for 6–8 hours.

4. Add the cherry tomatoes 2 hours before serving time.

5. When 30 minutes from cooked, season to taste. If the sauce is too runny, mix the cornflour with enough water to make a paste and stir it through. Add sour cream at this stage if using.

6. Serve with creamy mashed potato.

NOTE: Depending on the type of wine you use, you might need to add a bit of brown sugar to balance the acidity in the sauce.

Bromy Lines

Creamy Chicken

This is an adaptation of my husband's mother's recipe. She used to bring this casserole to cook for dinner when she and her husband stayed with us in the city. I have fond memories of Barb when I make this for the family.

Serves 4–6 • Preparation 15 mins • Cook 6–8 hours • Cooker capacity 4–6 litres

1 red capsicum (pepper), chopped
½ green capsicum (pepper), chopped
1 large onion, chopped
4 sprigs of thyme
4 sprigs of parsley
6 rashers bacon, sliced
600 g (1 lb 5 oz) chicken thigh fillets or breast, diced
1 cup mushrooms, quartered
420 g (15 oz) tinned cream of chicken soup
1 teaspoon chicken stock powder
3 garlic cloves, minced
½ cracked pepper
1–2 tablespoons cornflour (cornstarch), if required
½ cup frozen peas
Steamed rice, to serve

1. Put the capsicum, onion, and two sprigs each of the herbs in a slow cooker. Add bacon, chicken then mushrooms on top.

2. In a bowl, combine the soup, stock powder, garlic, remaining herbs and cracked pepper, and mix until it is of pouring consistency. Pour the mixture over the chicken and vegetables making sure they are covered with the soup mixture.

3. Cover and cook on LOW for 6–8 hours.

4. When 45 minutes from serving, check the seasoning and add salt and pepper to taste. If the sauce is too runny, mix the cornflour with enough water to make a paste and stir it through. Add frozen peas at this stage

5. Serve with rice (I like jasmine rice).

NOTE: I make a gluten-free version by making my own cream of chicken soup or using a jar of gluten-free white sauce from the pasta aisle of the supermarket.

Bromy Lines

▬— Chicken Fricassee —●

A classic dish with a slow-cooked twist. My family loves the creamy mushroom sauce. Serve this on brown rice or on creamy mashed potato, with steamed vegetables.

Serves 5 • Preparation 15 mins • Cook 4–5 hours • Cooker capacity 6 litres

1 kg (2 lb 3 oz) skinless chicken thigh fillets
2 tablespoons plain (all-purpose) flour
1 tablespoon butter
1 onion, chopped
250 g (9 oz) button mushrooms, cut into quarters
2 garlic cloves, crushed
¼ teaspoon dried thyme
¼ teaspoon dried tarragon
½ cup chicken stock
½ cup white wine
1 tablespoon cornflour (cornstarch)
150 ml (5 fl oz) cooking cream

1. Place the chicken in a plastic bag with the flour and shake well to coat.

2. Heat the butter in the searing insert of a slow cooker or a frying pan over medium–high heat. Add the chicken and fry until browned. Transfer to the slow cooker.

3. Add the onion, mushroom, garlic, thyme and tarragon and season with salt and pepper. Combine the stock and wine, then pour into the slow cooker.

4. Cover and cook on LOW for 4–5 hours.

5. Remove the chicken with a slotted spoon and set aside to keep warm.

6. Return the searing insert to the stovetop (or transfer the sauce to a saucepan). Mix the cornflour with enough water to make a paste and stir into the sauce. Add the cream and cook over medium heat for about 5 minutes until the sauce is nice and thick.

7. Serve the chicken with the sauce poured over the top.

Paulene Christie

PORK

PORK

Simple 'n' Saucy Pork Chops

I decided I wanted to do a pork chop recipe as I so rarely cook pork and I wanted to expand my repertoire. This is a no-fuss dish that takes only minutes to whip up. I'm a die-hard barbecue sauce fan, as is everyone in my family, so we love this recipe. We serve it with crunchy French fries and a large side salad.

Serves 4 • Preparation 5 mins • Cook 4 hours • Cooker capacity 6 litres

4 pork chops
1 onion, diced
1 cup tomato sauce (ketchup)
½ cup barbecue sauce
½ cup light brown sugar, lightly packed

1. Put the pork chops into a slow cooker (in a single layer, if possible) and put the onion on top.

2. In a bowl, combine the sauces and brown sugar, then pour over the chops.

3. Cover and cook on LOW for 3 hours.

4. Place a tea towel (dish towel) under the lid and continue cooking for 1 hour.

5. Serve the chops with the sauce spooned over.

NOTE: You can easily increase the number of chops for more serves, as the recipe makes plenty of sauce.

Paulene Christie

Tangy Mustard Pork Chops

I just made this up from scratch – as I do with most of my slow-cooker inventions – and it came out really well.

Serves 4 • Preparation 10 mins • Cook 4–6 hours • Cooker capacity 5 litres

4 pork chops, fat and bones removed
2 tablespoons wholegrain mustard
1 tablespoons English mustard or hot English mustard
2 onions, chopped
220 g (8 oz) tinned crushed pineapple in juice (half a tin)
1–2 tablespoons cornflour (cornstarch), if required
Steamed rice or vegetables, to serve

1. Put all of the ingredients except the cornflour into a slow cooker with ½ cup of water, season with salt and pepper and stir well to combine.

2. Cover and cook on LOW for 4–6 hours.

3. When 30 minutes from cooked, check the thickness of the sauce. If it is too runny, mix the cornflour with enough water to make a paste and stir it through the sauce.

4. Serve with rice or veg.

sam schmaling

Marinated Pork Tenderloin in Plum Sauce

When we go to our local Chinese restaurant, I always order pork in plum sauce. I just love it. So, I thought I would create my very own version – I hope you enjoy it.

Serves 6–8 • Preparation 30 mins • Cook 1½ hours • Cooker capacity 5 litres

400 g (14 oz) piece pork tenderloin
1 large carrot, julienned
1 large onion, sliced
1 cup snow peas (mange tout), trimmed
1–2 tablespoons cornflour (cornstarch), if required
Boiled or fried rice, to serve

MARINADE
¼ cup soy sauce
1 tablespoon honey
1 tablespoon light brown sugar
1 teaspoon crushed garlic
1 teaspoon red food colouring

SAUCE
2 tablespoons tomato sauce (ketchup)
2 tablespoons plum sauce
1 tablespoon oyster sauce
1 teaspoon Worcestershire sauce
1 teaspoon sugar
¼ teaspoon Chinese five-spice

1. In a bowl, combine the marinade ingredients. Cover the pork loin with the marinade and refrigerate for at least 4 hours or overnight.

2. 1 hour before cooking, place the pork into the freezer.

3. In a bowl, combine the sauce ingredients with ¼ cup of water. Pour into a slow cooker. Add the carrot and onion.

4. Remove the pork from the freezer and cut into very thin slices. Add to the slow cooker and stir gently to combine.

5. Cover, putting a tea towel (dish towel) under the lid, and cook on HIGH for 1½ hours or until cooked to your liking.

6. When 15–20 minutes from cooked, check the thickness of the sauce. If it is too watery, mix the cornflour with enough water to make a paste and stir through the stew to thicken. Add the snow peas (mange tout).

7. Serve with boiled or fried rice.

Carol Wilkinson

VJ's Sticky Pork Ribs

I first made this about a year ago and have made it at least once or twice a month since.

Serves 2–4 • Preparation 10 mins • Cook 7–7½ hours • Cooker capacity 5 litres

800 g–1 kg (1 lb 12 oz–2 lb 3 oz) pork rib racks
1½ cups barbecue sauce (I use a combination of a sweet, sticky sauce and a
    brown-sugar bourbon sauce)
½ cup sweet chilli sauce

1. Put all of the ingredients into a slow cooker and mix well to combine.

2. Cover and cook on LOW for 7 hours.

NOTE: For a crispy finish, preheat an oven to very hot (I turn mine up as hot as it will go), take the ribs out of the slow cooker after 7 hours, and bake in the oven for 30 minutes or until crisp.

Vince Johnson

 Swineapple

This is a fun recipe that can be tailored to any taste, using fresh ingredients and delivering something a little different.

Serves 4 • Preparation 20 mins • Cook 5¾ hours • Cooker capacity 5 litres

1 large pineapple
400 g (14 oz) pork loin or chicken fillets, cut into strips
4 tablespoons marinade of your choice
¼ red capsicum (pepper), sliced
¼ green capsicum (pepper), sliced
¼ red onion, sliced
600 g (1 lb 5 oz) middle bacon rashers
Barbecue sauce, to coat

1. Chop off the top of the pineapple and hollow it out (keep the top of the pineapple). Shave off the spines on the outside, taking care to leave a 1.5 cm (½ in) wall intact on all sides.

2. In a bowl, mix together the meat, marinade, capsicums and onion, then transfer the filling to the cavity of the pineapple.

3. Put the top back on the pineapple and secure with skewers.

4. Make a bacon weave (see note) and wrap it tightly around the pineapple. Secure it with toothpicks or skewers.

5. Coat the bacon in barbecue sauce, place the pineapple seam-side down in a slow cooker and cook on LOW for 5½ hours.

6. Meanwhile, preheat the oven to 220°C (430°F).

7. Transfer the pineapple to the oven and bake for 5–10 minutes, until the bacon is crisp. Rest for 2 minutes before carving to serve.

NOTE: A bacon weave is a square mat of rashers woven in a crosshatch pattern. YouTube can be really helpful for tutorials.

Jaime Caillot de Chadbannes

Bacon-wrapped Volcano Potatoes

I always look for new, interesting ways to serve vegetables to the kids. Mention 'volcano' and they can't wait to see the cheese oozing from the top and spilling over the crispy bacon!

Serves 4–6 • Preparation 10 mins • Cook 5¼ hours • Cooker capacity 3+ litres

4 large potatoes, washed
400 g (14 oz) grated cheese
400 g (14 oz) shredded ham or diced bacon
4 tablespoons sweet chilli sauce
8 rashers bacon
1 cup barbecue sauce
Sour cream and chopped chives, to serve

1. Wrap the potatoes individually in foil and put in a slow cooker.

2. Cook on LOW for 3 hours.

3. Unwrap the potatoes and cut a slice off the bases so the potatoes will stand up. Hollow out the potatoes using an apple corer or small spoon. Stuff with layers of cheese, ham or bacon, and sweet chilli sauce. Wrap each potato in 2 rashers of bacon and secure with toothpicks.

4. Put the wrapped potatoes into the slow cooker and cook on HIGH for 2 hours.

5. Meanwhile, preheat the oven to 220°C (430°F).

6. Carefully transfer the potatoes to a baking tray. Coat the bacon in barbecue sauce and bake in the oven for 5–10 minutes, until the bacon is crispy.

7. Serve topped with sour cream and chives.

Jaime Caillot de Chadbannes

Stuffed Potatoes

I learned this recipe in French class at high school. I have since adapted it to suit my family's taste. This is one of their favourite dinners.

Serves 4 • Preparation 20 mins • Cook 2–3 hours • Cooker capacity 6 litres

4 large potatoes
4 tablespoons milk
1 tablespoon butter
1 onion, chopped
2 rashers bacon, diced
1 cup corn kernels
1 cup grated cheese

1. Cook the potatoes in a microwave for 10–15 minutes on HIGH until cooked through.

2. Cut the potatoes in half and scoop out the flesh, transferring the scooped out potato to a bowl and setting the skins aside.

3. Mash the potato with the milk and butter. Mix in the onion, bacon, corn and cheese. Spoon the potato mix back into the skins and place in a slow cooker.

4. Cover, putting a tea towel (dish towel) under the lid, and cook on HIGH for 2–3 hours until heated through and cheese has melted.

NOTE: You can add whatever you like to the filling to suit your preference.

Narelle Youngs

Span's No-bake Bacon & Egg Pie

I'm not gonna lie, I make good pie! I just threw this all together one day and was surprised how well it turned out – I didn't even need to crisp it in the oven. The pastry came out beautiful and golden, and with no soggy bottom. The inside was lovely and moist, not dried out like the oven does. I'll never cook a pie in the oven again. This recipe is now a fave in my household, and quickly became a weekly meal. It even went down a treat with the in-laws!

Serves 4–6 • Preparation 20 mins • Cook 3½ hours • Cooker capacity 6.5 litres

1 brown onion, diced
2–4 sheets savoury shortcrust pastry
1 tablespoon crushed garlic
120 g (4½ oz) baby spinach, chopped
12 eggs, 6 lightly beaten
250 g (9 oz) bacon, chopped
Grated cheese (as much as you like)
Chopped spinach and bacon with Caesar dressing, to serve

1. Heat a large frying pan sprayed with cooking oil over medium–high heat. Add the onion and fry until softened. Set aside.

2. Line a shop-bought foil tray (small enough to fit inside your slow cooker) with baking paper and then with 1–2 sheets of pastry.

3. Lightly smear the pie base with half the garlic and top with half the onion and half the spinach. Crack the 6 whole eggs onto the spinach and season with pepper. Sprinkle over half the bacon and some cheese.

4. Repeat the layers with the remaining ingredients, starting with dots of crushed garlic and ending with the beaten egg. Cover with 1–2 sheets of pastry, sealing the edges well and poking a few holes in the top with a sharp knife. Place carefully into a slow cooker.

5. Cover, putting a tea towel (dish towel) under the lid, and cook on LOW for 3½ hours.

6. Serve with chopped spinach and bacon with Caesar dressing.

Anna Jane Macdonald

Pork Parcels in Asian Broth

I was sitting and thinking about something I could make for dinner that was a bit different – and this is what came to mind! I put a twist on Asian wontons. It turned out perfectly, and my hubby loved it too. I hope you enjoy!

Serves 8–10 • Preparation 1 hour • Cook 2 hours • Cooker capacity 5 litres

BROTH
1 litre (34 fl oz/4 cups) chicken stock
½ cup finely sliced spring onions (scallions)
1 small carrot, finely sliced
1 tablespoon soy sauce
1 tablespoon balsamic vinegar
1 tablespoon cooking wine
2 teaspoons sesame oil
1 teaspoon minced ginger

PORK PARCELS
450 g (1 lb) minced (ground) pork
½ cup finely sliced spring onions (scallions)
115 g (4 oz) tinned water chestnuts, chopped
1 egg, lightly beaten
3 teaspoons soy sauce
1½ teaspoons crushed garlic
1 teaspoon sesame oil
½ teaspoon minced ginger
Store-bought wonton wrappers

1. Put all of the broth ingredients into a slow cooker and stir well to combine.

2. Cover and cook on HIGH for about 2 hours.

3. Meanwhile, about 1 hour before serving, combine all of the pork parcel ingredients except the wonton wrappers in a bowl. Season with salt and pepper.

4. Working with just a few at a time, lay the wonton wrappers out on a clean work surface. Moisten the edges of the wrappers with water. Place 1 teaspoon of the pork mixture in the middle of each wrapper then fold in half and crimp the edges to seal. Set aside under a damp cloth to stop them drying out. Repeat with the remaining pork mixture.

5. Cook the wontons in batches. Heat a large frying pan filled with about 1.5 cm (½ in) of water over high heat. Add wontons, cover and cook until the water is absorbed and the bottoms of the wontons are browned. Turn the wontons over, add another 1.5 cm (½ in) of water and cook until the water is absorbed and the second side is browned. Set aside. Repeat until all of the wontons are cooked.

6. Transfer to the slow cooker and cook for 30 minutes.

Carol Wilkinson

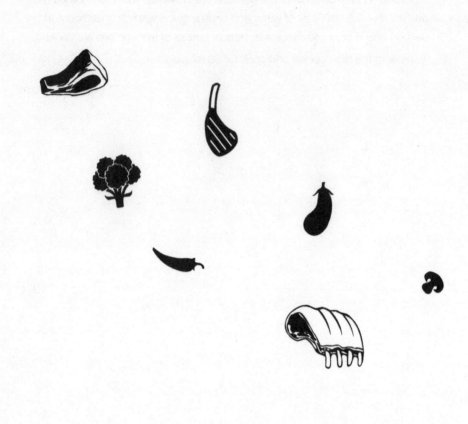

LAMB & GAME

Balinese Lamb Chops

My family loves this mild-tasting flavoursome meal. It is also delicious made using chicken thighs or pork chops. We serve it with rice or mashed potatoes and vegetables.

Serves 4–6 • Preparation 5 mins • Cook 6–8 hours • Cooker capacity 5 litres

400 ml (13½ fl oz) tinned coconut cream
1 brown onion, finely chopped
4 tablespoons crunchy peanut butter
2 tablespoons kecap manis (sweet soy sauce)
2 tablespoons sweet chilli sauce
8 lamb forequarter chops

1. In a jug or bowl, combine the coconut cream, onion, peanut butter, kecap manis and sweet chilli sauce.
2. Arrange the chops in the bowl of a slow cooker and pour the sauce mixture over the top. Turn the chops over a few times to coat in the sauce mixture.
3. Cover and cook on LOW 6–8 hours.

Megan Milligan

Chutney Chops

A family favourite that my mum used to make when I was growing up. These are delicious served with mashed potato and vegetables. The chops can be marinated in the sauce for a few hours or overnight for extra flavour.

Serves 4–6 • Preparation 5 mins • Cook 6–8 hours • Cooker capacity 5 litres

½ cup fruit chutney
1 tablespoon light brown sugar
3 teaspoons curry powder
1 teaspoon soy sauce
1 teaspoon mustard powder
8 lamb forequarter chops

1. Mix all of the ingredients except the chops in a jug or bowl with ½ cup of water. Stir well to combine.

2. Arrange the chops in the slow cooker bowl and pour the sauce mixture over the top. Turn the chops over a few times to coat in the sauce mixture.

3. Season with salt and pepper. Cover and cook on LOW for 6–8 hours.

NOTE: If marinating the chops before cooking, put them into a container after step 1 and pour over the sauce, turning the chops to coat with the mixture. Refrigerate until needed. When ready to cook, proceed from step 2 to finish.

Megan Milligan

Savoury Lamb Chops

This was my brother's favourite when we were kids, and it is now one of my kids' favourites. I love coming home when the house smells of this casserole.

Serves 4 • Preparation 10 mins • Cook 6 hours • Cooker capacity 3.5 litres

6–8 lamb chops
2 tablespoons tomato sauce (ketchup)
2 tablespoons vinegar
2 tablespoons plain (all-purpose) flour
1 tablespoon sugar
¼ teaspoon ground ginger
¼ teaspoon mustard powder
¼ teaspoon curry powder
¼ teaspoon mixed spice
1 cup chicken or vegetable stock
Mashed potato and vegies, to serve

1. Put the chops into a slow cooker. Combine the remaining ingredients except the stock in a bowl and stir to break up any lumps.

2. Add the stock and pour the mixture over the chops.

3. Cover and cook on LOW for 6 hours. Add extra stock if needed.

4. Serve with mashed potato and vegies.

NOTE: The chops can be marinated overnight for extra flavour.

Christine Meade

⊫— Slow-cooked Lamb Shanks —●

After having lamb shanks at a restaurant one night I wanted to make them at home. This is the recipe I came up with and my whole family loved it.

Serves 4 • Preparation 10 mins • Cook 8 hours • Cooker capacity 5.5 litres

4 lamb shanks
2 cups beef stock
¾ cup red wine
¼ cup maple syrup
2 teaspoons rosemary
2 teaspoons mixed herbs
1 teaspoon cornflour (cornstarch)
½ cup thin (pouring) cream

1. Put the lamb shanks into a slow cooker. Combine the remaining ingredients except the cornflour and cream in a bowl and pour over the lamb shanks.

2. Cover and cook on LOW for 7½ hours.

3. Mix the cornflour with enough water to make a paste and stir it through the sauce. Continue cooking for 30 minutes.

4. Remove the lamb shanks to serving plates, stir the cream through the sauce then spoon over the top of the lamb.

Stacey Goodall

French Lamb Casserole

Just a recipe I put together randomly. I had a lot of lamb in my freezer so I tried it with ingredients I thought would go together. It turned out beautifully.

Serves 6 • Preparation 5 mins • Cook 3–6 hours • Cooker capacity 6 litres

1 kg (2 lb 3 oz) lamb chops, fat trimmed
40 g (1½ oz) French onion soup mix, dry
425 g (15 oz) tinned crushed tomatoes with herbs and garlic
6 carrots, halved
Mashed potatoes and vegetables, to serve

1. Put all of the ingredients into a slow cooker and stir well to combine.

2. Cover and cook on LOW for 6 hours or on HIGH for 3–4 hours.

3. Serve with mashed potatoes and vegetables

Trinity Simmons

⇒— Sweet Lamb Casserole —●

This casserole is based on an oven-baked recipe I used many years ago. It is sweet and tasty, and you could use any cut of lamb and it would work beautifully. I usually use diced leg or shoulder, but you can use forequarter chops, lamb shanks, or even a whole leg of lamb if you want to. Shredded lamb would taste fantastic with this same sauce as well.

Serves 4 • Preparation 10 mins • Cook 6–8 hours • Cooker capacity 5 litres

420 g (15 oz) tinned tomato soup
¼ cup brown sugar
2 tablespoons soy sauce
2 tablespoons minced ginger
1 tablespoon Worcestershire sauce
500 g (1 lb 2 oz) diced lamb leg or shoulder, or cut of your choice
1 onion, diced
2 carrots, sliced
2 celery stalks, sliced
Steamed white rice, to serve

1. In a bowl, combine the soup, sugar, soy sauce, ginger and Worcestershire sauce with ½ cup of water.

2. Put the lamb, onion, carrot and celery in a slow cooker and pour the sauce over the top.

3. Cover and cook on LOW for 5–7 hours. Remove the lid and continue cooking, uncovered, for 1 hour to thicken the sauce.

4. Serve with steamed white rice.

Ellie Kerr

Sweet Lamb Curry

This dish came about when I was handing out meals to patients at my work and they were all enjoying a sweet lamb curry. It smelled so good! I'd never even eaten one before as I don't usually like fruit in cooked meals – but I set myself the challenge to make one of my own and the minute I tasted it I was hooked! After 'lamb obsession' (see *Slow Cooker Central 1*), this is now my second-favourite slow-cooked meal of all time. We have this regularly in our house now and it's not too spicy for all the family to enjoy – even my toddler loves it. We serve ours with creamy mashed potato or rice and crusty bread rolls to mop up all the delicious sauce.

Serves 6 • Preparation 5 mins • Cook 5 hours • Cooker capacity 5 litres

1 kg (2 lb 3 oz) diced lamb (I have a butcher debone and dice a leg piece)
1 large onion, diced
2 small green cooking apples, peeled, cored and diced
½ cup beef stock
½ cup fruit chutney
3 teaspoon mild curry powder
2 garlic cloves, crushed
½ teaspoon minced ginger
2–3 tablespoons cornflour (cornstarch)

1. Put all of the ingredients except the cornflour into a slow cooker and stir well to combine.

2. Cover and cook on HIGH for 2 hours then LOW for 3 hours, or on AUTO for 5 hours. (If you're not around to adjust the temperature, just start on LOW and cook for 7 or more hours.)

3. When 30 minutes from cooked, mix the cornflour with enough water to make a paste and stir into the curry. Leave the lid slightly askew to help the sauce to thicken.

Paulene Christie

Fragrant Lamb Curry with Kale

My gorgeous husband is the reason behind this recipe – he asked me to make a curry using lamb and that's how this recipe was created. I love to cook this on a cold winter's day and the best part is sitting down at the table with my little family and seeing how much they all enjoy my cooking.

Serves 6–8 • Preparation 15 mins • Cook 6 hours • Cooker capacity 5 litres

1 cinnamon stick
1 bay leaf
2¼ teaspoons cumin seeds
1½ teaspoons coriander seeds
¾ teaspoon ground turmeric
6 cardamom seeds, crushed with a spoon
6–8 lamb chops
3 cups chopped kale
700 g (1 lb 9 oz) passata (puréed tomato)
2 large potatoes, chopped into large pieces
2 onions, finely chopped
1 cup chicken stock
2 carrots, chopped into large pieces
2 teaspoons minced ginger
3 garlic cloves, chopped
1 teaspoon curry powder
Rice, mashed potato or naan bread, to serve

1. Place all the spices in a dry frying pan over medium–high heat and toast for 3 minutes or until fragrant (you could also do this in a pre-heated slow cooker). Transfer to a slow cooker.

2. Heat a large frying pan sprayed with cooking oil over medium–high heat. Add the lamb and sear quickly to brown. Transfer to the slow cooker. (You can skip this step and put the lamb straight into the slow cooker if you wish.)

3. Put all the remaining ingredients into the slow cooker and stir well to combine. Season with salt and pepper.

4. Cook on LOW for 6 hours.

5. Remove the cinnamon stick and bay leaves and serve with rice, mashed potato or naan bread.

NOTE: You can use spinach instead of kale. Just add the spinach leaves to the slow cooker 10 minutes before serving.

NOTE: If you find the sauce becomes oily, place some bread over the top before serving and this will soak up the excess oil.

NOTE: This isn't a spicy curry – if you like your curry with a bit of heat, just add some chilli.

Jarrah King

Lamb & Barley Hotpot

I first made this as a soup as a way to use the bits and pieces I had in the fridge, freezer and pantry before shopping day. It's so comforting and hearty it became a staple in our soup repertoire. It morphed into a hotpot one night when I didn't have enough stock to make it a soup. I thought, 'Oh well, I'm sure it could still be good,' and decided to add some gravy at the end. Now it's on the repeat menu. It's so easy to make, the ingredients are readily available and adjustable to suit your requirements, and best of all, it's budget-friendly.

Serves 2+ • Preparation 15 mins • Cook 3–8 hours • Cooker capacity 3.5 litres

2–3 cups vegetable or chicken stock (I use 2 concentrated stock pods with
    2 cups of water)
½ cup pearl barley
4 lamb forequarter chops, fat trimmed
1 brown onion, chopped
1 clove garlic, crushed
1 potato, chopped
1 stalk celery, chopped
1 carrot, chopped
½ cup frozen peas
2 tablespoons gravy powder

1. Put the stock and the barley in a slow cooker.
2. Heat a large frying pan sprayed with cooking oil over medium–high heat. Season the lamb with salt and pepper and sear quickly on all sides to brown. Transfer the lamb to the slow cooker. Fry the onion and garlic until soft, then transfer to the slow cooker.
3. Put all remaining ingredients except the peas and gravy powder into the slow cooker.
4. Cover and cook on LOW for 7–8 hours or on HIGH for 3–4 hours.
5. When 10–15 minutes from cooked, stir in the frozen peas and the gravy powder.

Melissa Warman

Greek Lamb Souvlaki

I have a family of boys (even the cat and dog are males!) and meals like this are a favourite. I learnt the tzatziki from a lovely lady I used to work for. I played around with ingredients and this is the version that got rave reviews from the family.

Serves 10+ • Preparation 10 mins • Cook 8+ hours • Cooker capacity 3 litres

1 boneless lamb leg or shoulder (about 2 kg/4 lb 6 oz)
2 teaspoons crushed garlic
1 bunch fresh oregano
Zest and juice of 2 lemons

TZATZIKI SAUCE
1 Lebanese cucumber
500 ml (17 fl oz/2 cups) Greek yoghurt
1 teaspoon crushed garlic
Juice of 1 lemon

TO SERVE
Lebanese flat bread
Grated cheese
Shredded lettuce
Sliced tomato
Thinly sliced onion

1. Put the lamb, garlic, oregano and lemon zest and juice into a slow cooker.

2. Cover and cook on HIGH for 4 hours, then reduce the temperature and cook on LOW for 4 hours (larger pieces may need longer). When the lamb is cooked, slice or shred the meat.

3. Meanwhile, make the tzatziki. Grate the cucumber and squeeze all the liquid out of it. Place it in a bowl and mix in the yoghurt, garlic and lemon juice. Set aside in the fridge.

4. To serve, spread the tzatziki onto the flat bread then sprinkle with grated cheese. Put some lamb down the centre of the bread then top with lettuce, tomato and onion and roll. Toast in a sandwich press until nice and toasted.

Maria Peterson

Saucy Pulled Lamb & 'Slaw Sliders

Lamb is great to pull or shred and this recipe makes a great easy weekend dinner. Beef or chicken work well too. Serve it with crunchy 'slaw and soft bread rolls. So yummy!

Makes 10 sliders • Preparation 5 mins • Cook 8 hours • Cooker capacity 5 litres

1–1.5 kg (2 lb 3 oz–3 lb 5 oz) boneless lamb leg or shoulder roast
420 g (14 oz) tinned diced or crushed tomatoes
1 small onion, finely diced
¼ cup hoisin sauce
3 tablespoons sweet chilli sauce
2 packed tablespoons light brown sugar
1½ tablespoons fish sauce
1 tablespoon cornflour (cornstarch)
1 heaped teaspoon crushed garlic
1 heaped teaspoon minced ginger
Crunchy 'slaw and soft bread rolls, to serve

1. Put the lamb into a slow cooker.

2. Combine the remaining ingredients in a bowl, then pour into the slow cooker.

3. Cover and cook on AUTO for 7 hours, or on HIGH for 2 hours and then LOW for 5 hours.

4. Remove the lamb from the slow cooker and shred or 'pull' the meat using two forks or tongs.

5. Combine the cornflour with enough water to make a paste and stir through the sauce. Mix the shredded lamb back into the sauce and continue cooking for 1 hour.

6. To serve, pile the lamb and 'slaw into soft bread rolls.

Paulene Christie

Maple Roast Lamb

This recipe is really easy. There's not much preparation, and it's very tasty.

Serves 8–12 • Preparation 5 mins • Cook 8–9 hours • Cooker capacity 7 litres

2–4 kg leg of lamb
3–4 tablespoons dijon mustard
1 cup chicken stock
1 cup maple syrup
Sprig of rosemary, leaves picked
120 g (4½ oz) gravy powder (I use lamb and rosemary flavour)

1. Coat the lamb with the mustard and put it into a slow cooker. Add the stock. Drizzle the maple syrup over the lamb, sprinkle with rosemary and season with salt and pepper.

2. Cover and cook on LOW for 8–9 hours.

3. Take the lamb out, cover and allow to rest for 30 minutes.

4. Strain the juices from the slow cooker into a small saucepan and bring to the boil over medium–high heat. Add the gravy powder and whisk until thick.

5. To serve, carve the lamb – it will fall apart beautifully.

Donna Mott

━ Duck Delight ━

This dish contains all of my favourite flavours and is a really easy way to cook duck. I like to serve this with steamed rice and Chinese vegetables.

Serves 4 • Preparation 5 min • Cook 4 hours • Cooker capacity 3.5 litres

2 duck breasts (or another cut of duck)
2 tablespoons honey
Juice of 1 orange
1 tablespoon soy sauce
1 teaspoon sesame oil
1 teaspoon crushed garlic

1. Put all of the ingredients into a slow cooker and stir well to combine.

2. Cover and cook on LOW for 4 hours.

NOTE: You can crisp up the skin at the end in a hot frying pan if you like.

Geoff Tapp

Lemon Rabbit

I had been out hunting rabbits and needed a new way to cook them. My partner trawled through some non-slow-cooker books and I got inspired by a couple of the recipes that we found. I decided to adapt them for the slow cooker and this delicious recipe is what I came up with. I'm now allowed out to hunt rabbits more often thanks to this recipe!

Serves 2–3 • Preparation 15–20 mins • Cook 4–6 hours • Cooker capacity 3.5 litres

500 g (1 lb 2 oz) rabbit, chopped into pieces (use more if any of the pieces have bones)
4 tablespoons olive oil
2 tablespoons mustard powder
1 teaspoon ground nutmeg
1 teaspoon ground allspice
½ teaspoon chilli powder
6 garlic cloves, crushed with the back of a knife
1 large or 2 small lemons, cut into wedges
1 tablespoon honey
1 tablespoon fresh thyme, leaves picked
2 tablespoons plain (all-purpose) flour
2 teaspoons light soy sauce
1 teaspoon Moroccan seasoning
Mashed potato or couscous and steamed vegetables, to serve

1. Put the rabbit pieces into a bowl. Drizzle with 2 tablespoons of the oil and add the mustard, nutmeg, allspice and chilli. Season with salt and pepper and mix well to coat.

2. Heat the remaining oil in a frying pan over medium–high heat. Add the coated rabbit pieces and the garlic and fry until the meat is browned all over. Transfer to a slow cooker.

3. Add the lemon wedges, honey and thyme and pour in enough water to come up to the top of the meat.

4. Cover and cook on LOW for 4–6 hours.

5. Remove the rabbit from the slow cooker and set aside to keep warm.

6. Add the flour, soy sauce and Moroccan seasoning to the liquid in the slow cooker and combine to make a gravy.

7. Serve with mashed potato or couscous and steamed vegetables.

Brad Hill

Slow-cooked Venison

I simply could not find a good slow-cooker venison recipe, so I had to improvise. A good recipe for those with hunting husbands!

Serves 4–6 • Preparation 15 mins • Cook 8 hours • Cooker capacity 3.5 litres

¼ cup barbecue sauce
3 tablespoons cranberry sauce
2 tablespoons Worcestershire sauce
2 tablespoons soy sauce
1 teaspoon crushed garlic
¼ cup plain (all-purpose) flour
500 g (1 lb 2 oz) diced venison
1 tablespoon olive oil
400 g (14 oz) tinned chopped tomatoes
1 brown onion, sliced
Creamy mashed potato, sweet potato and garlic mash or rice, to serve

1. Put the sauces and garlic into a slow cooker and stir well to combine.

2. Put the flour in a bowl and season well with salt and pepper. Add the venison and toss to coat.

3. Heat the oil in a frying pan over medium–high heat. Add the venison and cook until browned. Transfer to the slow cooker along with the tinned tomato and the onion. Mix well.

4. Cover and cook on LOW for 8 hours.

5. Serve with creamy mashed potato, sweet potato and garlic mash or rice.

NOTE: This recipe makes a great pie filling.

Danielle Atkinson

SEAFOOD

Mud Crab & Mango Chilli Tuna Soup

I first made this trying to be creative with new ingredients and great flavours. My experimental soup turned out just the way I was hoping. I hope you enjoy my creation as much as I do.

Serves 4 • Preparation 15 mins • Cook 2 hours • Cooker capacity 2 litres

1 tablespoon butter
1–2 teaspoon crushed garlic
½ cup chicken stock
½ teaspoon curry powder
1 small tin mango chilli tuna
2 spring onions (scallions), chopped
1 small chilli
1 mud crab, shelled, claw meat left in large pieces, body and leg meat shredded
400 ml (13½ fl oz) tinned coconut cream
Parsley and chives, to garnish

1. Put the butter and garlic into a slow cooker.

2. Cover and cook on HIGH for 5 minutes.

3. Add the chicken stock and curry powder and season with salt and pepper. Add the tinned mango chilli tuna, spring onions and whole small chilli and stir through.

4. Cover and cook on HIGH for 10 minutes.

5. Add the coconut cream and the crab except the claw meat and stir though.

6. Cover and cook on LOW for 1½–2 hours, stirring every 30 minutes.

7. Transfer the soup to serving bowls and top with the reserved claw meat. Garnish with parsley and chives and serve.

Mareea Mernin

Salmon Fillets With Asian Glaze

I don't cook or eat a lot of fish so this was out of my comfort zone, but I was surprised at how easy and tasty it was! I'll now be cooking fish regularly for my family. I love Asian flavours so this was right up my alley. Serve it with a crunchy salad and potato wedges.

Serves 2+ • Preparation 5 mins • Cook 1½ hours • Cooker capacity 3 litres

2 x 240 g salmon fillets, skin on
¼ cup soy sauce (salt-reduced if you have it)
2 tablespoons sesame oil
1 tablespoon rice wine vinegar
2 teaspoons crushed garlic
2 teaspoons minced ginger
2 teaspoons cornflour (cornstarch)

1. Line a slow cooker with non-stick baking paper. Place the salmon fillets on top.

2. In a small bowl, combine the remaining ingredients, then pour over the fish.

3. Cover and cook on LOW for about 1½ hours, or until the salmon is cooked to your liking (the fish should pull apart easily with a fork – overcooked fish will flake into dry pieces).

NOTE: You can use increase the number of salmon fillets if you like – there will be plenty of glaze.

Paulene Christie

Salmon Parcels

This is a great quick dinner or lunch. It's super tasty with all my favourite flavours. It's so easy but always gets amazing comments.

Serves 4 • Preparation 10 mins • Cook 2 hours • Cooker capacity 6 litres

2 carrots, peeled and finely chopped
4 broccoli florets, chopped
4 shallots, thinly sliced
2 cm (¾ in) piece ginger, peeled and finely chopped
1 chilli, finely chopped
4 x 200 g (7 oz) salmon fillets
2 tablespoons soy sauce
1 tablespoon lime juice
2 teaspoons sesame oil

1. Place four large squares of baking paper on a clean bench top.

2. Divide the carrot, broccoli, shallot, ginger and chilli evenly among the baking paper squares. Place the salmon fillets on top.

3. Fold up the baking paper to make individual parcels, but don't close them up just yet.

4. In a small bowl, combine the soy sauce, lime juice and sesame oil. Pour this mixture over the parcels, ensuring that none of the liquid escapes.

5. Fold up the parcels to completely enclose the salmon. Put the parcels into a slow cooker.

6. Cover and cook on LOW for 2 hours.

7. Serve with steamed or fried rice.

Melodie Tapp

Salmon Wrapped in Bacon

Our anniversary was coming up and I wanted to make something different so I decided to make this. We both loved it, so I make it all the time now.

Serves 4 people • Preparation 20 mins • Cook 2 hours • Cooker capacity 5 litres

1 zucchini (courgette), sliced diagonally
1 potato, sliced
½ red capsicum (pepper), julienned
½ onion, sliced
4 cherry bocconcini, chopped
Garlic butter, for spreading
4 salmon fillets
4 rashers bacon
1 lemon, sliced

1. Place 4 large squares of baking paper on a clean bench top.
2. Divide the zucchini and potato slices evenly among the baking paper squares. Add the red capsicum and onion, and place the chopped cherry bocconcini on top.
3. Spread some garlic butter over each salmon fillet, then wrap tightly with a bacon rasher. Transfer the salmon to the vegetable parcels and place a slice of lemon on top of each piece of salmon.
4. Wrap the salmon tightly in the baking paper to create individual parcels. Put in a slow cooker.
5. Cover and cook on HIGH for 2 hours.

Lisa Casey

⊫— Creamy Mustard Marinara —●

After a very busy day, I was looking for something to throw in the slow cooker, something quick and easy to make. We now have this at least once a fortnight.

Serves 4–5 • Preparation 10 mins • Cook 4½ hours • Cooker capacity 3–5 litres

1 teaspoon olive oil
1 large onion, diced
2 cloves garlic, diced
1 tablespoon dijon mustard
1 red capsicum (pepper), diced
500 g (1 lb 2 oz) seafood marinara mix
600 ml (20½ fl oz) cooking cream
½ cup milk
1–2 tablespoons cornflour (cornstarch)
½ cup spring onions (scallions)
Cooked pasta of your choice, to serve

1. Heat the oil in a frying pan over medium heat. Add the onion and garlic and sauté until soft. Add the mustard and stir to combine. Put the mixture into a slow cooker and add the capsicum and marinara mix. Pour in the cooking cream and gently mix to combine.

2. Cover and cook on HIGH for 1 hour, then reduce the temperature to LOW and cook for 3 hours.

3. In a small bowl, mix together the milk and the cornflour. Stir into the sauce along with the spring onions and continue cooking for 10–15 minutes for the mixture to thicken. Season with salt and pepper.

4. Pour over the cooked pasta and serve.

Kaz Hooker

◼━ Tuna Mornay ━●

I used to cook this dish on the stovetop. It was time consuming because it had to be stirred constantly as the white sauce thickened. The main advantage of cooking this in a slow cooker is that it doesn't catch on the bottom and it doesn't need continuous stirring. Therefore, happy me!

Serves 6 • Preparation 15 min • Cook 2 hours • Cooker capacity 5 litres

50 g (1¾ oz) butter
425 g (15 oz) tinned tuna in olive oil
8 tablespoons plain (all-purpose) flour
1 tablespoon stock powder or 1 stock cube
4 cups milk
1 onion, finely diced
1–2 carrots, grated
1–2 zucchini (courgettes), grated
375 g (13 oz) spiral pasta, cooked to just al dente
1 cup grated cheese
Finely chopped chives and parsley, to garnish

1. Preheat a slow cooker to HIGH.
2. Put the butter and the drained oil from the tinned tuna in the slow cooker.
3. Once the butter is melted, add the flour and stock powder or stock cube and mix until well combined.
4. In a small pan, heat the milk and onion until warmed through. Slowly add this mixture to the slow cooker, stirring until combined and smooth. Add the carrot and zucchini and mix well.
5. Cover, putting a tea towel (dish towel) under the lid, and cook on HIGH for 1½ hours, stirring every 20–30 minutes.
6. Add the tinned tuna, pasta and cheese and gently stir to combine.
7. Continue cooking until the pasta is warmed through.
8. Serve with a tossed salad.

NOTE: You can vary the grated vegetables as desired.

Judy Maughan

Cheat's Seafood Chowder

This recipe is super easy and deceptively cheap to make, being mainly potatoes and marinara mix. Everyone who has eaten this asks me for the recipe, but it's so easy I'm a bit embarrassed!

Serves 6 • Preparation 10 mins • Cook 5½–7 hours • Cooker capacity 5–6 litres

1 kg (2 lb 3 oz) potatoes, cut into quarters
2 celery stalks, chopped
1 onion, chopped
1 handful chives, chopped, plus extra for garnish
¼ cup oyster sauce
800 g–1 kg (1 lb 12 oz–2 lb 3 oz) seafood marinara mix
300 ml (10 fl oz) cooking cream
Crusty bread, to serve

1. Put the potato, celery, onion, chives and oyster sauce into a slow cooker with 2 cups water. Stir gently to combine.

2. Cover and cook on HIGH for 1 hour, then reduce to LOW and cook for 4–5 hours.

3. Using a hand-held blender, purée until smooth. (Or transfer to a blender or food processor and return to the slow cooker when smooth.)

4. Add the marinara mix, cover, and continue cooking for 30–40 minutes, until the seafood is cooked (the prawns (shrimp) should be orange and the fish white).

5. Add a pinch of salt, stir through the cream and serve with a sprinkle of chives and some crusty bread.

Ann Turnbull

Seafood Green Curry

I like seafood and so do my children. And my husband loves any sort of curry. I made this dish one night when I was going out with my girlfriends, and when I came home I asked my husband if he'd liked it. His response was, 'I have put all the leftovers in the freezer. They are mine, so don't touch.' My husband is pretty fussy and doesn't like anything from a jar, so I knew I was onto a winner with this one.

Serves 6 • Preparation 5 mins • Cook 6 hours • Cooker capacity 5 litres

1.5 kg (3 lb 5 oz) seafood marinara mix
800 ml (27 fl oz) tinned coconut cream
2 large potatoes, diced
4 carrots, diced
2 onions, quartered
2 green curry sachets (approximately 250 g total)
2 chicken stock cubes
2 cups frozen mixed peas and corn
Steamed rice, to serve

1. Put all of the ingredients except the peas, corn and rice into a slow cooker and stir well to combine.
2. Cover and cook on HIGH for 4 hours.
3. Add the peas and corn and continue cooking for 1 hour.
4. Serve with steamed rice.

NOTE: The cooking time will vary depending on your cooker and the size of your potato pieces.

Rebecca Moyle

Seafood Stock

Seafood stock is used in a number of different dishes, predominately in Asian-style soups or curries, or simply eaten by itself as broth. Creating your own stock, rather than using store-bought, adds a rich and authentic flavour to dishes.

Makes 2.5–3 litres • Preparation 30 mins • Cook 8 hours • Cooker capacity 3.5 litres

1 tablespoon oil or butter
1 teaspoon crushed garlic
1 teaspoon minced ginger
Shells and heads from 1 kg (2 lb 3 oz) raw prawns (shrimp)
500 g (1 lb 2 oz) fish of your choice, roughly chopped
Any other seafood (optional)
1 tablespoon oyster sauce
3 litres (101 fl oz/12 cups) warm water or stock of choice

1. Preheat a slow cooker to HIGH.

2. Add the oil or butter, garlic and ginger, and let sit for 10 minutes.

3. Add the prawn heads, fish, other seafood, if using and oyster sauce. Roughly stir and crush the ingredients with a wooden spoon, pressing on the prawn heads to release the flavour. Pour in the water or stock.

4. Cook on HIGH for 2 hours, then reduce to LOW and continue cooking for 6 hours. The stock should be a deep orange colour.

5. Strain the stock through a colander or sieve, repeating if necessary until only broth is left.

6. At this point, if the flavour is too strong, you can add more liquid. If it's not strong enough, you can reduce it on the stove.

7. Use immediately or freeze for later use.

Duane Rasmussen

VEGETARIAN

⬛━ Quorn Vegetarian Lasagne ━●

Being a vegetarian, I'm always trying to find alternatives for recipes we love. Quorn, a meat substitute made from mycoprotein, is really versatile and works so well in this recipe that my carnivore hubby will go back for seconds and even requests it. He prefers it to the meat version I used to make, so that's a huge winner for me.

Serves 6 • Preparation 20 mins • Cook 3 hours • Cooker capacity 3 litres

1 teaspoon olive oil
300 g (10½ oz) Quorn pieces or Quorn mince
1 large onion, thinly sliced
2 carrots, grated
1 zucchini (courgette), grated
2 yellow squash, thinly sliced
3 mushrooms, thinly sliced
1 vegetable stock cube
1 teaspoon crushed garlic
1 teaspoon minced chilli
375 g (13 oz) fresh lasagne sheets
400 ml (13½ fl oz) tomato-based pasta sauce
320 g white sauce or cheese sauce
Grated cheese, for topping

1. Heat the oil in a large frying pan over medium heat. Add the Quorn, onion, vegetables, stock cube, garlic and chilli and cook, stirring frequently, for around 5 minutes, or until the vegetables soften a little.

2. Place one layer of lasagne sheets in the bottom of a slow cooker. Add a third of the Quorn and vegetable mix, about ½ cup of the pasta sauce and a quarter of the white sauce. Repeat with another two layers and finish with a final layer of lasagne sheets. Pour the remaining pasta sauce and white sauce over the top. Sprinkle over the grated cheese.

3. Cover, putting a tea towel (dish towel) under the lid, and cook on HIGH for about 3 hours, or until cooked through.

NOTE: You can add any vegetables you like. If you prefer to use dried pasta sheets, add an extra hour to the cooking time. Quorn is available from the freezer section of major supermarkets.

Victoria Duncan

Cauliflower Rice

This dish was inspired by similar cauliflower rice recipes I'd seen on the internet, combined with the method I normally use for fried rice, as I couldn't find any recipes that used a slow cooker. Any vegetables can be added; you could also include bacon or sliced omelette for a non-vegan version. We now use this in place of rice for any dish, as it's a great way to get extra vegetables in your diet. The taste and texture is very much like fried rice. I hope you enjoy it.

Serves 4 as a side dish • Preparation 10 mins • Cook 1½ hours • Cooker capacity 5.5 litres

½ head cauliflower, broken into florets
2 garlic cloves, crushed
½ cup corn kernels
1 celery stalk, chopped
½ capsicum (pepper), chopped
½ carrot, grated
1 teaspoon sesame or peanut oil
2 tablespoons sweet soy sauce

1. Put the cauliflower into a food processor and pulse until the cauliflower resembles rice (do this in three batches so you don't end up with mash).

2. Put all of the ingredients into a slow cooker and stir well to combine.

3. Cover and cook on HIGH for 1½ hours or until the vegetables are tender but still have a little crunch. Stir once or twice during cooking.

Karen Stuckings

Cauliflower Cheese

I was starting to use cauliflower to replace pasta and potato. I also wanted something tasty that I could serve as a side dish or as a main meal. This was just a cohesion of the idea of a really good cheese sauce and whatever vegetables I had left in the kitchen.

Serves 4 • Preparation 20 mins • Cook 6 hours • Cooker capacity 3.5 litres

2½ cups milk
4 tablespoons butter
¼ cup plain (all-purpose) flour
Mixed herbs, to taste
2 cups grated cheese
1 head cauliflower, broken into florets
1 onion, finely diced
1 cup frozen greens (such as peas, beans and broccoli)
1 cup shredded chicken (optional)

1. Heat the milk in a small saucepan over medium heat until hot (do not bring to the boil).

2. In another saucepan, melt the butter and then add the flour, stirring with a whisk. Whisk in the hot milk along with the herbs. Season with salt and pepper. Cook, stirring, until the mixture has thickened and is smooth (approximately 5 minutes).

3. Remove from the heat and add the cheese. Stir until smooth and combined.

4. Put the cauliflower, onion, greens and chicken (if using) into a slow cooker and pour the cheese sauce over the top. Stir well to coat everything in the sauce.

5. Cover and cook on LOW for 6 hours.

Morgan Jane

Garlic Butter Beans

Sure, you can cook straight steamed beans in your slow cooker, but why have normal beans when you could have garlic butter beans?

Serves 4 • Preparation 5 mins • Cook 45 mins–1 hour • Cooker capacity Any

300 g (10½ oz) green beans, trimmed
2 teaspoons butter
2 garlic cloves, finely chopped

1. Place a rectangular sheet of foil on your bench top. Place the beans in the centre of the foil and top with the butter and garlic.

2. Fold the foil around the beans into a parcel. Put the parcel into a slow cooker.

3. Cover and cook on HIGH for 45–60 minutes, or until the beans are cooked to your liking. (Be careful when opening the foil, as steam will escape.)

Paulene Christie

Stuffed Pumpkin

My husband loves my cob loaf and used to request it almost every weekend. On one occasion I didn't have a cob loaf available but did have a whole pumpkin (squash). I thought it would be interesting to see how it tasted and it was amazing! We do this almost every weekend now to accompany roast chicken or even a barbecue; it's a great side dish!

Serves 4–6 • Preparation 20 mins • Cook 5 hours • Cooker capacity 5–6 litres

1 whole pumpkin (squash)
300 ml (10 fl oz) sour cream
250 g (9 oz) cream cheese
250 g (9 oz) frozen spinach (defrosted and excess water squeezed out)
½–1 cup diced bacon (optional)
½ cup grated tasty cheese
30 g (1 oz) (dry) spring vegetable soup mix

1. Line a slow cooker with enough baking paper or foil to help you remove the pumpkin at the end of cooking.

2. Slice the top off the pumpkin and scoop out the seeds, leaving as much pumpkin flesh as possible.

3. In a bowl, combine the remaining ingredients and mix well. Spoon the mixture into the prepared pumpkin.

4. Put the pumpkin in the slow cooker. If the pumpkin doesn't touch the bottom, pour ½ cup water into the base of the slow cooker.

5. Cook on LOW for 5 hours.

Alycia Park

Slow-cooked Honey Carrots

Why have boring carrots when you could have these tasty honey carrots? This is an easy way to jazz up a sometimes ordinary vegetable.

Serves 5 • Preparation 5 mins • Cook 2 hours • Cooker capacity 1.5 litres

4 carrots, peeled and sliced
3 tablespoons honey
2 tablespoons butter
2 tablespoons light brown sugar
Juice of ½ a small lemon
2 teaspoons sesame seeds

1. Put the carrot in a slow cooker insert. Add the honey, butter, sugar and lemon juice. Stir to combine.

2. Cover and cook on HIGH for 2 hours, or until the carrots are tender.

3. Drain and reserve the cooking liquid.

4. Place the carrots in a serving bowl and spoon 2–3 tablespoons of the reserved liquid over the top. Sprinkle with sesame seeds and serve.

Paulene Christie

Asparagus with Garlic Butter

This recipe works well with other vegetables that cook in about the same time as asparagus – try yellow squash, zucchini, peas, spinach or kale.

Serves 4 as a side dish • Preparation 5 mins • Cook 2 hours • Cooker capacity 3 litres

1 bunch asparagus, trimmed
1 tablespoon butter
2 garlic cloves, minced

1. Line a slow cooker insert with baking paper.
2. Put the asparagus in the slow cooker and add the butter and garlic. Season with salt and pepper.
3. Cover and cook on LOW for 2 hours, or until soft.

NOTE: Larger slow cookers will cook the asparagus more quickly.

Paulene Christie

Honey-Mustard Corn Cobs

We eat a lot of fresh corn on the cob in our house. This recipe gives a lovely sweet touch to fresh corn and really lifts it above the normal.

Serves 1 cob per person (or half each if large cobs) • **Preparation 5 mins** • **Cook 1½ hours** • **Cooker capacity 7 litres**

Corn cobs, husks and fibrous hairs removed
1 teaspoon wholegrain mustard per cob
1 teaspoon butter per cob
1 teaspoon honey per cob

1. Place a rectangular sheet of foil on the bench top and place the corn on top.
2. Spread a little mustard on each cob, then top with some butter and a drizzle of honey.
3. Fold the foil around the corn into parcels. Put the parcel into a slow cooker.
4. Cover and cook on HIGH for 1½ hours. Open the parcel and turn the corn over halfway through. (Be careful when opening the foil, as steam will escape.)
5. Serve with the honey-mustard juices drizzled over the hot corn.

Paulene Christie

Spinach & Ricotta Scrolls

I LOVE spinach and ricotta in anything and everything! After seeing scrolls with other fillings (sweet or savoury) I thought I would try this.

Serves 10–12 • Preparation 20–30 mins • Cook 1½–2 hours • Cooker capacity 5.5 litres

3 cups self-raising flour, plus extra for dusting
100 g (3½ oz) butter or margarine, softened
1 teaspoon salt
1 cup milk

FILLING
500 g (1 lb 2 oz) frozen spinach (defrosted and excess water squeezed out)
1 kg (2 lb 3 oz) ricotta

1. Either grease your slow cooker or line it with baking paper.

2. Mix the flour, butter or margarine, and salt in a bowl until the mixture resembles breadcrumbs. Stir in the milk, then knead on a lightly floured bench top until you have a smooth dough (add a little extra flour if the dough is sticky). Roll the dough out to 5 mm (¼ in) thick.

3. To make the filling, combine the spinach and ricotta in a bowl, season to taste, then spread evenly over the dough. Roll the dough up into a sausage shape and cut into 2–3 cm (¾ in–1¼ in) thick slices. Put the slices in a single layer in the slow cooker. Leave ½ cm between them to allow them to expand.

4. Cover, putting a tea towel (dish towel) under the lid, and cook on HIGH for 1½–2 hours.

Nicole Bazzacco

Mushrooms with Parmesan & Thyme

This is a great way to enjoy mushrooms. The parmesan and thyme add delicious texture and flavour to the dish.

Serves 4 • Preparation 5 min • Cook 2 hours • Cooker capacity 6 litres

8 large mushrooms
¾ cup freshly grated parmesan
½ cup fresh thyme

5. Remove the stalks from the mushrooms and put the mushrooms in a slow cooker. Sprinkle the parmesan and thyme over the mushrooms and season with salt and pepper.

6. Cover, putting a tea towel (dish towel) under the lid, and cook on LOW for 2 hours.

Geoff Tapp

Garlic Butter Mushrooms

If you love mushrooms as much as I do, you could eat these on their own. The garlic infuses the mushrooms with a delicious flavour. This recipe can easily be doubled or increased to serve as many people as you wish.

Serves 3–6 • Preparation 5 mins • Cook 1 hour • Cooker capacity 1.5 litres

6 large flat mushrooms
1 teaspoon butter
1–2 garlic cloves, crushed

1. Brush or peel the mushrooms, if desired. I like to leave the skin on.

2. Put the mushrooms top side down in a slow cooker. Add the butter and as much garlic as you like.

3. Cover and cook on HIGH for 1 hour, stirring occasionally if you wish, but you don't really need to.

4. Serve drizzled with the garlic butter.

Paulene Christie

Mushroom Egg Cups

As a child I never liked mushrooms. It wasn't until adulthood that I realised what I was missing out on and now I eat them every chance I get! Mushrooms and eggs go well together at breakfast, so I thought, why couldn't one be cooked inside the other? These are perfect served with just a sprinkle of cracked black pepper.

Serves Variable • Preparation 5 mins • Cook 45 mins • Cooker capacity 3 litres or larger

- 1–2 large flat mushrooms per person
- 1–2 eggs per person

1. Line the insert of a slow cooker with baking paper.
2. Remove the stalks from the mushrooms. Peel the mushrooms, if desired. Put the mushrooms top side down into the slow cooker.
3. Carefully crack one egg into each upturned mushroom.
4. Cover, putting a tea towel (dish towel) under the lid, and cook on HIGH for about 45 minutes, or until the egg is set to your liking.
5. Serve with a sprinkle of cracked black pepper, if desired.

NOTE: Cook as many mushrooms and eggs as required or desired per serve.

Paulene Christie

⊨— Creamy Avocado & Egg Breakfast —●

I love avocado and eggs together at breakfast time. What better way to combine the two than to cook your eggs right inside a lush avocado bowl? Use a spoon to tuck right in.

Serves 2 • Preparation 5 mins • Cook 45 mins • Cooker capacity 5 litres

1 large avocado, cut in half, stone removed
2 eggs

1. Line a slow cooker with baking paper and preheat to HIGH.

2. Put the avocados on the baking paper, cut side up. Carefully crack an egg into the hollow of each avocado half and season with black pepper.

3. Cover and cook on HIGH for 45 minutes, or until the eggs are cooked to your liking.

Paulene Christie

Potato Nacho Bake

I made this recipe with my son, because I was trying to get him interested in cooking. He pulled all the ingredients out and I mixed them together.

Serves 4 • Preparation 20 mins • Cook 8–10 hours • Cooker capacity 7 litres

1 butternut pumpkin (squash), deseeded and cut into quarters
8–9 small potatoes cut into quarters
2 carrots, diced
2 cups crushed corn chips (any flavour you like)
1 cup diced ham
1 onion, diced
½ cup diced butter
1 tablespoon oil
Mixed seasonings, such as paprika and garlic powder
1 cup grated cheese, plus extra to taste (optional)

1. Line a slow cooker with enough foil to completely enclose the ingredients.

2. Put a layer of pumpkin, potato and carrot in the slow cooker, then add some corn chips and a little of the ham, onion, butter, oil and seasonings. Sprinkle over some cheese. Repeat this process until all the ingredients are used up. Wrap the dish securely in the foil.

3. Cover and cook on LOW for 8–10 hours, or until the potatoes are soft.

4. Top with more cheese halfway through cooking, if you wish.

Jasmine Klieve

Parsley Potatoes

This is an old Hungarian family favourite recipe.

Serves 4–6 • Preparation 10 min • Cook 5–6 hours • Cooker capacity 6.5 litres

1–2 kg (2 lb 3 oz–4 lb 6 oz) potatoes, peeled and diced
½ cup oil
1 bunch flat-leaf (Italian) parsley

1. Put the potatoes, oil and parsley in a slow cooker.

2. Cook on LOW for 5–6 hours, or until the potatoes are nice and tender.

3. Season with salt and serve. Enjoy!

Elena Kompar

Stump – Mash With Hidden Veg

A friend showed me how to make this once, and since then it has been a family favourite.

Serves 4–6 • Preparation 10 mins • Cook 6–7 hours • Cooker capacity 6.5 litres

1.5 kg (3 lb 5 oz) potatoes, peeled and chopped
2–3 carrots, peeled and chopped
2 onions, chopped
6 eggs

1. Put the potatoes, carrots and onions in a slow cooker and crack the eggs on top.

2. Cover and cook on LOW 6–7 hours.

3. Blend with a hand-held blender and enjoy.

Elena Kompar

Moroccan Vegetable Medley

This vegetable mix works well as a healthy, low-fat family meal or side dish.

Serves 2 as a main course or 4 as a side dish • Preparation 15 mins • Cook 3½ hours
• Cooker capacity 5 litres

3 potatoes, peeled and cut into 1 cm (½ in) dice
200 g (7 oz) pumpkin (squash), cut into 1 cm (½ in) dice
2 carrots, cut into 1 cm (½ in) dice
2 small onions, roughly chopped
1 garlic clove, crushed
2 teaspoons Moroccan seasoning
2 teaspoons olive oil
¼ cup dried peas
2 medium–large mushrooms, cut into 1 cm (½ in) dice
1 cup spring onions (scallions), cut into 1 cm (½ in) slices

1. Put the potato, pumpkin, carrot, onion, garlic, Moroccan seasoning and olive oil into a slow cooker and mix to combine.

2. Cover and cook on HIGH for 1½ hours, or until the potato is half cooked and softened around the edges.

3. Stir in the peas and mushrooms and continue cooking for 1 hour.

4. Stir in the spring onions and continue cooking for 1 hour.

Simon Christie

Tasty Tomato Juice

This superfood drink is something I ALWAYS turn to when those nasty viruses are going around. I stand by my belief that tomato juice keeps me flu- and cold-free during the winter months, year after year. I use 'roadside' home-grown tomatoes for this recipe. Tomato juice has LOTS of health benefits for your body.

Makes 600 ml (20½ fl oz) • Preparation 10 mins • Cook 4 hours • Cooker capacity 5 litres

1 kg (2 lb 3 oz) ripe tomatoes, halved
30 g (1 oz) celery, sliced
1 teaspoon salt
1 teaspoon cracked black pepper
1 teaspoon light brown sugar
⅛ teaspoon Tabasco sauce

1. Put the ingredients in a slow cooker.

2. Cover and cook on HIGH for 3 hours.

3. Transfer the mixture to a food processor and process until smooth.

4. Return the tomatoes to the slow cooker and continue cooking for 1 hour.

5. Transfer again to a food processor and process for 2 minutes.

6. Strain the juice through a fine sieve to remove any solids. Refrigerate and serve ice cold!

Simon Christie

CAKES

Chai-Spiced Carrot Cake

Ours is a family that enjoys cakes and slices, and never turns downs a dessert (our guilty pleasure, if you will!) This is a delicious spin on the average carrot cake. It's great with cream cheese icing.

Serves 12 • Preparation 15 mins • Cook 2 hours • Cooker capacity 6 litres

2 cups self-raising flour
1½ cups light brown sugar, lightly packed
1 cup grated parsnip
½ cup grated carrot
½ cup chopped walnuts
2 teaspoons ground cinnamon
1 teaspoon ground ginger
1 cup vegetable oil
4 eggs

1. Line a slow cooker with baking paper or line a cake tin that fits in your slow cooker with baking paper (see page 15 for hints on using cake tins in your slow cooker).

2. In a large bowl, combine the flour, sugar, parsnip, carrot, walnuts, cinnamon and ginger.

3. In a separate bowl, whisk the oil and eggs together.

4. Stir the egg mixture into the dry ingredients and mix until combined.

5. Pour the cake batter into the lined slow cooker or cake tin. If using a cake tin, transfer it to the slow cooker.

6. Cook on HIGH for 2 hours, or until a skewer inserted into the middle of the cake comes out clean.

Kahlia Price

Coconut Carrot Cake

I originally used this recipe to make lactation muffins: just add 2 tablespoons of flaxseed oil and 1 tablespoon of brewer's yeast. You could use wholemeal (wholewheat) self-raising flour instead of white flour and 1 cup of coconut sugar instead of brown sugar. This is my favourite cake to make when I have too many carrots!

Serves 8 • Preparation 20 mins • Cook 1½–2 hours • Cooker capacity 5 litres

2 eggs
1 cup light brown sugar, firmly packed
¾ cup melted coconut oil
1 teaspoon vanilla essence
1 cup self-raising flour
1 teaspoon ground cinnamon
½ teaspoon salt
300 g (10½ oz) grated carrot
250 g (9 oz) walnuts
½ cup desiccated coconut

ICING
1 cup icing (confectioner's) sugar
150 g (5½ oz) cream cheese, at room temperature
1 teaspoon lemon juice
zest of 1 lemon

1. Line a slow cooker with baking paper or line a cake tin that fits in your slow cooker with baking paper (see page 15 hints on using cake tins in your slow cooker).

2. In a large mixing bowl, whisk the eggs, sugar, coconut oil and vanilla until combined.

3. In a separate large mixing bowl, combine the flour, cinnamon and salt. Sift the dry ingredients into the egg mixture and mix to combine. Add the grated carrot, walnuts and coconut and mix until just combined.

4. Pour the cake batter into the lined slow cooker or cake tin. If using a cake tin, transfer it to the slow cooker.

5. Cook on HIGH for 1½–2 hours (depending on the size of your slow cooker), or until a skewer inserted into the middle of the cake comes out clean. Remove the cake from the slow cooker, using the baking paper to assist you.

6. While the cake is cooling, combine the icing ingredients in a bowl and mix well until the icing is creamy. Spread it over the cooled cake.

Kimberlee Webb

Delicious Lemon Cake

I first made this cake in a regular oven and decided to convert the recipe for a slow cooker, because it results in a much more moist cake. I class this as a very naughty cake because I can't stop at just one slice!

Serves 8–12 • Preparation 15 mins • Cook 1½–2 hours • Cooker capacity 3.7 litres

185 g (6½ oz) sugar
125 g (4½ oz) butter, at room temperature
2 large eggs
185 g (6½ oz) self-raising flour
4 tablespoons milk
Zest of 2 large lemons
6 tablespoons lemon juice
6 tablespoons icing (confectioner's) sugar

1. Line a cake or loaf tin that fits in your slow cooker with baking paper (see page 15 for hints on using cake tins in your slow cooker).

2. Using an electric mixer, beat the sugar and butter until light and fluffy. Add the eggs, one at a time, mixing until just combined. Add the flour, milk and lemon zest and mix well.

3. Pour the batter into the prepared tin and place in the slow cooker. Cover, putting a tea towel (dish towel) under the lid, and cook on HIGH for 1½–2 hours until a skewer inserted into the middle of the cake comes our clean.

4. In a bowl, mix together the lemon juice and icing sugar.

5. Prick holes in the top of the cake with a skewer then drizzle over the lemon syrup. Leave to cool completely before turning out of the cake tin.

Roselyn Chrisp

Orange & Poppy Seed Cake

This is a nice light cake, perfect for morning tea.

Serves 12 • Preparation 20 mins • Cook 2½ hours • Cooker capacity 6 litres

½ cup Greek yoghurt
125 ml (½ cup) orange juice
¼ cup poppy seeds
1¼ cups sugar
250 g (9 oz) butter, at room temperature
2 tablespoons grated orange zest
4 eggs
2¼ cups self-raising flour
2½ teaspoons baking powder

1. Line a slow cooker with baking paper or line a cake tin that fits in your slow cooker with baking paper (see page 15 for hints on using cake tins in your slow cooker).

2. In a small bowl, mix together the yoghurt, orange juice and poppy seeds.

3. Using an electric mixer beat the sugar, butter and orange zest until light and fluffy. Add the eggs, one at a time, mixing until just combined.

4. Sift in the flour and baking powder. Add the yoghurt mixture and mix with a large spoon until just combined.

5. Pour the cake batter into the lined slow cooker or cake tin. If using a cake tin, transfer it to the slow cooker.

6. Cover, putting a tea towel (dish towel) under the lid, and cook on HIGH for 2½ hours, or until a skewer inserted into the middle of the cake comes out clean.

Narelle Youngs

Berry Custard Cake

This is a beautiful and light dessert that combines cake and custard. I love experimenting with recipes, mixing them up and making use of seasonal fruit.

Serves 4–6 • Preparation 20 mins • Cook 2 hours • Cooker capacity 3–5 litres

BASE
1 packet vanilla cake mix
½ cup melted butter
1 egg
1 tablespoon lemon zest or orange zest
Few drops yellow food colouring (or another colour)

FILLING
3 eggs
1¼ cups caster (superfine) sugar
½ cup plain (all-purpose) flour
3 tablespoons cornflour (cornstarch)
¾ cup sour cream
1 cup berries of your choice
1 tablespoon lemon zest or orange zest

DECORATION
Mixed fresh berries

1. Grease a slow cooker and line it with baking paper.

2. In a large bowl, combine all the base ingredients and mix well with your hands. Press the base mixture into the slow cooker.

3. For the filling, beat the eggs in a large bowl and gradually add the sugar. Beat until light and fluffy then beat in the flours. Add the sour cream and mix. Fold in the berries and zest. Pour the mixture on top of the base.

4. Cover, putting a tea towel (dish towel) under the lid, and cook on HIGH for 1½ hours and then on LOW for about another 30 minutes.

5. The cake is ready when the edges are brown and the centre wobbles a little bit when you shake the cooker. Leave to cool in your cooker with the lid on for about 30 minutes. Remove the cake from the slow cooker, using the baking paper to assist you. Cut into slices and decorate with mixed fresh berries, to serve.

Robyn Clark

Banana Raisin Ring Cake

This is a lovely moist cake passed on to me from my mother. I have adapted it for the slow cooker.

Serves 6–8 • Preparation 20 mins • Cook 2 hours • Cooker capacity 3–5 litres

125 g (4½ oz) cup butter
¾ cup sugar, plus extra, for sprinkling
2 eggs
3 large bananas, mashed
¾ teaspoon bicarbonate soda (baking soda)
1 tablespoon milk
1 teaspoon vanilla
1½ cups self-raising flour
1 cup raisins
1 cup icing (confectioner's) sugar
1 tablespoon lemon juice
Ground cinnamon, for sprinkling

1. Grease a slow cooker and line it with baking paper, or grease a ring tin that fits inside your slow cooker and line it with baking paper (see page 15 for hints on using cake tins in your slow cooker).

2. In a large bowl, cream the butter and sugar until light and fluffy. Add the eggs one at a time and continue beating. Add the mashed bananas and mix well.

3. Dissolve the bicarbonate of soda in the milk and add the vanilla. Fold into the cake alternately with the flour. Finally, fold in the raisins.

4. If you are pouring the cake batter directly into the slow cooker, place a well-greased small glass in the centre of the slow cooker. Pour the batter around the glass or into the cake tin and spread evenly.

5. Cover, putting a tea towel (dish towel) under the lid, and cook on HIGH for 2 hours, or until a skewer inserted into the middle of the cake comes out clean. Remove the cake from the slow cooker, using the baking paper to assist you.

6. Ice the cake with a mixture of icing sugar and lemon juice. In a small bowl, combine some ground cinnamon with a little sugar and sprinkle over the cake.

Robyn Clark

Banana Date Loaf

I used to make this as a child and it's still a favourite today.

Serves 12 • Preparation 10 mins • Cook 2–3 hours • Cooker capacity 6 litres

90 g (3 oz) butter, at room temperature
¼ cup sugar
¼ cup light brown sugar, firmly packed
½ teaspoon ground cinnamon
2 eggs
1 teaspoon grated orange zest
3 ripe bananas, mashed
¾ cup chopped dates
2½ cups wholemeal (wholewheat) self-raising flour
⅓ cup orange juice
Butter, lemon butter or lemon icing, to serve

1. Grease a loaf tin (see page 15 for hints on using cake tins in your slow cooker).

2. Using an electric mixer, beat the butter, sugars and cinnamon until light and fluffy. Add the eggs, one at a time, beating well after each addition, and add the zest. Stir in the mashed bananas and dates, mixing well. Fold in the sifted flour alternately with the orange juice.

3. Pour the batter into the prepared tin. Put two egg rings in the bottom of a slow cooker and add 1 cup water to create a water bath. Place the loaf tin on top of the egg rings.

4. Cover, putting a tea towel (dish towel) under the lid, and cook on HIGH for 2–3 hours, or until a skewer inserted into the middle of the cake comes out clean.

5. Serve warm with butter or lemon butter, or ice with lemon icing and serve cold.

Narelle Youngs

⊯— Banana Custard Cake —●

A family favourite, this recipe is very adaptable as you can replace some ingredients with healthier alternatives, if you like. Swap white flour for wholemeal (wholewheat) flour, sugar for honey and custard for yoghurt.

Serves 6–8 • Preparation 10 mins • Cook 2 hours • Cooker capacity 6–7 litres

1½ cups self-raising flour or wholemeal (wholewheat) self-raising flour
1 cup low-fat custard or vanilla yoghurt
2 ripe bananas, mashed
2 eggs
1 tablespoon sugar or honey, plus extra sugar, for sprinkling
1 teaspoon bicarbonate of soda (baking soda)
1 teaspoon ground cinnamon

1. Line and grease a loaf tin that fits inside your slow cooker (see page 15 for hints on using cake tins in your slow cooker). Sit two egg rings in the base of the slow cooker.

2. In a large bowl, combine all of the ingredients except the extra sugar and the cinnamon and mix well. Pour the mixture into the prepared loaf tin and place in the slow cooker, on the egg rings.

3. Cover, putting a tea towel (dish towel) under the lid, and cook on HIGH for about 2 hours, or until a skewer inserted into the middle of the cake comes out clean. Remove the cake from the slow cooker, using the baking paper to assist you, and leave to cool in the tin.

4. Combine the cinnamon with a little sugar and sprinkle over the cake.

Robyn Clark

Easy Boiled Fruit Cake

This cake is yummy and doesn't cost a small fortune to make. It stores really well and you can also freeze it.

Serves 12–18 • Preparation 20 mins • Cook 2 hours • Cooker capacity 5 litres

375 g (13 oz) dried mixed fruit
1 cup sugar
1 tablespoon butter
1 tablespoon raspberry jam
1 teaspoon bicarbonate soda (baking soda)
1 teaspoon ground cinnamon
½ teaspoon freshly grated nutmeg
½ teaspoon mixed spice
1½ cups self-raising flour
2 eggs

1. Line a slow cooker with baking paper or line a cake tin that fits in your slow cooker with baking paper (see page 15 for hints on using cake tins in your slow cooker).

2. Place all of the ingredients except the flour and eggs in a saucepan with 1 cup of water and stir well. Bring to the boil then remove from heat and let the mixture sit for about 10 minutes.

3. Put the flour in a large bowl then pour in the fruit mixture and mix well. Add the eggs and mix well.

4. Pour the cake batter into the lined slow cooker or cake tin. If using a cake tin, transfer it to the slow cooker.

5. Cover, putting a tea towel (dish towel) under the lid, and cook on HIGH for 2 hours, or until a skewer inserted into the middle of the cake comes out clean. Check the cake after 1 hour and rotate the cake tin 180 degrees, if it looks like the cake is cooking unevenly.

Carol Wilkinson

Mel's Wholemeal Apple Sultana Cake

I wanted to make something yummy and healthy for my kids, and I didn't want to use tinned apples. I thought of this cake and they loved it.

Serves 6–12 • Preparation 10–15 mins • Cook 1 hour, 40 mins • Cooker capacity 6 litres

125 g (4½ oz) butter
¾ cup sugar
2 eggs
1½ cups stewed apples, mashed
1½ cups sultanas (golden raisins)
1 teaspoon vanilla essence
1 teaspoon ground cinnamon
2 cups wholemeal (wholewheat) self-raising flour

1. Line a slow cooker with baking paper or line a cake tin that fits in your slow cooker with baking paper (see page 15 for hints on using cake tins in your slow cooker).

2. In a mixing bowl, cream the butter and sugar. Beat in the eggs. Add the apples, sultanas, vanilla essence and cinnamon and beat until combined. Fold in the wholemeal (wholewheat) flour until combined.

3. Pour the cake batter into the lined slow cooker or cake tin. If using a cake tin, transfer it to the slow cooker.

4. Cover, putting a tea towel (dish towel) under the lid, and cook on HIGH for 1 hour and 40 minutes, or until a skewer inserted into the middle of the cake comes out clean.

Melissa Hardstaff

Upside-Down Pear Teacake

I came up with this cake in an effort to use up uneaten pears that I had bought. My kids always love this cake, and often ask me to buy pears, and then purposely not eat them so I will bake them a pear cake. It is always a hit in my house.

Serves 8–12 • Preparation 15 mins • Cook 2½ hours • Cooker capacity 5 litres

TOPPING
2 tablespoons caster (superfine) sugar
1 teaspoon ground allspice
½ teaspoon ground cinnamon
½ teaspoon freshly grated nutmeg
3–4 ripe pears, cored and thinly sliced

CAKE
125 g (4½ oz) butter
125 g (4½ oz) caster (superfine) sugar
2 eggs
500 g (1 lb 2 oz) self-raising flour
2 cups milk
1 teaspoon vanilla extract

1. Grease a slow cooker and line it with baking paper.

2. In a small bowl, mix the sugar and spices together and sprinkle over the baking paper. Arrange the pear slices over the sugar and spice mix in a pretty pattern.

3. Using an electric mixer, beat the butter and sugar until light and fluffy. Add the eggs and beat well. Alternately add the flour and milk, beating well between additions, until the mixture is combined. Add the vanilla extract and mix well.

4. Carefully pour the cake batter over the pear slices. Cover, putting a tea towel (dish towel) under the lid, and cook on HIGH for 2½ hours, or until a skewer inserted into the middle of the cake comes out clean.

5. Remove the cake from the slow cooker, using the baking paper to assist you, and turn out onto a wire rack to cool.

6. This cake can be served warm as a dessert with cream, ice cream or custard.

Ellie Kerr

Fruit with Cake Topping

This recipe is an old family favourite, which I used to cook in the oven. I've adapted it for the slow cooker.

Serves 4 • Preparation 10 mins • Cook 1–1½ hours • Cooker capacity 1.5–3.5 litres

425 g (15 oz) tinned fruit of your choice, or more, if desired
2 tablespoons custard powder
½ cup sugar
1 egg
4 tablespoons milk
1 cup plain (all-purpose) flour
1 tablespoon baking powder

1. Put the tinned fruit including the juice into a slow cooker. Add the custard powder and stir well. Preheat the slow cooker to HIGH.

2. In a large bowl, beat the sugar and egg together then add the milk and mix well. Add the flour and baking powder and mix until combined. Pour the cake batter over the fruit.

3. Cover and cook on HIGH for 1½ hours in a 1.5 litre slow cooker or for 1 hour in a 3.5 litre slow cooker.

Nikki Willis

≡— Fruit Juice Cake —●

Sometimes the simple things are the best. This recipe uses only fruit juice and cake mix.

Serves 10 • Preparation 5 mins • Cook 1½–2 hours • Cooker capacity 7 litres

340 g (12 oz) packet cake mix
160 ml (5½ fl oz/2/3 cup) fruit juice of your choice

1. Lightly grease a 13 x 23 cm (5 x 9 inch) silicone loaf tin.

2. Combine the ingredients in a mixing bowl then pour into the loaf tin.

3. Put the silicone tin into a slow cooker and cook on HIGH for 1½–2 hours, or until a skewer inserted into the middle of the cake comes out clean.

4. Allow to cool on a wire rack before serving.

5. Enjoy!

Simon Christie

One-pot Cookie Cake

This is not quite a cookie and not quite a cake … it's something in between. It has a cake-like centre and a chewy soft cookie exterior. DELICIOUS!

Serves 12 • Preparation 15–20 mins • Cook 1½ hours • Cooker capacity 5 litres

110 g (4 oz) butter (unsalted, if desired)
½ cup caster (superfine) sugar
½ cup light brown sugar, lightly packed
1 teaspoon vanilla essence
1½ cups plain (all-purpose) flour
½ teaspoon bicarbonate of soda (baking soda)
¼ teaspoon salt
3 tablespoons milk
1 egg
1 cup cooking chocolate chips
Ice cream or warm custard, to serve

1. Preheat a slow cooker to HIGH.

2. Melt the butter in the insert of the slow cooker then stir in the sugars and vanilla essence. Add the flour, bicarbonate of soda and salt and stir well to combine. Pour in the milk and crack in the egg and stir well. Pour the chocolate chips over the dough and mix thoroughly.

3. Cover, putting a tea towel (dish towel) under the lid, and cook on HIGH for about 1½ hours or until a skewer inserted into the middle of the cake reveals sticky crumbs. Remove the insert from the slow cooker and gently pull away the cookie cake edges from the insert. Remove the cookie cake by carefully inverting it onto a tea towel (dish towel).

4. Serve with ice cream or warm custard.

Simon Christie

Snickers Cake

My family love Mars bar cake, so I thought I would give this a try and it's a real hit. I like to cook it when we have a Sunday roast, and it's always so good to eat warm in winter with some cream!

Serves 4–6 • Preparation 10 mins • Cook 2½ hours • Cooker capacity 1.5 litres

200 g (7 oz) light brown sugar
190 g (6½ oz) plain (all-purpose) flour
180 ml (6 fl oz/¾ cup) milk
125 g (4½ oz) melted butter
3 eggs
50 g (1¾ oz) unsweetened cocoa powder
1 teaspoon baking powder
3–4 Snickers bars, cut into pieces

1. Line a slow cooker with baking paper or line a cake tin that fits in your slow cooker with baking paper (see page 15 for hints on using cake tins in your slow cooker).

2. In a large bowl, mix all of the ingredients except the Snickers bars until well combined.

3. Pour the cake batter into the lined slow cooker or cake tin. If using a cake tin, transfer it to the slow cooker. Top with pieces of Snickers bar.

4. Cover and cook on HIGH for 1½ hours and then on LOW for 1 hour.

Lisa Pittaway

Chocolate Baileys Mudcake

I've had this recipe for years and never thought it could be done in a slow cooker, but now it is the only way I will cook it! The result is a much more fudgy cake than one cooked in the oven, and it is ten times better the next day!

Serves 8 • Preparation 20 mins • Cook 1½–2 hours • Cooker capacity up to 5 litres

180 ml (6 fl oz/¾ cup) Baileys Irish Cream
150 g (5½ oz) unsalted butter
100 g (3½ oz) dark chocolate
100 g (3½ oz) caster (superfine) sugar
100 g (3½ oz) light brown sugar
50 g (1¾ oz) unsweetened cocoa powder
3 eggs, at room temperature
170 g (6 oz) plain (all-purpose) flour
1½ teaspoons baking powder
½ teaspoon bicarbonate of soda (baking soda)
½ teaspoon salt

CHOCOLATE BAILEYS GANACHE
200 g (7 oz) dark chocolate, chopped
100 ml (3½ fl oz) Baileys Irish Cream
100 ml (3½ fl oz) cream
Pinch of sea salt
1 tablespoon unsalted butter, softened

1. Line a slow cooker with baking paper or line a cake tin that fits in your slow cooker with baking paper (see page 15 for hints on using cake tins in your slow cooker).

2. For the cake, heat the Baileys, butter, chocolate, sugars and cocoa powder in a saucepan over low heat until the chocolate and butter are melted. Whisk to remove any lumps. Remove from the heat and set aside to cool for 5 minutes.

3. Add the eggs to the slightly cooled mixture and mix well. Combine the flour, baking powder, bicarbonate of soda and salt in a large bowl then fold into the cooled mixture.

4. Pour the cake batter into the lined slow cooker or cake tin. If using a cake tin, transfer it to the slow cooker.

5. Cover, putting a tea towel (dish towel) under the lid, and cook on HIGH for 1½–2 hours (depending on the size of your slow cooker), or until a skewer inserted into the middle of the cake comes out clean.

6. While the cake is cooking, put the chopped chocolate for the ganache in a bowl. In a small saucepan, bring the Baileys, cream and salt to the boil. Pour over the chocolate and let sit for 1 minute. Gently stir and add the butter. Set aside at room temperature to cool, stirring occasionally, until the ganache is thick and spreadable.

7. Remove the cake from the slow cooker, using the baking paper to assist you. Turn out onto a wire rack to cool. Spread the ganache over the cooled cake.

NOTE: You can omit the cream and use all Baileys, if you prefer a boozier ganache. Alternatively, replace the Baileys with cream for a virgin ganache.

Kimberlee Webb

Trinity's Slow-Cooked Chocolate Lava Cake

I was experimenting one day and made a lava cake. It was OK, but not quite right, so I didn't make it again. Then, after about 2 years, I thought, I'll try it again but this time I'll make it in the slow cooker. It was so much better, and since then I've made it again and again – it's beautiful.

Serves 6–8 • Preparation 10 mins • Cook 2–2½ hours • Cooker capacity 6 litres

3½ cups brown sugar
2 cups plain (all-purpose) flour
6 tablespoons unsweetened cocoa powder
4 teaspoons baking powder
1 teaspoon salt
1 cup milk
4 tablespoons butter, melted
1 teaspoon vanilla extract
3 cups boiling water
Vanilla ice cream or cream, to serve

1. Grease a slow cooker and line it with baking paper.

2. In a large bowl, mix together 2 cups of the sugar, the flour, half the cocoa powder, and the baking powder and salt. Stir in the milk, melted butter and vanilla. Combine the remaining brown sugar with the remaining cocoa powder and add to the mixture. Pour the cake batter into the prepared slow cooker.

3. Pour the boiling water over the top of the cake batter and resist all temptation to stir. Do not stir!

4. Cover, putting a tea towel (dish towel) under the lid, and cook on HIGH for 2–2½ hours (depending on the size of your slow cooker), or until a skewer inserted into the middle of the cake comes out clean.

5. Remove the slow cooker lid and set the cake aside to cool for 30 minutes before serving. Serve with vanilla ice cream or cream.

Trinity Simmons

Choc-caramel Self-Saucing Cake

Here is a recipe for those searching for that little sweet something after their main evening meal. There's no chance of leftovers – it is THAT good.

Serves 4–6 • Preparation 15 mins • Cook 2 hours • Cooker capacity 5 litres

CAKE
1½ cups self-raising flour
½ cup light brown sugar, lightly packed
½ cup sweetened condensed milk
¼ cup milk
100 g (3½ oz) butter, softened
3 tablespoons unsweetened cocoa powder
1 tablespoon vanilla essence
1 teaspoon salt

CARAMEL SAUCE
2 cups boiling water
¾ cup light brown sugar, lightly packed
¾ cup sweetened condensed milk

1. In a large bowl, combine all of the cake ingredients and mix well with a wooden spoon, removing all lumps. Pour the mixture into a casserole dish that will fit inside your slow cooker.

2. In a separate bowl, combine the caramel sauce ingredients and stir until the sugar is dissolved. Gently pour the sauce over the cake batter.

3. Cover the casserole dish with aluminum foil, pressing around the edges to seal well. Alternatively, you can use your casserole lid, if it fits in your slow cooker.

4. Place the dish directly into the slow cooker insert and cover, putting a tea towel (dish towel) under the lid. If you have a ceramic insert, cover the base with water.

5. Cook on HIGH for two hours, or until a skewer inserted into the middle of the cake comes out clean.

6. Serve alone or with ice cream.

NOTE: The total amount of sweetened condensed milk in this recipe is 1 tin.

Simon Christie

DESSERTS & SWEETS

Hasselback Apples

After making hasselback potatoes, I started to think about what else you could apply this method to. Apples, sugar and cinnamon are a match made in heaven and, being a lover of desserts, I though why not try hasselback apples and put a new spin on apple crumble? The apples are deliciously soft and the brown sugar caramelises beautifully. Enjoy!

Serves 2 • Preparation 15 mins • Cook 2½ hours • Cooker capacity 3 litres

4 tablespoons light brown sugar
2½ tablespoons butter, melted
1½ teaspoons ground cinnamon
2 large apples (I like to use Granny Smith), peeled, cored and cut in half vertically
2 tablespoons rolled traditional (not instant) porridge oats
1 teaspoon plain (all-purpose) flour
¼ teaspoon salt
Ice cream, to serve (optional)

1. Grease the base of a slow cooker and preheat to HIGH.

2. In a bowl, combine 1 tablespoon of the sugar, 1 tablespoon of the butter and ½ teaspoon of the cinnamon.

3. Place the apples in the slow cooker, cut side down, and coat the apples with the butter mixture using a pastry brush.

4. Cover, putting a tea towel (dish towel) under the lid, and cook on HIGH for about 1½ hours, or until just soft.

5. In a bowl, combine the remaining sugar, butter and cinnamon with the oats, flour and salt.

6. Carefully remove the apples from the slow cooker and make vertical cuts about 3 mm (⅛ in) apart into the tops of the apples, being careful you don't cut all the way through. Fan out and press the oat mixture into the cuts.

7. Return to the slow cooker and continue cooking for 1 hour.

8. Serve with ice cream.

Alyssa Green

➤— Apple Windsor – Fast 'n' Easy —●

An old-time recipe with a slow-cooker twist. Our goal was to make this version fast and easy by using packet cake mix. However, you can certainly replace the mix with your favourite homemade cake batter. This is perfect served with vanilla ice cream or a drizzle of thickened cream.

Serves 8 • Preparation 5 mins • Cook 1½ hours • Cooker capacity 5 litres

800 g (1 lb 12 oz) tinned apple pie filling (see note)
Ground cinnamon, for sprinkling
340 g (12 oz) packet vanilla cake mix and associated ingredients

1. Put the apple pie filling directly into a slow cooker or in a cake tin that fits in your slow cooker (see page 15 for hints on using cake tins in your slow cooker), and sprinkle generously with ground cinnamon.

2. Mix the cake according to the packet instructions.

3. Pour the batter over the apples, trying to cover the apples completely.

4. Cover, putting a tea towel (dish towel) under the lid, and cook on HIGH for 1½ hours, or until a skewer inserted into the middle of the cake comes out clean.

5. Serve with cream or ice cream.

NOTE: Look for a pie filling with soft, almost mashed apples, without a lot of liquid.

Paulene Christie

Caramel & Apple Plait

A lovely light and flaky pastry dessert that only needs a few ingredients, but looks great! You could serve this as it is with just a dusting of icing (confectioner's) sugar, or with a scoop of creamy vanilla ice cream.

Serves 4 • Preparation 15 mins • Cook 1 hour 10 mins • Cooker capacity 7 litres

1 sheet puff pastry
4 tablespoons caramel (ready-made or slow-cooked)
½ cup tinned apple pie filling
Ground cinnamon, for sprinkling
Beaten egg, for brushing

1. Line a slow cooker with non-stick baking paper.

2. Using the point of a knife, score the pastry into thirds. Cut each outer third into horizontal strips approximately 2 cm (¾ in) wide, leaving the ends attached to the middle third. Your pastry sheet will now have ribbons on each side.

3. Spread the middle third of the pastry with caramel and top with the tinned apple. Sprinkle with cinnamon.

4. Plait the pastry by folding each ribbon over the centre – one from the left, then one from the right – and keep going until you have reached the bottom. You will now have a plaited pastry parcel.

5. Brush a little egg wash lightly over the pastry. Carefully transfer the pastry to the slow cooker.

6. Cover, putting a tea towel (dish towel) under the lid, and cook on HIGH for about 1 hour and 10 minutes, or until cooked through.

Paulene Christie

Bananas in Caramel Sauce

I made this recipe in an oven for years, but it translates perfectly to the slow cooker. The result is caramelised bananas in the most decadent sauce. It's lovely served with creamy vanilla ice cream to balance the sweetness of the caramel.

Serves 4 • Preparation 5 mins • Cook 40 mins • Cooker capacity 7 litres

4 bananas, peeled and sliced lengthways
50 g (1¾ oz) butter
½ cup light brown sugar, lightly packed
1 tablespoon apple juice

1. Line a slow cooker with baking paper and add the bananas cut side down.

2. In a heatproof bowl, melt the butter in a microwave. Add the brown sugar and apple juice and stir to combine well. Pour the mixture over the bananas.

3. Cover, putting a tea towel (dish towel) under the lid, and cook on HIGH for about 40 minutes, or until the banana is soft and the syrup, thick.

Paulene Christie

Blueberry Butter

I first made this when I came across it in a family recipe book, so I thought I would try it and it was delicious. I like to make this all the time and eat it on my toast.

Makes 4–5 cups • Preparation 15 mins • Cook 5–6 hours • Cooker capacity 5 litres

5 cups blueberries, puréed
1 cup sugar
2 teaspoons ground cinnamon
½ teaspoon freshly grated nutmeg (optional)
¼ teaspoon ground ginger (optional)
Zest of 1 lemon

1. Put the puréed blueberries in a slow cooker.

2. Cover and cook on LOW for 1 hour.

3. Stir the blueberry purée and prop open the slow cooker lid with a spatula or wooden spoon. Continue cooking for 4 hours.

4. Add the sugar, spices and lemon zest and stir well to combine.

5. If the mixture is still a little runny, remove the lid and cook, uncovered, on HIGH for 1 hour or until thickened.

6. Pour into a blender or food processor and process until smooth.

7. Store in airtight containers or sterilised jars in the fridge.

Trinity Simmons

Passionfruit & Lemon Custard

This is so scrumptious. I make this recipe when I'm making pavlova, to use up the egg yolks. It is a yummy pavlova topping, but you could also serve it with tinned fruit or on its own, or freeze it in ice cream moulds to make frozen treats. You can add as much passionfruit or lemon juice as you like to suit your taste. I hope you enjoy this recipe.

Serves 6–8 • Preparation 30 mins • Cook 2 hours • Cooker capacity 3 litres

600 ml (20½ fl oz) milk
¾ cup caster (superfine) sugar
6 egg yolks, lightly beaten
2 tablespoons cornflour (cornstarch)
Pulp of 4 passionfruit
1 tablespoon butter, melted
Juice of 2 lemons

1. Warm the milk in the microwave and pour into a slow cooker. Stir in the sugar, egg yolks, cornflour, passionfruit pulp, butter and lemon juice.

2. Cover, putting a tea towel (dish towel) under the lid, and cook on HIGH for 2 hours, stirring after 40 minutes, and then every 15–20 minutes until cooked.

Carol Wilkinson

Bread & Butter Pudding

This is a favourite my grandmother used to make.

Serves 6–8 • Preparation 20 mins • Cook 2–2¾ hours • Cooker capacity 3.5–5.5 litres

6 hot dog rolls, sliced open
Butter, for spreading
Strawberry jam, for spreading
5 large eggs
2½ cups full-cream milk powder
200 ml (7 fl oz) tinned coconut milk
¾ cup sugar
2 teaspoons vanilla extract
1 teaspoon ground cardamom
2 teaspoons freshly grated nutmeg

1. Grease the insert of a slow cooker.

2. Spread the rolls with as much butter and jam as you like. Arrange the rolls, spread side up, in the slow cooker.

3. Using an electric mixer, beat the eggs with 1 litre (34 fl oz/4 cups) water. Mix in the milk powder. Add the coconut milk, sugar, vanilla and cardamom and mix well.

4. Ladle the egg mixture evenly over the rolls, then sprinkle with nutmeg.

5. Cover, putting a tea towel (dish towel) under the lid, and cook on HIGH for 2–2¾ hours until it is just set with a slight wobble in the middle.

6. Remove the insert bowl from the slow cooker and set aside to cool completely so the pudding can set. When cool, invert the bread and butter pudding onto a plate and serve.

Yvonne Chapman

━ French Custard Crumpet Bake ━

This dish is similar to bread and butter pudding, but the crumpets don't get as soggy as bread. It's a really yummy twist.

Serves 4–6 • Preparation 15 mins • Cook 2–4 hours • Cooker capacity 4 litres

1 cup milk
4 eggs, lightly beaten
2 tablespoons custard powder
2 tablespoons caster (superfine) sugar
1 teaspoon vanilla essence
6 round crumpets, chopped into bite-sized pieces
½ cup sultanas (golden raisins)
Freshly grated nutmeg, for sprinkling
Ice cream, to serve

1. In a large bowl, whisk the milk, eggs, custard powder, sugar and vanilla until combined.

2. Place half of the crumpets in a slow cooker and sprinkle over half of the sultanas. Pour the egg mixture over the top and mix well. Layer the remaining crumpets on top. Finally, sprinkle over a little grated nutmeg and the remaining sultanas.

3. If you like, leave the mixture to soak into the crumpets for a while, or cook straightaway.

4. Cover and cook on LOW for 2–4 hours. Serve with ice cream!

sam schmaling

Roly-Poly Pudding

My nana used to make this recipe when I was little, and I now enjoy making it for my family – it's a popular choice in my household.

Serves 3–4 • Preparation 30 mins • Cook 3 hours • Cooker capacity 5 litres

1½ cups plain (all-purpose) flour, plus extra for dusting
2 teaspoon baking powder
Pinch of salt
30 g (1 oz) butter
1 tablespoon sugar
2 teaspoon lemon zest (optional)
About ⅓ cup milk
6–8 tablespoons of your favourite jam

SYRUP
½ cup sugar
1 tablespoon honey
1 tablespoon butter
2 tablespoons lemon juice

1. To make the syrup, place the sugar, honey, butter and 1 cup water into a saucepan and bring to the boil. Add the lemon juice and set aside.

2. Sift the flour, baking powder and salt in a large bowl, then rub the butter in until the mixture forms soft crumbs. Add the sugar and lemon zest (if using), then as much milk as needed to form a soft dough.

3. Lightly dust a clean bench top with flour, then roll the dough to roughly a 25 cm (10 in) square. Spread over your jam of choice, then roll the dough into a log and gently pinch the ends together.

4. Place the roll, seam side down, into a slow cooker and pour the syrup over the roll.

5. Cover and cook on LOW for 3 hours.

Lacey-Anne Noyer

Caramel Dumplings

I often see requests for caramel dumpling recipes on the Slow Cooker Central website, so I took a few different recipes and made my own from there.

Serves 2–4 • Preparation 10–15 mins • Cook 1 hour 10 mins • Cooker capacity 3.5 litres

CARAMEL SAUCE
1½ cups boiling water
1 cup light brown sugar, lightly packed
1 tablespoon butter

DUMPLINGS
¾ cup plain (all-purpose) flour
1½ teaspoons baking powder
1 tablespoon sugar
1 tablespoon cold butter, chopped
⅓ cup milk

1. To make the caramel sauce, place all of the sauce ingredients in a slow cooker.
2. Cover and cook on HIGH for about 30 minutes.
3. Meanwhile, make the dumplings. Mix together the dry ingredients in a large bowl. Using your fingertips, rub the butter into the flour until the mixture resembles breadcrumbs. Add the milk and mix well.
4. With damp hands, roll the dough into 12 small dumplings.
5. Carefully place the dumplings into the caramel sauce. Cover, putting a tea towel (dish towel) under the lid, and cook on HIGH for 40 minutes.

NOTE: A triple quantity of dumplings requires only a double quantity of sauce.

Nikki Willis

Chocolate Risotto

When everyone was cooking rice pudding in their slow cookers, I didn't have any long-grain rice to try it out! I did, however, have arborio rice and thought that a sweet risotto could work. It took a little tinkering, but eventually after four or five attempts I perfected the recipe and shared it on the website.

Serves 4–6 • Preparation 5–10 mins • Cook 3 hours • Cooker capacity 5–6 litres

2 cups boiling water
1½ cups arborio rice
395 g (14 oz) tinned sweetened condensed milk
2 cups milk
¼ cup light brown sugar, lightly packed
1 tablespoon unsweetened cocoa powder
1½ teaspoons vanilla essence
⅛ teaspoon salt
200 g (7 oz) chocolate chips

1. Put the water, rice and condensed milk in a slow cooker and stir well to combine.

2. Cover and cook on HIGH for 2 hours.

3. Stir in 1½ cups of the milk along with the sugar, cocoa powder, vanilla and salt. Continue cooking for 1 hour.

4. Stir in the remaining milk and the chocolate chips. Let sit uncovered for 15 minutes to thicken slightly.

Alycia Park

Nutella Pudding in a Mug

I love cooking desserts, so I thought I would try a Nutella pudding in a mug. It tasted amazing and is a big hit with friends and family.

Serves 4 • Preparation 10 mins • Cook 1 hour 20 mins • Cooker capacity 6 litres

1½ cups self-raising flour, sifted
¾ cup milk
½ cup white sugar
2 tablespoons unsweetened cocoa powder, sifted
2 tablespoons melted butter
2 eggs
250 g (14 oz) Nutella

1. In a large bowl, mix together the flour, milk, sugar, cocoa, butter and eggs powder.

2. Divide the mixture evenly among 4 coffee mugs and top each mug with 3 tablespoons Nutella.

3. Pour just enough boiling water into a slow cooker to cover the base and put the mugs inside.

4. Cook, covered, on HIGH for 1 hour 20 minutes, or until the puddings spring back when touched. Serve with cream or custard.

Brendan Hill

Chocolate-Dipped Caramel Spoons

I was looking for a more sophisticated way to eat caramel from the tin! These caramel spoons look so pretty all done up, and they make great gifts, party favours or sweet treat with your coffee.

Makes 20 • Preparation 10 mins + setting time • Cook 6 hours • Cooker capacity 6 litres

395 g (14 oz) tinned sweetened condensed milk
300 g milk/dark/white chocolate melts
Crushed nuts, crushed biscuits and/or sprinkles, to decorate

1. Place the tin of condensed milk into a slow cooker, completely submerged in water. Cover and cook on HIGH for 6 hours. Turn off and allow the tin to cool before removing from the water. You now have a tin full of caramel.

2. Once the caramel is completely cool, open the tin and spoon the caramel onto your serving spoons. Place the spoons on a sheet of baking paper. Refrigerate for 1 hour until completely chilled.

3. Prepare the chocolate by melting it in a glass or metal bowl over hot/simmering water, stirring with a metal spoon, until melted.

4. Dip the caramel-filled spoons into the melted chocolate and completely cover the caramel. Tap the spoons on the side of the bowl a few times to remove any excess chocolate. Return to the baking paper and set aside in the fridge to set.

5. Once set, dip the spoons back in the chocolate, then decorate with your choice of crushed nuts, crushed biscuits or sprinkles before the chocolate sets. Set aside in the fridge to set.

Holly Ware

Choc-Mint Coconut Rough

I love peppermint-flavoured chocolate, so I thought I would join the fudge craze and vary a plain-flavoured recipe.

Serves 6–10 • Preparation 5 mins + setting time • Cook 1 hour • Cooker capacity Any

400 g (14 oz) mint-flavoured chocolate, broken into pieces
395 g (14 oz) tinned sweetened condensed milk
¾ cup toasted desiccated coconut
1 teaspoon vanilla essence
1 teaspoon butter

1. Put all the ingredients in a slow cooker and stir well to combine.

2. Cover and cook on HIGH for one hour, stirring every 10 minutes or so.

3. Grease a slice tray (bar tray) and line it with baking paper. Pour the mixture into the prepared tin and refrigerate for at least 2 hours to set. Slice into squares and store in an airtight container in the fridge.

Sherrie Vigar

➤— Peanut Butter Slice —●

I came up with this recipe when I was trying to use up bits and pieces from the pantry. It's a great treat to make for school lunches and snacks, and for coffee with friends.

Serves 8 • Preparation 10 mins + setting time • Cook 1–1½ hours
• Cooker capacity 6.5 litres

1 cup crunchy peanut butter
1 cup sugar
3 cups cornflakes
Melted chocolate (optional), for drizzling

1. Line a slice tray (bar tray) with baking paper.

2. Combine the peanut butter and sugar in a slow cooker with 2 tablespoons water.

3. Cover and cook on high for 1–1½ hours, stirring frequently.

4. Stir through the cornflakes then press the mixture into the prepared tin. If desired, drizzle melted chocolate over the top. Refrigerate for at least 2 hours to set. Slice into squares and store in an airtight container in the fridge.

Melissa Walton

Mars Bar Slice

One day, instead of making the normal chocolate crackles, I thought it might be nice to try using my favourite chocolate in the recipe. I haven't looked back since.

Serves 30–40 pieces • **Preparation** 5 mins + setting time • **Cook** 20 mins
• **Cooker capacity** 3 litres

18 fun-size Mars bars, plus extra, sliced, to decorate
2 tablespoons butter or margarine
4 cups Coco Pops (Cocoa Krispies)

1. Put the Mars bars and butter in a slow cooker.

2. Cover and cook on LOW for 20 minutes, stirring, until the mixture is melted. Add the Coco Pops and stir until combined.

3. Grease a slice tin (bar tray) and press the mixture firmly into the tin.

4. Decorate the top of the slice with the extra Mars bar slices.

5. Refrigerate for at least 20 minutes to set. Slice into squares and store in an airtight container in the fridge.

Cheree Bone

Caramel Brownie Slice with Cookies-and-Cream Topping

This is a recipe my son and I made up while I was driving him to school one morning. We were talking about our favourite food combos. My partner loves brownies, I love caramel and my son loves anything cookies-and-cream, so we decided to experiment and add the three elements together to make one decadent slice. It's rich and delicious.

Serves 8 • Preparation 20 mins + setting time **• Cook** 3 hours **• Cooker capacity** 6.5 litres

185 g (6½ oz) unsalted butter
185 g (6½ oz) dark chocolate, broken into pieces
275 g (9½ oz) caster (superfine) sugar
3 large eggs
90 g (3 oz) plain (all-purpose) flour
40 g (1½ oz) unsweetened cocoa powder
100 g (3½ oz) milk chocolate chips

CARAMEL
395 g (14 oz) tinned sweetened condensed milk
½ cup light brown sugar, firmly packed
60 g unsalted butter
3 tablespoons golden syrup
3 tablespoons thickened (whipping) cream

COOKIES-AND-CREAM TOPPING
200 g (7 oz) block of white chocolate, broken into pieces
1 tablespoon copha
130 g (4½ oz) packet Oreo biscuits, crushed

1. Line a 20 cm (8 in) cake tin with baking paper (see page 15 for hints on using cake tins in your slow cooker).

2. In a large saucepan, melt together the butter and chocolate over low heat until smooth. Set aside for 2 minutes to cool slightly. Add the caster sugar and mix well. Add the eggs one at a time, mixing well after each addition.

3. In a large bowl, sift together the flour and cocoa, then fold through the chocolate and egg mix, using a metal spoon. Add the chocolate chips and gently mix until evenly distributed through the batter. Pour the mixture into the prepared cake tin and place directly into a slow cooker.

4. Cover, putting a tea towel (dish towel) under the lid, and cook on HIGH for 2 hours, or until a skewer inserted into the middle of the cake comes out clean. Remove the tin from the slow cooker and set aside to cool.

5. For the caramel, put the condensed milk, brown sugar, butter, golden syrup and cream in the slow cooker and cook, uncovered, for 1 hour, stirring every 10 minutes until the caramel is thick and golden. Pour the caramel over the cooled brownie base and set aside in the fridge to cool completely.

6. To make the topping, put the white chocolate and copha in a microwave-safe bowl and microwave for 20-second bursts, stirring in between each burst, until melted and smooth. Stir through the crushed Oreos and pour the mixture over the caramel. Refrigerate until set.

7. Cut into wedges and serve.

Alanna Williams

Peanut Butter & Oreo Brownies

After seeing a similar oven-cooked recipe online, I decided there must be a way to make these brownies in a slow cooker. I used silicone muffin cases to help the brownies cook evenly, plus they are the perfect portion size. No guarantee you'll be able to stop at just one 'portion' though!

Makes 16 • Preparation 20 mins • Cook About 45 mins • Cooker capacity 7 litres

48 mini Oreo biscuits (about 5 packets)
1 packet brownie mix and associated ingredients
Peanut butter

1. Layer 3 mini Oreos biscuits in a stack with a generous smear of peanut butter between each layer and on top. Place each stack in an individual silicone cupcake case.

2. Prepare the brownie mix according to the packet instructions. I add an extra 1–2 tablespoons water to make the mix easier to work with.

3. Gently spoon the brownie mixture around and on top of each Oreo stack.

4. Put the silicone cases in a slow cooker. Cover, putting a tea towel (dish towel) under the lid, and cook on HIGH for about 45 minutes or until the brownie mixture is set.

5. Cool on a wire rack before removing the silicone cases.

Paulene Christie

⬛━ Scottish Tablet ━●

My husband is Scottish and Scottish tablet is his favourite treat, so I came up with a slow-cooker version. It is so much easier to make in the slow cooker than on the stovetop.

Serves 20 • Preparation 2 mins + setting time • Cook 5–6 hours • Cooker capacity 6 litres

125 g (4½ oz) salted butter
1 kg (2 lb 3 oz) sugar
250 ml (8½ fl oz/1 cup) full-cream milk
395 g (14 oz) tinned sweetened condensed milk

1. Put everything except the condensed milk into a slow cooker.

2. Cook on HIGH for 3 hours with the lid off, stirring occasionally (about every 30 minutes).

3. Add the condensed milk. Mix well and continue cooking for 2 hours with the lid off, stirring more frequently (about every 15–20 minutes). The mixture will turn a nice caramel colour.

4. Grease a slice tin (bar tray) and set aside.

5. Whisk the mixture vigorously for 10 minutes (this is very important as it helps the tablet to set) then pour into the prepared tray.

6. Leave to set on the kitchen bench top (no refrigeration required). Once set, cut into squares and store in an airtight container in the pantry.

Bel Ruddy

Bubblegum Banana Fudge

I was inspired to make this fudge after reading all the lovely creations by the fantastic slow-cooker group members.

Serves 20 • Preparation 10 mins + setting time **• Cook** 1½ hours **• Cooker capacity** Any

600 g (1 lb 5 oz) white chocolate, broken into pieces
395 g (14 oz) tinned sweetened condensed milk
1 tablespoon butter
85 g (3 oz) bubblegum-flavoured jelly (gello) crystals
160 g (5½ oz) banana lollies (candies/sweets), roughly chopped

1. Put the chocolate, condensed milk, butter and half of the jelly crystals in a slow cooker.

2. Cook on HIGH for 1 hour, stirring every 15 minutes or so until the mixture is smooth and a skin starts to form on the top.

3. Grease a slice tin (bar tray) and line it with baking paper. Stir the bananas through the fudge mix and pour into the prepared tin. Sprinkle with the remaining jelly crystals.

4. Refrigerate for at least 2 hours to set. Slice into squares and store in an airtight container in the fridge.

Corrina Conlan

Rum Ball Fudge

I like both fudge and rum balls, so I decided to combine the two – and it is yummy.

Makes 48 pieces • Preparation 5 mins + setting time • Cook 1½ hours
• Cooker capacity 1.5 litres

750 g (1 lb 11 oz) milk chocolate, broken into pieces
395 g (14 oz) tinned sweetened condensed milk
75 ml (2½ fl oz) rum
1 cup raisins
1 cup desiccated coconut
100 g (3½ oz) crumbled sponge cake

1. Line a slice tray (bar tray) with baking paper.

2. Put the chocolate and half of the condensed milk in a slow cooker. In a bowl, mix the rum with the remaining condensed milk and add to the slow cooker.

3. Cook on HIGH for about 1½ hours, stirring every 10–15 minutes, until a crust forms on top between stirring.

4. Mix in the raisins, coconut and sponge cake.

5. Pour the mixture into the prepared tin and refrigerate for at least 2 hours to set. Slice into squares and store in an airtight container in the fridge.

Narelle Youngs

Bounty or Mars Bar Fudge

I love this recipe – it's so simple to make and delicious. You can't have just one piece!

Serves 24 • Preparation 5 minutes + setting time • Cook 1 hour • Cooker capacity 6 litres

- 500 g (1 lb 2 oz) milk chocolate, broken into pieces
- 395 g (14 oz) tinned sweetened condensed milk
- 1 tablespoon butter
- 1 tablespoon vanilla essence
- 30 fun-size Bounty or Mars bars

1. Place all of the ingredients except the chocolate bars into a slow cooker.
2. Cook, uncovered, on HIGH for 1 hour, stirring every 15 minutes, until a crust forms on top between stirring.
3. Line a slice tin (bar tray) with baking paper and add the chocolate bars.
4. Pour the fudge into the prepared tin and place in the fridge overnight to set.
5. Cut into slices and enjoy.

Angela Beswick

Choc Milo Fudge

After seeing the rise in popularity of slow cooker fudge recipes on the Slow Cooker Recipes for Families Facebook page, I decided to try my hand at making fudge. My first attempt was the cookies-and-cream fudge, which was a massive hit, so I decided to create some of my own flavours. This choc Milo fudge is my family's favourite fudge recipe.

Serves 25 • **Preparation** 3 mins + setting time • **Cook** About 1 hour • **Cooker capacity** Any

500 g (1 lb 2 oz) milk chocolate, broken into pieces
395 g (14 oz) tinned sweetened condensed milk
1 tablespoon butter
½ cup Milo

1. Put the chocolate in a slow cooker.

2. Pour the sweetened condensed milk over the top, then add the butter.

3. Cover and cook on LOW, stirring every 10–15 minutes, for about 1 hour, or until the fudge forms a slight crust between stirring. Stir through the Milo.

4. Transfer the fudge to a baking dish lined with baking paper and refrigerate overnight until set.

5. Cut into squares and serve.

Erin Athanassiou

White Chocolate Cookie-dough Fudge

I love the way fudge allows you to be creative with whatever sweet ingredients you have available. I saw a cookie dough recipe and thought cookie dough would be amazing with a white chocolate based fudge! I created this recipe and it must have been a great hit, as it only lasted a couple of days. What I love about this recipe is that you can tweak it to your liking: use dark chocolate for the fudge or add M&Ms to the cookie dough, for example.

Serves 8–12 • Preparation 10 mins + setting time • Cook 1–2 hours
• Cooker capacity 1.5 litres

395 g (14 oz) tinned sweetened condensed milk
220 g (8 oz) block white chocolate, broken into pieces
180 g (6½ oz) block Milky Bar Cookies and Cream,
    broken into pieces
2 teaspoons vanilla essence
65 g (2¼ oz) butter, softened, plus 2 teaspoons extra
¾ cup light brown sugar, firmly packed
¼ cup milk
1¼ cups plain (all-purpose) flour
½ cup mini chocolate chips

1. Put the condensed milk, chocolate, 1 teaspoon of the vanilla and the 2 teaspoons butter in a slow cooker. Cook, uncovered, on HIGH for 1–2 hours, stirring every 10–15 minutes, until a skin forms on top. Remove from the heat and set aside.

2. Meanwhile, place the softened butter and brown sugar in a medium bowl and cream together until smooth. Add the milk and remaining vanilla and mix until combined. It may appear lumpy but this is OK. Add the flour and chocolate chips and mix until combined.

3. Spread out the cookie dough on a baking sheet or baking tray lined with baking paper and set aside in the fridge for 1–2 hours until slightly set.

4. When the fudge and cookie dough are ready, take little pieces of dough and gently fold through the fudge, reserving some pieces for decoration.

5. Line a 10 cm x 20 cm (4 in x 8 in) slice tin (bar tray) with baking paper and transfer the fudge to the tin. Decorate the top with the remaining cookie dough pieces.

6. Refrigerate for at least 2 hours to set. Slice into squares and store in an airtight container in the fridge.

Alicia Lowe

Caramel Chocolate Fudge

This recipe is my absolute favourite. I make it over and over again, that's how amazing it is!

Serves 10–12 • Preparation 10 mins + setting time • Cook 1–1½ hours
• Cooker capacity 5 litres

395 g (14 oz) tin sweetened condensed, unopened
1 tablespoon butter
660 g (1 lb 7 oz) chocolate, broken into pieces
1 tablespoon vanilla essence
Sprinkles, to decorate
Jelly beans or other confectionary, to decorate

1. To make the caramel, place the unopened can of sweetened condensed milk into your slow cooker. Cover the can completely with water. Make sure there are at least 5 cm (2 inches) of water over the top of the can. (It is very important that the can remains completely covered.)

2. Put the lid on the slow cooker and cook on HIGH for 4–5 hours or on LOW for 7–8 hours. The longer you leave it, the thicker the caramel will be. Check the water level regularly.

3. Allow the can of caramel to cool completely before opening (very important). The caramel is under pressure in the tin and you don't want molten caramel to explode at you from a hot tin!

4. Once the caramel is cool, put it and all the other ingredients (except the sprinkles and jelly beans) in the slow cooker and stir well to combine.

5. Cover and cook on LOW for 1–1½ hours, stirring every 10–15 minutes.

6. Spread the fudge into a slice tin lined with baking paper. Decorate with the sprinkles, jelly beans and other confectionary. Refrigerate until set.

7. Slice into squares and store in an airtight container in the fridge.

Kayla Fels

Hazelnut Fudge

I wanted to create a fudge for my nut-loving husband, who, not-so-coincidently also loves fudge. Using hazelnut chocolate made it so easy!

Makes 50 pieces • Preparation 5 mins + setting time • Cook 1½ hours • Cooker capacity 1.5 litres

600 g (1 lb 5 oz) hazelnut chocolate, broken into pieces
395 g (14 oz) tinned sweetened condensed milk
1 tablespoon butter
1 tablespoon vanilla essence

1. Put all of the ingredients into a slow cooker.
2. Cook, uncovered, on LOW for about 1½ hours, stirring every 15 minutes with a silicone or metal spoon.
3. Line a baking tin with baking paper and pour in the fudge. Refrigerate for at least 2 hours to set.
4. Slice into squares and store in an airtight container in the fridge.

Paulene Christie

White Chocolate Fudge

I created this recipe (and many other fudges) one week when I had a book signing and fudge-tasting event for our first *Slow Cooker Central* book. I had to create a different fudge for every night of the week prior to the event, and as a white chocolate lover I knew I had to make this one. Of all the fudges I made that week, this one was my favourite.

Makes 50 pieces • Preparation 5 mins + setting time • Cook 1½ hours • Cooker capacity 1.5 litres

600 g (1 lb 5 oz) white chocolate, broken into pieces
395 g (14 oz) tinned sweetened condensed milk
1 tablespoon butter
1 tablespoon vanilla essence

1. Put all of the ingredients into a slow cooker.

2. Cook, uncovered, on LOW for about 1½ hours, stirring every 15 minutes with a silicone or metal spoon.

3. Line a baking tin with baking paper and pour in the fudge. Refrigerate for at least 2 hours to set.

4. Slice into squares and store in an airtight container in the fridge.

Paulene Christie

▰▬ Choc Honeycomb Fudge ▬●

As a child I loved choc-coated honeycomb squares. There was something so good about the combination of sweet honeycomb and silky chocolate. This choc honeycomb fudge is no exception. Yummy from go to woah!

Makes 50 pieces • Preparation 10 mins + setting time • Cook 1½ hours • Cooker capacity 1.5 litres

600 g (1 lb 5 oz) milk chocolate, broken into pieces
395 g (14 oz) tinned sweetened condensed milk
1 tablespoon butter
1 tablespoon vanilla
400 g (14 oz) chocolate-coated honeycomb pieces

1. Put all of the ingredients except the honeycomb pieces into a slow cooker.

2. Cook, uncovered, on LOW for about 1½ hours, stirring every 15 minutes with a silicone or metal spoon.

3. Meanwhile, place the honeycomb in a clean plastic bag or under a tea towel on a bench top. Using a rolling pin, smash the honeycomb into small pieces.

4. When the fudge is cooked, stir through half of the honeycomb pieces.

5. Line a baking tin with baking paper and pour in the fudge. Scatter over the remaining honeycomb pieces and press them gently into the fudge. Refrigerate overnight to set.

6. Slice into squares and store in an airtight container in the fridge.

NOTE: If you have any leftover honeycomb, it can be sprinkled over ice cream.

Paulene Christie

Homemade 'Ice Magic'

I first made this as a cheap alternative to the store-bought equivalent, but it has become a huge hit with the family.

Serves 4+ • Preparation 5 mins • Cook 1–1½ hours • Cooker capacity 1.5 litres

500 g (1 lb 2 oz) chocolate, broken into pieces
2 tablespoons coconut oil

1. Put the chocolate and coconut oil in the slow cooker.
2. Cook, uncovered, on LOW for 1–1½ hours, stirring occasionally.
3. Once the chocolate mix is smooth, remove from the slow cooker and set aside to cool to room temperature.
4. Store in an airtight container at room temperature in the pantry. If it hardens, just warm in the microwave to soften again.
5. Serve drizzled over cold desserts.

NOTE: If you want to thin out the mixture, add more coconut oil, and if you want it thicker, add more chocolate. You can flavour it with any essence you like, for example, try orange essence.

John Walter

SLOW COOKER SURPRISE

You can cook what!?

If you're the owner of a slow cooker, you probably already know that they are amazingly versatile appliances. Casseroles, roasts, soups, curries, cakes and desserts: not only can a slow cooker cope with these culinary challenges, in most cases they are the *superior* choice when compared with oven or stovetop methods. But could they be good for more than helping you create easy, delicious meals? Well, yes, they can! Read on to discover how your slow cooker can entertain the kids, fill up the dog and light up the house!

Pet Food Casserole

I adapted this from my mother's recipe. Our dog seemed to get sick from so many different foods – I was exasperated, so my mum gave us a recipe that she's always used for the family's dogs. I now feed this to both my dogs, and I recommend it to anyone looking for a cheaper alternative for their dog's food. I have checked all of the ingredients with an animal dietician and a veterinarian.

Makes About 14 portions • Preparation 5 mins • Cook 3–6 hours • Cooker capacity 5.5 litres

2 kg (4 lb 6 oz) budget beef mince
1 kg (2 lb 3 oz) diced frozen mixed vegetables
2 cups brown rice
1 cup 12-grain soup mix
½ cup rolled oats
2 tablespoons Vegemite
2 tablespoons honey
Sprinkle of herbs (optional)

1. Put all of the ingredients into a slow cooker, cover with boiling water and stir well to combine.

2. Cover and cook on LOW for 6 hours or on HIGH for 3 hours.

Tabatha Wendell

Slow-cooker Finger Paints (Non-toxic)

We are always trying to occupy the minds of our little ones, and what better way than to let their imagination run wild with these groovy paints? These are perfectly safe for the children, our homes and our environment. So, what are you waiting for?

Makes About 500 ml (17 fl oz/2 cups) • **Preparation** 5 mins • **Cook** 30–45 mins • **Cooker capacity** 1.5 litres

2/3 cup cornflour (cornstarch)
3 tablespoons caster (superfine) sugar
½ teaspoon salt
Liquid food colouring – red, yellow, blue, green

1. In a bowl, combine the cornflour, caster sugar, salt and 2 cups water. Pour into a slow cooker.

2. Cover, putting a tea towel (dish towel) under the lid, and cook on HIGH for about 30 minutes, or until thickened, stirring occasionally.

3. When the mixture reaches a paint consistency, spoon into storage bottles (baby-food jars are great). Add 6 drops of food colouring to each jar, except for red, which needs 25 drops to achieve a rich colour. Screw the lids on tightly and shake each bottle vigorously to mix the colour through the paint.

4. Store, sealed, in the fridge. If the paint gets too thick over time, just add a dash of water and shake vigorously to disperse.

NOTE: You can create additional colours by combining different food colours in each jar. Add glitter for extra sparkle!

Simon Christie

➤── Basic Recycled Candles ──●

Most of us have some old, not-so-pretty-anymore candles hidden around the house. Well, here is something you can try out at home to revamp those candles! Just another quirk of the slow cooker.

Preparation 30 mins • Cook 2 hours • Cooker capacity 6 litres

Used candles, still in their holders (if applicable)
Cheap candles with long wicks
1 x 375 ml (12½ fl oz/1½ cups) glass jar or several smaller jars
Candle moulds
Scents, such as essential oils (optional)

1. Using a screwdriver, knife or spoon, very carefully pry away the wax from any old candle holders along with the wax from your old and cheap candles. Keep the colours separate or combine them. Discard all the old wicks. Set aside the new wicks from the cheap candles.

2. Soak the candle moulds in hot soapy water.

3. Put the recovered wax into jars. Use a separat jar for each colour or mix different colours together.

4. Put the jars into a slow cooker insert and fill with warm water to halfway up the side of your smallest jar.

5. Cover, putting a tea towel (dish towel) under the lid, and cook on HIGH for 2 hours, or until the wax has melted.

6. Drain the candle moulds and pat dry with paper towel.

7. Cut the new wicks into lengths to fit your candle moulds, plus an additional 2 cm (¾ in) for burning. Spear a toothpick through one end of each wick length as a 'support'.

8. Very carefully, as the wax will be extremely hot, remove the jars from the slow cooker and pour the wax into the moulds. If you want to add any scents, do so now.

9. Place one wick into the centre of each wax-filled mould, resting the 'support' across the rim.

10. Allow to cool in a safe place for a few hours until set. Remove the toothpicks, unmould the candles and light the candles in a safe environment.

simon Christie

Slow-cooker Play Dough

The texture of this play dough is incomparable to any other. It is silky smooth and non-greasy, and is sure to be a hit with children of all ages.

Makes 1 kg (2 lb 3 oz) • **Preparation** 10 mins • **Cook** 45–60 mins • **Cooker capacity** 5 litres

2 cups plain (all-purpose) flour
½ cup salt
⅓ cup cream of tartar
2 tablespoons vegetable oil
1–2 teaspoons liquid food colouring

1. In a bowl, combine the flour, salt and cream of tartar. In a separate bowl, combine the oil and 2 cups water.

2. Put the dry ingredients into a slow cooker, add the wet ingredients and mix to combine.

3. Cover, putting a tea towel (dish towel) under the lid, and cook on HIGH for 45–60 minutes, stirring often for the first 30 minutes of cooking time, and then once or twice for the remaining cooking time.

4. The dough is ready when it no longer sticks to the sides of the slow cooker. You can test this by rolling a small amount of dough into a ball and placing it in the freezer for a few minutes. If the dough doesn't stick to your fingers when you remove it from the freezer, it is ready.

5. Remove the dough from the slow cooker, knead until smooth and set aside in an airtight container in the fridge to cool.

6. Divide the play dough into four equal pieces and add food colouring a few drops at a time to each piece, kneading thoroughly to mix. Keep adding and kneading until the play dough is the colour you want.

7. Store the play dough in the fridge.

NOTE: You can add glitter for sparkle, if desired.

Simon Christie

INDEX

THANK YOU

I would like to give special thanks to those who have made this journey possible.

I couldn't do what I do without the help of my incredible admin team, who help with the massive job of keeping our Facebook group running smoothly day and night. Simon, Felicity, Nikki, Victoria, Denise, Karen, and Rozi ... I'm forever in your debt x And to Melodie, Cassandra, Narelle and Kris ... you may no longer admin in our group, but your contributions will never be underestimated or forgotten x

To Brigitta Doyle of ABC Books – I would not be writing this without you. Your vision for this book series and your never-ending encouragement along the way have literally changed my life. You did that for me. 'Thank you' will never be enough for the impact you have had on my life x

Thanks also to Lachlan McLaine, Matthew Howard, Camellia Yildirim, Amy Kusuma and the whole team at ABC Books and HarperCollins Publishers who led me through the publishing process and never tired of my endless questions along the way.

To Sarah Dennis of Fresh Marketing, who guides me through every turn on my journey to build the Slow Cooker Central brand and share it with the world. You are so good at what you do and it is inspirational to watch you work. Because of you I am chasing dreams I never thought possible.

To my family, my friends and loved ones who support and encourage me along the way – thank you! It takes a lot of work, and a lot of sacrifice to achieve my goals, and you give me the support I need to keep going and never give up. To my sisters Vicki and Debbie – I hope I make you proud of your little sister and that our mum is looking down on us, smiling at the women we became. To my dearest friend Julie – who always cares, always asks and always listens – you truly are an inspiration to me in so many ways x

To our amazing, spirited children who I laugh to overhear telling others about their 'famous author' mummy with such pride, and who shower me with love and adoration every day of my life – Mummy loves you to the moon and back xx I'm so proud of all three of you and the amazing kind and caring souls you are!

Simon, you push me to always keep going, to never give up, to achieve anything I set my mind to. You are my biggest supporter in every way! You have no shame in bending the ear of anyone you come across to tell them with such pride and enthusiasm about me and about our slow cooking journey! Like me, you work many hours a day with the Facebook group, as well as in recipe development and statistics management, and still you are always looking for new ideas or new ways to help me do what I do. This book may have my name on the cover but yours is right there beside mine in spirit. I'd never ever be here where I am today without you and your unconditional love and that of our children. Thank you my groom xx

And last but in no means least – I'd like to give a special thanks to every member of our Facebook group 'Slow Cooker Recipes 4 Families' and of our website www.slowcookercentral.com. Without you none of this would be possible. Your support of our first book was overwhelming and I hope this book delivers everything you hoped it would. I'm inspired by the amazing dishes you create every day and I am thankful that you share your recipes, your advice, your experiences and your conversations with me and with each other. It's what makes us unique – that community spirit – united in our slow cooking adventures.

Thanks for being a part of it x

Paulene Christie

Slow-cooking internet sensation Paulene Christie is a busy working mum with a passion for sharing new and exciting recipes for the slow cooker. She now has more than 430,000 members in her Facebook group, Slow Cooker Recipes 4 Families, and a hugely successful website, Slow Cooker Central. The Facebook page is so popular Paulene has a team of seven people (including her husband, Simon) to help her administer the thousands of recipes and comments that are posted each day. Paulene lives in Queensland with Simon, their three young children and seven slow cookers.

www.slowcookercentral.com
www.facebook.com/groups/SlowCookerRecipes4Families

SLOW
COOKER
CENTRAL

**More than 250 recipes
from the hugely popular
online community**

Paulene Christie

If you'd like more recipes,
be sure to get your hands on

SLOW
COOKER

CENTRAL

The first book in the series is a fantastic collection of
over 250 delicious and easy recipes from Paulene Christie
and the Slow Cooker Central community.